AF278862

The Enshittification of America

How Private Equity Destroyed the Things We Love

Richard Lowe

The Writing King

Enemies of You Series

https://enemiesofyou.com

The Enshittification of America: How Private Equity Destroyed the Things We Love

Copyright © 2026 by Richard G Lowe

All rights reserved. No part of this publication may be reproduced, stored in a retrieval system, or transmitted by any means – electronic, mechanical, photographic (photocopying), recording, or otherwise – without prior permission in writing from the author.

Although every precaution has been taken to verify the accuracy of the information contained herein, the author and publisher assume no responsibility for any errors or omissions. No liability is assumed for damages that may result from the use of information contained within.

Trademarked names appear throughout this book. Rather than use a trademark symbol with every occurrence of a trademarked name, names are used in an editorial fashion, with no intention of infringement of the respective owner's trademark.

Disclaimer

This book presents the author's analysis and opinions based on publicly available information, documented business practices, and industry observations. While every effort has been made to ensure accuracy, some company details and timelines may have changed since publication. The examples cited represent patterns observed across industries rather than comprehensive assessments of individual companies. Readers should conduct their own research before making business or investment decisions. The author has no financial interest in promoting or disparaging any specific companies mentioned. Views expressed are solely those of the author and do not constitute financial, legal, or business advice.

Table of Contents

See books by Richard Lowe at

https://masterofworlds.com

Get free publishing insights and industry updates at

https://thewritingking.substack.com

For ghostwriting and book coaching services see

https://thewritingking.com

Enemies of You Series

https://masterofworlds.com/enemies-of-you

The Death of Thinking
The Enslavement of Humanity

The Birth of the Augmented Human
The Freeing of Humanity

Turn Off The TV, Get Off Your Ass, and Do Something

Stuck in the Middle
Wars, Weapons, and the Forces That Will Shape the Next Thirty Years

The Enshittification of America
How Private Equity Destroyed the Things We Love

The Emasculation of America
How Russia's Long War Against the American Male Is Destroying the Nation From Within

The Villainization of America

———

See the full series description at the back of this book.

All books available at masterofworlds.com

Preface

I never set out to write a book about the decline of American business. I was perfectly happy ghostwriting memoirs and helping executives tell their success stories. But after twenty years managing technology at Trader Joe's and then a decade listening to business leaders share their real stories, I started noticing patterns that kept me awake at night.

The same private equity playbook destroying one industry after another. The same optimization algorithms that could improve customer service getting repurposed to maximize fee extraction. The same executives who built great businesses explaining how they were pressured to dismantle what made those businesses great.

I watched companies I'd shopped at my whole life turn into hollow shells of themselves. Airlines that once made flying feel special now treat passengers like cattle. Department stores that anchored communities became real estate plays. Local newspapers that held mayors accountable got strip-mined by hedge funds that wouldn't know journalism if it sued them for libel.

The turning point came during a client conversation in 2023. A Fortune 50 executive was explaining how his company had "optimized customer interactions" by replacing human service representatives with chatbots designed to frustrate callers into giving up. He said it with the detached professionalism of someone describing weather patterns. No malice, no awareness of what he was describing. Just systems working exactly as designed.

That's when I realized we weren't just witnessing random business failures. We were watching the systematic transformation of American commerce from a system designed to serve customers into one designed to extract maximum value from them. The same balance-sheet techniques, the same consulting playbooks, the same private equity strategies, deployed across industry after industry.

This isn't a book about individual bad actors or isolated corporate greed. It's about a system that consistently produces outcomes we call failures but which are working exactly as intended. When you optimize for extraction rather than service, you get extraction. When you reward quarterly performance over long-term value creation, you get short-term thinking. When you structure businesses to maximize cash flow to investors rather than value to customers, you get enshittification.

The most frustrating part is how preventable this all was. The businesses that escaped this fate prove it every day. They're not miraculous outliers or lucky accidents. They're companies that made different choices about ownership, optimization, and what success means.

I wrote this book because I'm tired of pretending that widespread business degradation is just how markets work. It's not. It's how these particular markets work, structured by these particular incentives, optimized for these particular outcomes. We built these systems, which means we can rebuild them.

The stories in this book come from two decades of watching systems work and a decade of listening to the people who run them. Some details have been changed to protect client confidentiality, but the patterns are real, the data is documented, and the outcomes speak for themselves.

A note on ghostwriting: my professional work involves helping business leaders write books they have the knowledge and experience to write but not always the time or inclination to write alone. That collaboration is as old as publishing. What this book criticizes is not expertise assisted by craft, but institutions hollowed out so that the people with genuine expertise are replaced entirely by cheaper substitutes. The distinction matters, and I'd rather name it than leave it for someone else to point out.

We can do better. We just have to decide we want to.

A Note on Sources

The financial figures, employment statistics, fee disclosures, and corporate chronologies in this book are drawn from public sources: SEC filings, bankruptcy court documents, congressional testimony, regulatory agency reports, and named journalism from the publications that originally broke the stories. Where worker and executive experiences are described without attribution, names and identifying details have been changed to protect people who spoke candidly about their employers.

No company or individual paid to appear in this book, positively or negatively. The counter-examples cited as resistant to enshittification are included because the evidence supports them, not because they supported this project.

Readers who want to trace specific claims to their sources will find the most useful starting points are the bankruptcy filings for Toys"R"Us, Sears, and Steward Health Care; the Wells Fargo Senate hearing transcripts from 2016; the American Medical Association's annual prior authorization surveys; and the FTC's 2024 report on pharmacy benefit manager practices.

Introduction: The Great Degradation

Remember when getting on an airplane felt like an adventure? When the stewardess (they called them that then) wore a crisp uniform and a genuine smile, and your seat had enough legroom for an actual human being? When restaurants had names like "Mel's Diner" and "The Blue Moon Café," each one a little universe with its own personality, its own stories scrawled on the walls in decades of coffee stains and laughter?

That America didn't just disappear. It was murdered.

This book has a point of view and you should know it up front. Private equity, as currently practiced in the cases documented here, is not a neutral economic force or a misunderstood tool occasionally misapplied. It is a system deliberately designed to extract wealth from productive businesses, transfer it to a small number of already-wealthy people, and leave the wreckage for everyone else to deal with. The executives who implement it are not stupid or ignorant. They know exactly what they are doing. This book names them, documents what they did, and calls it what it is.

A note on what this book is arguing about. The phenomenon documented here has at least three components, and they are not the same phenomenon, even though they often appear together and reinforce each other.

The first is deliberate financial extraction via leverage. A private equity firm acquires a profitable business with borrowed money, charges that business for the privilege of being acquired, sells off its assets, replaces its experienced workers with cheaper ones, and exits with returns that come from the dismemberment rather than from any improvement to operations. This is the primary subject of the book. It is what most of the case studies document. It has a specific mechanism, specific actors, and specific consequences that respond to specific policies.

The second is structural displacement. Newspapers lost most of their advertising revenue to Facebook and Google not because Alden Capital bought them but because the advertising business itself migrated. Department stores faced Amazon. Travel agents faced Expedia. Some industries had genuine structural pressure that would have produced decline regardless of who owned the businesses. Some of what looks like enshittification is closer to disruption. The distinction matters because the responses are different.

The third is ordinary management decline. Companies age. Founders retire. Boards make bad decisions. Markets shift in ways that punish slow adaptation. Some of what looks like enshittification is just the long-running phenomenon of businesses getting worse for reasons that have nothing to do with private equity or platform displacement.

What this book argues is that the first phenomenon, deliberate financial extraction via leverage, has been operating across American business for forty years at a scale that dwarfs the others, that it frequently combines with structural displacement and management decline in ways that make all three worse, and that it is the only one of the three that responds to the kind of policy reform that produced Glass-Steagall and other twentieth-century corrections. The second and third are real. The first is what this book is about.

Walk through any American city today and you'll find the crime scene. Strip malls stretch like suburban graveyards, filled with identical gray boxes that could house a Subway or a tax preparation service with equal enthusiasm. The bones of old department stores, once grand as cathedrals, sit picked clean and left to rot while their former owners count tax write-offs. Airlines have turned the miracle of human flight into livestock transport.

This isn't progress. This isn't the invisible hand of the market doing its mysterious work. This is enshittification, and it's eating America alive.

Cory Doctorow gave us the word to describe what happens when digital platforms start good, then gradually abuse their users to benefit advertisers, then eventually abuse everyone while the owners cash out and run. But enshittification has crawled out of our screens and into every corner of American life. Your bank. Your hospital. Your grocery store. The place where you buy your morning coffee. All infected with the same disease: the relentless pursuit of extractable value over everything else that once made life worth living.

The pattern is heartbreakingly simple once you see it. Private equity vultures spot a profitable business with loyal customers, the kind of place where the owner knew your name and your usual order. They swoop in with borrowed money, load the business with crushing debt, then strip everything that made it special. Cut the staff. Cheapen the ingredients. Raise the prices. Extract every possible dollar until there's nothing left but a hollow brand name stuck to the front of another gray box.

And now they have algorithms to help them do it faster.

The same artificial intelligence that could help a chef create better recipes instead powers systems that calculate exactly how much they can charge you before you storm out in disgust. The same automation that could help airline mechanics prevent delays instead manages overbooking systems designed to squeeze every last seat full. Customer service chatbots don't exist to serve customers. They exist to exhaust you into giving up.

Technology turned into a weapon against the very people it was supposed to help.

Saddest of all isn't what we lost. It's that we're forgetting we ever had it. Kids today think airline delays and hospital billing nightmares and phone trees from hell are just how the world works. Like weather. Like gravity. Something you endure, not something you can change.

But scattered across America, a few stubborn holdouts refuse to surrender. Trader Joe's still treats its workers like human beings and its customers like friends. In-N-Out still makes burgers the way burgers are supposed to be made. Costco still believes that taking care of customers and employees might be good business. These companies have access to the same soul-crushing technologies as everyone else. The difference is they use computers to help their people do better work, not to replace their people with cheaper machines.

The secret isn't mysterious. Companies that resist enshittification tend to be owned by families or cooperatives or people who plan to stick around for a few decades. They optimize for customer loyalty and employee happiness because they'll still be here next year to face the consequences of their choices. When they buy new technology, they ask: "How can this help us serve people better?" Not: "How can this help us eliminate people entirely?"

This book visits thirteen industries that once made America proud, now hollowed out by financial strip-mining. We'll meet the companies that sold their souls and the stubborn few that kept theirs. We'll see how the same technologies can either accelerate the decay or help rebuild what we lost, depending on who's holding the controls and what they're trying to accomplish.

Each industry chapter follows a similar structure: what it was, what happened to it, who did it, and who refused to let it happen to them. The repetition is intentional. Private equity playbook doesn't change because it doesn't have to. The same moves work on toy stores and newspapers and hospital chains and airlines because the underlying logic is always identical: extract, exit, repeat. Seeing the pattern across thirteen industries is the point.

This isn't just a catalog of corporate crimes. It's a love letter to the America we lost and a blueprint for getting it back. Because once you understand how enshittification works, how it spreads, what feeds it, what starves it, you can start to imagine an economy that serves people instead of devouring them.

The choice is still ours. We can keep accepting degradation as inevitable, shrugging our shoulders while the last good places get picked apart by spreadsheet jockeys. Or we can remember what we're fighting for: businesses that treat customers like neighbors, workers like family, and communities like something worth preserving.

The America that built things to last and took pride in serving people well isn't buried yet. But if we want to save it, we'd better start digging fast.

So maybe the question isn't whether what this book documents is evil. Maybe the question is whether we want to keep operating systems that consistently produce results we consider evil.

Because systems do not design themselves. We designed them. Which means we can redesign them.

The choice isn't between accepting enshittification or abandoning markets entirely. The choice is between markets that serve communities and markets that serve extraction.

When you put it that way, evil starts to seem like the right word. Not the cartoonish evil of villains plotting world domination. The banal evil of normal people implementing systems they know cause harm because those systems reward them personally.

The tools exist. The examples exist. The knowledge exists. The title of this book is its thesis. All we need is the will to admit that treating human beings like extraction opportunities isn't just bad business.

It's wrong.

Take a Drive with Me

I remember what Route 66 was like in the late 1960s and early 1970s, riding with my father on business trips when the Mother Road still pulsed with authentic American life. What I saw during those childhood journeys wasn't just a highway. It was a living demonstration of how businesses could thrive while serving their communities, how owners could prosper while taking pride in their work, and how commerce could create gathering places that strengthened the social fabric.

The gas stations alone told the story of a different America. Pull into a Sinclair or Phillips 66, and three attendants would materialize before you'd even turned off the engine. One checked your oil, another cleaned your windshield until it sparkled, and the third filled your tank while asking about your journey and offering directions to local attractions. These weren't minimum-wage workers going through corporate-mandated motions. They were employees of local franchise owners who lived in the community, men who took genuine pride in keeping your car running and sending you safely down the road.

The station owner himself might emerge from the service bay, wiping grease from his hands, to chat about road conditions ahead or recommend his wife's favorite diner in the next town. His kids probably went to school with the kids whose parents ran that diner. The mechanic fixing transmissions in the back bay had learned his trade from his father and would pass it on to his son. These weren't gig workers rotated through by corporate algorithms designed to minimize labor costs. They were craftsmen, neighbors, stakeholders in their community's prosperity.

Compare that to today's gas stations. Pump your own gas at a pump that may or may not work. Swipe a credit card through a reader that demands your ZIP code for unstated security reasons. Shuffle inside to pay a clerk behind bulletproof glass who can't leave the register to help you find anything. The "service" consists of surveillance cameras and a loudspeaker telling you to see the cashier if you need assistance. The message is clear: you're not a valued customer on a journey. You're a potential shoplifter conducting a reluctant transaction.

The diners and cafés of the Mother Road operated on an entirely different philosophy. Walk into Velma's Diner outside Tucumcari or the Route 66 Cafe in Barstow, and you'd find more than food. You'd find theater. The waitress knew the truckers by name and their usual orders by heart. She'd pour coffee before you asked, remember that you liked your eggs over easy from your last visit six months ago, and somehow keep track of eight different conversations while serving twenty tables during the lunch rush.

The pie case wasn't a display of mass-produced desserts shipped from a corporate bakery. It showcased the work of someone who'd gotten up before dawn to make coconut cream and apple crumb from family recipes passed down through generations. The cook wasn't following a laminated instruction sheet designed by food scientists to minimize ingredient costs. He was an artist who took pride in his chicken fried steak and knew his reputation traveled with every customer who left satisfied.

These weren't "restaurant concepts" designed by marketing committees and rolled out across identical locations. Each place had personality, quirks, local history embedded in every corner. The walls held photos of local high school football teams, newspaper clippings about the town's centennial celebration, business cards from traveling salesmen who'd become friends over the years.

Today's roadside dining tells a different story. Chain restaurants dominate highway exits, their beige interiors designed by corporate headquarters to minimize cleaning costs and maximize table turnover. The server works from a tablet that tracks movements and suggests upsells based on algorithms. The food arrives pre-portioned and reheated, designed not to delight but to meet the lowest acceptable standard while maximizing profit margins.

The real magic of Route 66 lived in its roadside attractions, those wonderfully bizarre monuments to American entrepreneurialism. In Cabazon, California, you could stop for gas next to a concrete brontosaurus the size of a building, built by Claude Bell as an advertisement for his Wheel Inn Restaurant. The dinosaur wasn't focus-grouped or market-tested. It was pure American folk art, the vision of one man who figured that if you're going to sell hamburgers in the middle of the desert, you might as well do it next to something memorable.

Holbrook, Arizona had the Wigwam Motel, where you slept inside concrete tepees that Chester Lewis built in 1950 because he thought travelers would get a kick out of the novelty. Each wigwam was a fully functional motel room decorated with Native American motifs, not because some corporate committee decided it would test well with focus groups, but because Lewis genuinely believed his guests deserved something special to remember.

Near Oro Grande, the Bottle Tree Ranch featured thousands of colored glass bottles hung on metal trees, creating a forest that sang in the desert wind. Elmer Long didn't build it because market research suggested roadside art installations would drive traffic. He built it because he thought it was beautiful and wanted to share that beauty with travelers.

Albuquerque had the Dog House Drive-In, shaped like an enormous hot dog, complete with mustard squiggles painted on the sides. The owner wasn't following architectural guidelines developed by corporate branding departments. He was making a statement: this is what we sell, this is who we are, and we're proud enough of both to build a monument.

None of these places exist in their original form anymore. Some have been preserved as historical curiosities, sanitized and stripped of their commercial purpose. Others were demolished to make way for strip malls and chain restaurants that could have been built anywhere. The few survivors operate as tourist attractions rather than functioning businesses.

Today's roadside architecture follows strict branding guidelines enforced across thousands of identical locations. McDonald's golden arches look the same in Missouri as they do in California. Walmart stores follow identical floor plans whether they're in small towns or suburbs. The regional character, local pride, and entrepreneurial creativity that once made every mile of American highway a potential adventure have been eliminated in favor of efficiency and brand recognition.

The motor courts and tourist cabins of Route 66 represented hospitality as an art form. The owners lived on the property, often in a house connected to the office. They knew their business depended on word-of-mouth from satisfied travelers, so they maintained their cabins like they were expecting relatives to stay. Fresh paint, clean linens, maybe a small refrigerator stocked with cold drinks. The proprietor would personally show you to your room, point out the best local restaurants, and warn you about road construction ahead.

Now there is a Hampton Inn or Holiday Inn Express, designed to be instantly recognizable and identically mediocre anywhere in America. The desk clerk follows scripts created by corporate trainers. The breakfast consists of mass-produced items in warming trays. The room feels designed for easy cleaning and maximum occupancy turnover rather than human comfort.

The trading posts told stories through their merchandise. The owner had personally selected every item, often knowing the artisan who made it. He could tell you the difference between Hopi and Navajo pottery, explain why this turquoise came from the Sleeping Beauty mine while that piece was from Royston. These weren't imported knockoffs designed to fool tourists. They were authentic expressions of regional culture, sold by people who understood and respected their origins.

Today's highway exits are dominated by the same corporate chains regardless of location. The gift shops, when they exist at all, sell mass-produced items manufactured overseas and decorated with generic "Route 66" logos that have no connection to local history. The entrepreneurial network that once supported hundreds of small business owners has been replaced by franchise operations that extract profits from local communities and send them to distant corporate headquarters.

What I witnessed as a child on Route 66 was America operating on fundamentally different principles. Business owners were community stakeholders. Employees were skilled craftsmen. Customers were valued guests. The entire system was designed around long-term relationships and sustainable prosperity.

Route 66 in its prime represented everything that enshittification destroys: craftsmanship over cost-cutting, relationships over transactions, community investment over wealth extraction, local character over corporate standardization. When you drove the Mother Road in 1970, you experienced an America that still believed business could build communities rather than hollow them out.

That America didn't disappear because it was inefficient or unprofitable. It was bypassed by federal infrastructure decisions, replaced by chains managed for short-term returns, and what survived got loaded with debt and stripped for parts. Different mechanisms operating on the same kind of place. What we lost wasn't just a highway or a collection of businesses. We lost a model for how American commerce could serve American communities.

Part I: The Mechanism of Decay

The Private Equity Playbook

Remember the Mafia? Not the Hollywood version with pinky rings and cement shoes, but the real thing. The way they'd roll into a neighborhood, spot the most successful businesses, and make them an offer they couldn't refuse. "Nice restaurant you got here. Shame if something happened to it."

The beauty of the racket was its simplicity. You didn't have to burn anything down or break kneecaps. You just made it clear that cooperation was the only path to survival. Pay us our monthly cut, and we'll make sure nothing bad happens. Refuse, and accidents happen. Equipment breaks. Suppliers get nervous. Customers stop coming.

The modern American economy runs on the same principle, except now the guys in expensive suits call it "private equity," and somehow that makes it respectable.

Walk into any business school today and they'll tell you private equity is the peak of financial innovation. Smart money identifying underperforming assets and optimizing them for maximum returns. Creative destruction in action. The invisible hand of the market doing its beautiful work.

What they won't tell you is that "optimization" is just a fancy word for the same protection racket that used to get you arrested.

The playbook hasn't changed much. PE firms still target successful businesses with loyal customers and steady cash flow. Places that have been around long enough to build something worth stealing. But instead of showing up with baseball bats, they arrive with

PowerPoint presentations and something called a "leveraged buyout."

Here's how it works, and it's so elegant a wise guy from Brooklyn would weep with admiration.

First, you identify your mark. Maybe it's a regional restaurant chain that's been family-owned for three generations. Maybe it's a newspaper that's served the same community for a century. Maybe it's a toy store where every kid in America spent Saturday afternoons turning birthday wishes into reality. Find something profitable, something beloved, something that took decades to build and would be almost impossible to replace.

Then you make them an offer they can't refuse. Not because you'll hurt them if they say no, but because you'll offer them so much money they can't imagine saying no. Who wouldn't want to cash out for ten times what their business is worth on paper?

Here's the beautiful part: you don't even use your own money. You borrow most of it from banks, promising to pay them back with the very cash flow you're about to destroy. It's like buying a house with a mortgage, except instead of paying the mortgage yourself, you make the house pay its own mortgage. And then you charge the house rent for the privilege of living in itself.

The banks love this arrangement because they get their money back either way. If the business thrives, great! If it collapses under the debt load, that's not their problem anymore. They've been paid. The only ones who lose are the customers, the employees, and the communities that depended on the business. But those people don't have lobbyists in Washington.

Once you own the business, the real fun begins. Remember, you've just loaded it with more debt than a gambling addict on his third mortgage. Every month, enormous debt payments come due, payments that would make a loan shark blush. The business that was profitable last week is now bleeding money, not because it's selling fewer hamburgers or newspapers or toys, but because it's paying interest on the money someone else borrowed to buy it.

So you do what any rational person does when faced with impossible financial pressure: you start cutting. Not the debt payments, of course. Those are sacred. You cut everything else.

First to go are the employees. Why pay three people to do a job when two people can do it badly? Why pay two people when one exhausted, stressed-out person can do it terribly? Fire the experienced workers who know how things are supposed to work. Replace them with part-timers who cost less and know less. Automate everything you can, not because automation improves the customer experience, but because robots don't get sick days or health insurance.

Next, you cut the quality. Why use real ingredients when artificial ones cost half as much? Why maintain equipment when you can run it into the ground and replace it later (or better yet, let the next owner worry about it)? Why invest in training when you're planning to sell the business in five years anyway?

Then you raise prices. After all, what are customers going to do? Go to your competitors? You've probably bought them too. And even if you haven't, they're all playing the same game now.

The final step is the most elegant: you sell everything that isn't nailed down. That real estate the business owns? Sell it to yourself through another company you control, then charge the business rent to use its own building. That fleet of delivery trucks? Lease them back at a premium. Those warehouses full of inventory? Liquidate them and switch to just-in-time delivery, which sounds efficient until you realize it means customers wait longer and pay more for everything.

Every dollar you squeeze out goes straight into your pocket, justified as "management fees" and "consulting expenses" and "special dividends." You're not stealing, after all. You're optimizing shareholder value. You're maximizing returns. You're making the business more efficient.

And when the customers finally revolt? When the workers finally quit? When the community finally realizes that the beloved local institution has been gutted and left to die? You're already gone, counting your profits and looking for the next target.

The business you leave behind is a zombie. It still has the same name, the same logo, maybe even the same locations. But everything that made it special, everything that made customers love it, everything that took generations to build has been stripped away and sold for parts.

Take Toys"R"Us. For sixty years, it was the place where childhood dreams came true. Geoffrey the Giraffe with his dopey smile and bow tie. The Big Book catalog that kids would memorize cover to cover, folding down page corners next to the things they wanted most. "I don't want to grow up, I'm a Toys"R"Us kid."

Remember that jingle? Remember pushing those oversized shopping carts through aisles that seemed to stretch forever, filled with every toy a kid could ever imagine? Remember the way the store smelled like new plastic and possibility, the way your parents would set a budget and you'd spend an hour agonizing over whether to get the Lego set or the action figure, knowing that whatever you chose would be the center of your universe for months?

In 2005, Bain Capital, KKR, and Vornado Real Estate bought the company for $6.6 billion, loading it with $5.3 billion in debt. Almost overnight, a profitable business that had survived recessions, changing trends, and the rise of Walmart was drowning in interest payments. The new owners extracted over $470 million in fees for themselves while the company struggled to stock its shelves and keep its stores clean.

When Amazon started eating into toy sales, Toys"R"Us couldn't adapt. It couldn't invest in better websites or improve its stores because every spare dollar was going to service the debt its owners had saddled it with. By 2017, the company was bankrupt. By 2018, all 735 stores were closed.

The vultures had moved on. Bain and KKR were already busy destroying other beloved brands. But 33,000 people lost their jobs. Kids lost their wonderland. America lost another institution that had brought families together for generations.

The most maddening part? Toys"R"Us didn't fail because people stopped buying toys. It failed because a handful of financial engineers figured out how to extract more value from killing it than from keeping it alive.

This is the private equity playbook in its purest form. Identify something people love. Buy it with borrowed money. Bleed it dry. Walk away rich. Repeat.

And somehow, we've decided this is not only legal but admirable. Business schools teach case studies on these "turnarounds." Financial journalists write breathless profiles of the "innovators" who pulled them off. Politicians take campaign contributions from the very people strip-mining their communities.

It's the perfect crime because the victims don't even realize they're being robbed until it's too late. The cancer spreads slowly, one cost-cutting measure at a time. The local newspaper starts running more wire stories and fewer local investigations. The restaurant's food gets a little blander, the service a little slower. The department store's shelves get a little emptier, the staff a little more harried.

By the time customers notice something's wrong, the people responsible are long gone, and the customers are left wondering why everything seems to be getting worse at the same time.

The answer is simple: because the same people are making everything worse, using the same playbook, for the same reason. Not to build anything or improve anything or serve anyone, but to extract maximum value in minimum time and move on to the next target.

The Puppet Masters

Who's Really Behind the Great Extraction

"Behind every great fortune lies a great crime." — Honoré de Balzac

A note before we go further. Cataloging billionaire spending sounds like resentment, and resentment is not the point. Stephen Schwarzman is allowed to spend his money however he wants. The problem is how the money was made: by buying healthy companies, loading them with debt, charging the companies for the privilege of being acquired, and walking away while those companies collapse. The parties matter because every dollar of them was paid for, line by line, by what got destroyed. Every camel rented for a Palm Beach lawn is a closed Toys"R"Us store. Every Picasso on a Park Avenue wall is a thousand laid-off employees no longer in the middle class. That is the connection the next several pages are going to insist on.

Meet Stephen Schwarzman. Worth roughly $40 billion, he throws birthday parties that cost more than most people will earn in their lifetimes. His 60th birthday bash in 2007 featured Rod Stewart, reportedly paid $1 million for a half-hour performance, plus Patti LaBelle singing "Happy Birthday" in a replica of Schwarzman's $30 million Park Avenue apartment built inside the Park Avenue Armory. The party cost between $3 and $5 million for 500 guests. A decade later, his 70th in Palm Beach featured Gwen Stefani, trapeze artists, live camels, and a custom Chinese-temple cake, with cost estimates ranging from $7 million to $20 million.

Schwarzman isn't a tech entrepreneur who built something the world wanted. He's not an inventor whose patents changed how we live. He's the co-founder and CEO of Blackstone, the world's largest private equity firm, and his fortune comes from buying healthy companies, loading them with debt, stripping out everything valuable, and walking away with billions while leaving destroyed businesses and unemployed workers behind.

If you want to understand who's behind the enshittification of America, start with people like Schwarzman. The destruction of American business isn't some invisible hand of the market or inevitable economic evolution. It's not Chinese manipulation or technological disruption. It's a small group of extraordinarily wealthy people who discovered they could make more money tearing things apart than building them up.

The Billionaire Demolition Crew

The private equity industry is dominated by a handful of mega-firms, each controlled by a small group of people who've become some of the wealthiest people in human history by perfecting legal extraction schemes. These aren't household names like Bezos or Musk, because their business model requires staying in the shadows. But their impact on daily American life dwarfs almost any other force.

Leon Black built Apollo Global Management into a $700 billion asset manager by buying distressed companies and squeezing every possible dollar out of them. His personal art collection, valued at over $1 billion, includes Edvard Munch's "The Scream" (purchased for $119.9 million), plus works by Picasso, Cézanne, and van Gogh, all bought with money extracted from companies like Caesars Entertainment, which Apollo loaded with so much debt it eventually filed for bankruptcy.

Henry Kravis and George Roberts, cousins who founded KKR, pioneered many of the techniques now standard across private equity. They figured out how to use borrowed money to buy companies, then make the companies themselves pay back the loans even when those loans funded KKR's massive fees. Kravis owns a 26-room penthouse at 625 Park Avenue that he bought for $15 million in 1995 and spent another $7 million decorating, now worth an estimated $80 million.

These people didn't get rich by creating value. They got rich by capturing value created by others. The difference is essential.

The Three-Card Monte of Modern Finance

The private equity model works like an elaborate shell game. The firms raise money from institutional investors (pension funds, university endowments, insurance companies) by promising higher returns than public markets can deliver. Then they use that money, plus massive amounts of borrowed cash, to buy companies.

Here's where it gets interesting. Once they own a company, the private equity firm pays itself three different ways: management fees (usually 2% of assets under management), carried interest (usually 20% of profits), and transaction fees charged to the companies they own. So even if the company they bought fails, the private equity executives still get paid.

Apollo collected over $300 million in fees from Caesars Entertainment while the casino company was struggling with the debt Apollo had loaded onto it. When Caesars finally filed for bankruptcy, Apollo had already extracted more in fees than its original investment. The bankruptcy was someone else's problem: Caesars' employees, customers, and creditors.

This isn't a bug in the system. It's the feature. Private equity firms have designed a business model where they win regardless of whether the companies they buy succeed or fail. The only requirement is that they extract cash faster than the companies collapse.

The Enablers

The billionaires at the top of private equity firms couldn't accomplish this wealth transfer alone. They need enablers, and they've found plenty in America's most respected institutions.

University endowments and public pension funds have poured trillions of dollars into private equity, chasing the higher returns promised by firms like Blackstone and Apollo. Harvard's endowment has invested billions with private equity firms, using tuition dollars and taxpayer-supported research funding to bankroll the destruction of American businesses. CalPERS, the California public pension fund, has invested over $30 billion in private equity, meaning California teachers and firefighters are unknowingly funding the very firms eliminating good middle-class jobs.

The cruel irony: pension funds representing workers are providing the capital used to eliminate those same workers' jobs. The chickens decided to invest their retirement savings with the fox.

The consulting industry provides intellectual cover for the carnage. McKinsey, Bain, and Boston Consulting Group have become the private equity industry's willing accomplices, providing supposedly objective analysis that almost always recommends cost-cutting, workforce reductions, and operational "efficiency" improvements. These firms charge millions to tell companies they should fire thousands of workers, then charge more millions to implement the firings.

McKinsey alone has worked with at least 90 of the top 100 Fortune 500 companies, spreading the gospel of shareholder value maximization. When Valeant Pharmaceuticals was systematically destroying the drug industry by buying companies and jacking up prices, McKinsey was there to help with "strategic planning." When Purdue Pharma was flooding the country with opioids, McKinsey provided advice on how to "turbocharge" sales.

The China Distraction

Politicians love to point fingers at Beijing when American companies move jobs overseas or when communities lose their economic anchors. It's a convenient distraction from the real culprits.

China didn't force private equity firms to load Toys"R"Us with debt until it collapsed. China didn't make Bain Capital gut KB Toys or force Apollo to extract billions from Caesars Entertainment. Chinese investors didn't create the leveraged buyout model or the carried interest tax loophole that allows private equity executives to pay lower tax rates than teachers and firefighters.

American-owned private equity firms have done more damage to American communities than any foreign power could dream of accomplishing. While politicians rail about Chinese economic warfare, firms like Blackstone and Apollo are systematically dismantling American businesses using American capital provided by American institutions.

The real threat to American business culture comes from inside the house.

The Academic Indoctrination Machine

None of this wealth concentration happened by accident. It required a sustained ideological campaign to convince Americans that greed was good, that corporations existed solely to maximize shareholder value, and that any consideration of workers, communities, or long-term sustainability was economically naive.

The intellectual foundation was laid in business schools, particularly at the University of Chicago, where economists like Milton Friedman taught that a corporation's only social responsibility was to increase profits for shareholders. This wasn't economic science. It was ideology dressed up as scholarship. But it provided the intellectual cover needed to justify systematic extraction of value from American companies.

Harvard Business School, Wharton, and Stanford became factories for producing MBAs trained to see businesses as collections of assets to be optimized instead of institutions serving multiple stakeholders. These graduates flooded into consulting firms and private equity shops, armed with spreadsheets and PowerPoint presentations that reduced complex human institutions to numbers on a page.

The academic capture was so complete that obviously destructive practices got rebranded as innovations. "Leveraged buyouts" sounded more sophisticated than "debt loading." "Operational efficiency" masked mass layoffs. "Strategic restructuring" disguised asset stripping. The language of business education became a euphemism machine, turning predation into expertise.

The Media Cheerleaders

The financial media played an essential role in normalizing what was organized looting. CNBC,

Bloomberg, and the Wall Street Journal turned private equity executives into celebrities, profiling their homes, their art collections, and their philanthropic activities while barely mentioning the trail of destroyed businesses they left behind.

Forbes' annual billionaire rankings became scorecards for the extraction economy, celebrating wealth accumulation regardless of how that wealth was generated. Business magazines ran breathless profiles of "visionary" private equity executives who were "revolutionizing" industries by applying "market discipline" to "underperforming assets."

The coverage created a mythological narrative where private equity firms were portrayed as efficiency experts saving bloated companies from themselves. The human cost (lost jobs, shuttered stores, abandoned communities) was treated as an unfortunate but necessary side effect of economic progress.

When Mitt Romney ran for president in 2012, his background at Bain Capital was largely portrayed as business experience rather than training in wealth extraction. The media treated his role in loading companies with debt and stripping out value as evidence of his qualifications to run the economy, not as a disqualifying conflict of interest.

The Government Revolving Door

What is most troubling is how smoothly private equity executives have moved between Wall Street and Washington, using government positions to shape policies that benefit their industry and then returning to private equity to profit from those policies.

Henry Paulson went from CEO of Goldman Sachs to Treasury Secretary, where he orchestrated the 2008 financial bailouts that rescued many of the same firms he'd worked with throughout his career. Timothy Geithner moved from the New York Federal Reserve to Treasury Secretary to private equity, where he became president of Warburg Pincus.

Steven Mnuchin, Donald Trump's Treasury Secretary, was previously a partner at Goldman Sachs and had his own investment fund. Before joining the Trump administration, he was involved in the purchase and controversial management of IndyMac Bank during the foreclosure crisis.

This revolving door ensures that financial industry priorities get embedded in government policy. The carried interest tax loophole, which allows private equity executives to pay capital gains rates on what is labor income, has survived multiple attempts at reform partly because of this influence network.

The Scale of the Heist

Private equity firms currently manage over $4 trillion in assets globally, with American firms controlling the majority of that total. That's more than the GDP of Germany, and it's money invested in buying companies for the purpose of extracting maximum value in minimum time.

Blackstone alone manages over $1 trillion in assets, more than the market capitalization of most Fortune 500 companies. Apollo manages over $700 billion. KKR manages over $600 billion. These aren't investment funds in any traditional sense. They're extraction engines designed to strip value from the real economy and concentrate it in the hands of a few hundred people.

Stephen Schwarzman's $40 billion fortune makes him richer than most countries. Leon Black, who stepped down from Apollo in 2021 after disclosures of his $158 million in payments to Jeffrey Epstein, is worth over $10 billion. Henry Kravis and George Roberts each have fortunes exceeding $5 billion.

This isn't wealth created through innovation or entrepreneurship. It's wealth extracted from businesses that other people built, using money provided by pension funds and endowments that other people contributed to. A massive upward transfer of wealth disguised as investment management.

Not Random Market Forces

None of this was inevitable. The enshittification of American business didn't happen because of technological change or global competition or shifting consumer preferences. It happened because a group of people designed and implemented systems to extract wealth from productive businesses.

The private equity model isn't a natural evolution of capitalism. It's a deliberate perversion of it. Traditional capitalism, for all its flaws, was supposed to reward people who built valuable businesses that served customers and employed workers. Private equity rewards people who destroy valuable businesses while extracting maximum cash in minimum time.

This distinction matters because it means the problem is solvable. If the destruction of American business culture came from people making choices, then different people can make different choices. The system wasn't broken by mysterious economic forces. Identifiable people rigged it. It can be unrigged.

The Human Cost

Behind every private equity "success story" are thousands of people whose lives were upended by leveraged buyouts. When Sports Authority liquidated, 14,500 employees were laid off so that private equity investors could recover their investments.

These aren't abstract economic statistics. They're real people who lost their careers, their health insurance, their retirement savings, and their communities' gathering places so that billionaires could add more zeros to their net worth.

The human cost extends beyond immediate job losses. When private equity firms gut local businesses, they destroy the social fabric of communities. The local newspaper that gets stripped for parts was often the only source of information about city council meetings and school board elections. The department store that gets liquidated was often the anchor that kept downtown areas alive.

The Real Enemy

The enemy of American prosperity isn't China or immigrants or technological change. It's a small group of extraordinarily wealthy Americans who've figured out how to get rich by making everyone else poorer. They've created a system where financial engineering trumps productive investment, where quarterly extraction matters more than long-term value creation, and where the wealth of communities gets systematically transferred to a handful of billionaires.

Stephen Schwarzman can afford a $10 million birthday party because thousands of businesses have been stripped for parts to fund his lifestyle. Leon Black can collect billion-dollar art because communities across America have lost their economic anchors. Henry Kravis can live in an $80 million penthouse because the companies that employed millions of Americans have been loaded with debt until they collapsed.

This isn't conspiracy theorizing. It's pattern recognition. The same names appear again and again in the destruction of American businesses. The same firms use the same playbook to extract wealth from different industries. The same people move between Wall Street and Washington, ensuring that the policies remain tilted in their favor.

The enshittification of America has authors, and their names are on the letterhead of every major private equity firm. They're not shadowy figures operating in secret. They're public billionaires who give interviews to financial magazines and donate wings to hospitals and universities. They're hiding in plain sight, using their wealth and influence to ensure that the operation keeps running while American communities pay the price.

The first step toward stopping the destruction is knowing who's behind it. The men running these firms are not anonymous. They serve on hospital boards, donate wings to universities, give interviews to financial magazines, and run advisory councils for whichever administration is in office. Their business model depends on public ignorance and political protection. Once Americans understand who is actually responsible for the enshittification of their economy, the political cover those billionaires have always relied on may stop being so reliably available.

From Ownership to Extraction

There was a time when owning a business meant something. Not just having your name on letterhead or showing up to cut ribbons, but genuinely owning it. Caring about its future past next quarter, knowing your employees' kids' names, giving a damn about whether customers left happy. That era is as dead as the dodo, and we killed it with spreadsheets and debt instruments that would make a loan shark blush.

The transformation from ownership to extraction didn't happen overnight. Like watching your favorite neighborhood slowly turn into a strip mall, the change crept in gradually until one day you looked around and realized everything good was gone. Stewardship got replaced by balance-sheet manipulation. Businesses stopped existing to create value and started existing to extract it.

The old ownership model operated on a simple premise: you put money into a business, nurtured it, helped it grow, and eventually reaped rewards that matched your investment of time and capital. Success was measured in decades, not fiscal quarters. The Walton family didn't build Walmart by loading it with debt and stripping out everything valuable. Ray Kroc didn't turn McDonald's into a global empire by cutting corners until the experience became miserable. These founders understood that their wealth was tied to their companies' long-term health.

But somewhere along the way, we discovered we could make more money by breaking things than by building them. The financial wizards on Wall Street realized that a mediocre business with terrible customer service could generate spectacular returns if you knew how to milk it properly. Enter the era of extraction.

The extraction model flips the traditional ownership script. Instead of investing capital to improve operations, you load the business with debt and use that borrowed money to pay yourself massive dividends upfront. Customer experience becomes an afterthought because customers don't show up on the quarterly earnings call. Debt holders do.

This shift represents more than just a change in business strategy. It's a fundamental reordering of priorities that puts leveraged buyouts ahead of operational excellence. When Apollo Global Management bought Claire's Stores in 2007, they weren't interested in revolutionizing teenage jewelry retail. They wanted to extract maximum value from the brand before the inevitable collapse. Load the company with $2 billion in debt, cut costs to service that debt, extract management fees, repeat until the patient dies.

The mechanics of this extraction operate through what financial professionals euphemistically call "leverage." Leverage is a polite word for debt, and debt is a weapon that transforms businesses into extraction vehicles. When a private equity firm buys a healthy company for $100 million and immediately loads it with $300 million in debt, they haven't improved anything. They've created a ticking time bomb that must be defused through radical cost-cutting or face detonation.

This debt load creates a perverse incentive structure where short-term cash generation becomes the only metric that matters. Employee training becomes an unnecessary expense. Equipment maintenance gets deferred. Customer service representatives get replaced with automated phone trees designed to exhaust callers into giving up. Every decision gets filtered through a single question: does this generate cash in the next ninety days?

The result is what economists politely call "efficiency gains" but what customers experience as systematic degradation. When a restaurant chain fires experienced managers and replaces them with undertrained kids making minimum wage, that's not efficiency. That's extraction. When airlines pack more seats into planes and charge for carry-on bags, they're not optimizing the flying experience. They're extracting value from a captured customer base.

The technology revolution promised to make this extraction more palatable by automating away the rough edges. Instead, it became a force multiplier for customer abuse. Artificial intelligence gets deployed to create more sophisticated barriers between customers and actual human assistance. Machine learning algorithms get turned toward maximizing revenue through dynamic pricing schemes that would make carnival barkers proud.

Consider the two paths that customer service technology could take. The service enhancement path uses chatbots to handle simple requests instantly while connecting complex issues to knowledgeable humans faster than ever before. AI analyzes customer interaction patterns to identify frustration points and proactively address them. Automated systems learn customer preferences to personalize experiences without creepy surveillance.

The extraction path deploys these same technologies as customer exhaustion weapons. Chatbots get programmed to cycle through endless loops of unhelpful responses, wearing down customers until they abandon legitimate complaints. AI optimizes hold times not for customer satisfaction but for the perfect balance between cost savings and retention. Automated systems collect personal data to enable more sophisticated price discrimination and targeted manipulation.

The choice between these paths isn't technical. It's philosophical. The same neural network that could help a customer solve their problem faster can be trained to make problem-solving so frustrating that they give up. The difference lies in who benefits from the optimization: customers or shareholders.

Most insidious is how the extraction model masquerades as normal business operations. When customer service deteriorates, companies blame market forces or consumer preferences. When quality declines, they point to cost pressures and competitive dynamics. The extraction is hidden behind layers of financial complexity that make it nearly impossible for outsiders to understand what's happening.

The human cost of this extraction goes far beyond financial statements. When a business shifts from ownership to extraction mode, employees stop being colleagues and become cost centers. Customers transform from relationships to be nurtured into resources to be mined. Communities lose institutions that once provided stability and local identity.

Saddest of all isn't just what we're losing. It's how much better things could be. The same technological advances that enable sophisticated extraction could create genuinely better customer experiences. The same financial innovations that enable debt loading could support long-term business building. The same data analytics that optimize revenue extraction could identify and solve customer problems before they become complaints.

But building requires patience, and extraction demands immediate results. In a world where private equity funds promise their investors returns in five to seven years, patience becomes a luxury that businesses can't afford. The long-term health of companies, communities, and customers gets sacrificed on the altar of IRR targets and fund performance metrics.

This is the fundamental choice facing American business today: optimization for customer value or optimization for capital extraction. Technology amplifies whichever choice companies make, but it can't make the choice for them. Every business decision becomes a referendum on whether the company exists to serve customers or to generate returns for financial engineers.

The extraction model works brilliantly for the extractors. Private equity partners get rich, management consulting firms collect enormous fees, and debt holders receive their interest payments. Everyone wins except the customers, employees, and communities that these businesses were originally created to serve.

This dynamic matters because once you see it, you can recognize enshittification when it happens. The degradation isn't accidental or inevitable. It's the predictable result of systematic optimization for extraction over service. Once you recognize the pattern, you start seeing it everywhere: the extra fees, the reduced staffing, the automated systems designed to frustrate rather than help, the subtle erosion of quality that happens so gradually you barely notice until it's too late.

The next time a beloved business suddenly gets worse for no apparent reason, look for the debt load. Check for new ownership structures. Follow the money flowing out of operations and into management fees. Nine times out of ten, you'll find the same extraction playbook being executed with ruthless efficiency.

We built an economy that mistakes extraction for value creation, and then we act surprised when everything starts falling apart. The miracle isn't that enshittification is happening. It's that anything good survives at all.

The Strongest Case for Private Equity

Anyone arguing against private equity should be able to articulate the strongest case for it. The case exists. It is not stupid. It deserves engagement.

The first defense is that distressed companies sometimes do need new capital and new management. A company that has been mismanaged for years, that has lost its competitive position, that cannot raise public equity because public markets have lost confidence in it, may genuinely benefit from private capital willing to take a position no one else will take. The PE firm that buys a company nobody else will buy and turns it around is not extracting. It is investing.

The second defense is that some PE deals produce stable, profitable, going-concern businesses. The PE firm that bought Hilton and worked with management through the financial crisis to position the company for growth, eventually taking it public again, is not the firm that loaded Toys"R"Us with debt and walked away. The category contains both cases. Treating all of PE as the destructive variant is a category error.

The third defense is that pension funds need returns to pay benefits, that public markets have produced volatile returns over the past two decades, and that PE has historically delivered higher returns than public alternatives. The teachers and firefighters whose retirement security depends on those returns benefit from PE existing as an investment vehicle, even if the businesses being extracted from suffer.

The fourth defense is that the market for corporate control imposes useful discipline on management. Public companies have well-documented agency problems.

Managers prioritize their own interests over shareholders. Board oversight is weak. Accountability is diffuse. The threat of being acquired and dismantled is a real disciplining force on management. Even the PE firms that do not acquire a particular company affect how that company runs by existing as a possibility.

These arguments are not absurd. They have been made by serious people in serious venues, including by economists who have studied the data carefully and concluded that PE on net produces value. The book has spent two hundred pages making the opposite case. Honesty requires naming the strongest version of the case the book is arguing against.

The rebuttal is straightforward when the arguments are stated clearly.

The first defense, that distressed companies sometimes benefit from new capital, is true and uncontroversial. The book is not arguing against private capital investment in distressed companies. It is arguing against the leveraged buyout structure that loads acquisition debt onto the target company and extracts management fees regardless of operational performance. Those are different things. A PE firm that puts its own capital at risk and shares in upside and downside through a non-leveraged investment is doing something the book has no quarrel with.

The second defense, that some PE deals produce stable companies, is true. It is also a survivorship argument that ignores the base rate. The companies that emerge from PE ownership intact are visible. The companies that died on the way are also visible if you look. The pattern documented in this book, Toys"R"Us, Sears, Red Lobster, Caesars, Sports Authority, Brookstone, Payless, Steward Health Care, and dozens more, is not a collection of edge cases. It is the modal outcome for businesses acquired through leveraged buyouts of a certain size and structure. The successful exits are the exception, not the rule.

The third defense, that pension funds need PE returns, requires examining whether the returns are real. Multiple pension fund analyses, including CalPERS, have found that PE returns net of fees, properly adjusted for risk and illiquidity, do not significantly exceed public market alternatives. The promised premium is largely illusory once the full fee structure is accounted for. The pension funds that have been chasing PE returns have, on average, paid more in fees than they have earned in excess returns. The teachers and firefighters whose retirements depend on those returns are not being well served. They are being told they are.

The fourth defense, that the threat of acquisition disciplines management, is the most defensible. There is a real argument that public companies need external discipline. The form of that discipline matters. The PE model imposes discipline through extraction, which incentivizes the destruction documented in this book. Other forms of discipline, regulatory enforcement of fiduciary duties, stronger antitrust enforcement, greater shareholder rights, board reform, are available and produce better outcomes. The choice is not between PE-driven discipline and no discipline. It is between discipline that produces extraction and discipline that produces accountability. The book is arguing for the latter.

None of these rebuttals invalidates the strongest defense of PE. The strongest defense remains that, in some cases, PE adds value. The book's argument is that the cases where PE destroys value substantially outnumber the cases where it adds value, that the destruction is concentrated in industries that affect ordinary people's lives most directly, that the regulatory framework that would constrain the destruction has been systematically weakened over forty years, and that the time has come to restore it. That argument is not refuted by acknowledging that the opposing argument exists and has merit at the edges. The argument is strengthened by it.

The Algorithmic Layer

Before walking through the industries, one element appears in every chapter that follows and deserves treatment first. The financial mechanism documented in the preceding chapters is the why of modern extraction. This chapter is the how, the layer of software that makes extraction operable at the scale and velocity the industries demonstrate.

Everything in this book runs on software. The mechanisms documented in the previous chapters do not work without it. The leveraged buyout that destroys a restaurant chain depends on financial modeling that calculates the maximum extractable cash flow before bankruptcy. The dynamic pricing that charges different customers different prices for the same product depends on real-time analysis of behavioral signals. The customer service system that exhausts callers into giving up depends on machine learning that optimizes the exhaustion. The credit denial that the small business owner cannot get explained depends on an algorithm that produces decisions without explanations.

Software is the connective tissue of modern extraction. It enables operations that would be impossible at human scale. The industries documented in this book have been transformed not just by ownership changes but by the specific deployment of software that allows extraction to happen faster, more cheaply, and at higher resolution than any previous era of business permitted.

The pattern is consistent across industries. Identify a customer behavior that previously required human discretion. Replace the discretion with an algorithm. Optimize the algorithm against a metric that benefits the institution. Hide the optimization from customers. Charge the customers more. Repeat.

Dynamic Pricing as the Default

Dynamic pricing is the most legible example. Airlines, hotels, ride-sharing services, online retailers, and increasingly grocery chains and physical retailers, deploy systems that adjust prices in real time based on demand patterns, customer browsing history, device type, location, and signals of urgency. The price you see for an airline ticket is not the result of a market discovery process. It is the result of an algorithm that has determined how much it can extract from a customer fitting your profile in your specific moment of need.

The algorithms learn. The customer who searches for a flight three times in twenty minutes signals urgency. The price adjusts upward. The customer who searches from a hotel WiFi network in a major city signals business travel. The price adjusts upward. The customer searching for the last available seat on a route signals desperation. The price adjusts upward. None of this is illegal. None of it is even openly dishonest. It is the application of behavioral economics to pricing in a way that captures more value from the customers least equipped to detect what is happening.

Surveillance pricing extends the model further. Companies now have access to data about individual customers that was previously available only to retailers who knew them personally. The sophisticated retailer of 1985, the corner grocer who knew who could afford what, who was likely to grumble about prices, who paid in cash and who had a tab, was operating with a level of customer-specific information that the modern algorithmic pricing system replicates at scale. The difference is that the corner grocer used the information to maintain relationships. The algorithmic system uses it to extract more from the customers it can identify as least able to resist.

Algorithmic Decision-Making in Daily Life

Algorithmic decision-making in lending, insurance, healthcare, and criminal justice operates on the same principles. The credit score that determines whether you can get a mortgage. The algorithmic underwriting that determines your insurance premium. The utilization review system that determines whether your hospitalization gets covered. The risk assessment that determines your bail or sentencing. All of these are software systems that have replaced human discretion with computational decisions. The systems are sold as objective. They are not. They optimize against whatever metric the institution deploying them has chosen, which is rarely the metric the affected person would have chosen.

The asymmetry of information that these systems produce is the operational core of modern extraction. The institution knows everything about you. You know nothing about the institution. The credit denial does not come with reasons. The insurance premium does not come with itemized inputs. The healthcare denial does not come with the algorithm's training data. You are subject to a decision that you cannot evaluate, contest, or understand. The decision producer takes no responsibility for the decision because the algorithm produced it, and the algorithm is proprietary, and the proprietary nature is justified by competitive concerns that conveniently coincide with the institution's interest in opacity.

Customer Service as Engineered Frustration

Customer service algorithms operationalize a particular kind of contempt. The phone tree that routes you through eight menus before disconnecting you was not designed by accident. It was designed to minimize the cost of customer service while maintaining the appearance of providing it. The chatbot that cycles through the same three suggestions regardless of your problem is not malfunctioning. It is functioning exactly as designed. The metric the system optimizes is not customer satisfaction. It is contact resolution per cost, and the most efficient resolution is the one where the customer gives up before reaching a human.

Algorithmic auditing of these systems is largely absent. The systems produce decisions. The decisions affect millions of people. No one is responsible for whether the decisions are fair, accurate, or even consistent with the institution's stated policies. When auditors do get access, the results are damning. The nH Predict system that UnitedHealthcare uses for post-acute care decisions has been alleged in court filings to carry a 90 percent error rate. Credit scoring algorithms have been documented to discriminate by race, gender, and zip code in ways that violate the spirit if not the letter of fair lending laws. Dynamic pricing systems have been documented to charge higher prices in lower-income zip codes for identical products.

The Choice the Technology Reflects

The technology is not neutral. The technology has been built specifically to do what it does. The institutions deploying it have chosen to deploy it this way. The choices are documented. The harm is documented. The remedy is not to ban the technology. The remedy is to require accountability for what the technology does, which means transparency about what the systems optimize for, audit rights for the people affected, and legal liability for the harms the systems cause.

The technology that could be used to make products better, services more available, and decisions fairer is being used instead to extract value from customers who do not understand what is being done to them. The choice between the two paths is not technical. The same machine learning that powers a recommendation system that helps you find what you want can power a recommendation system that manipulates you into buying what the system was paid to surface. The same data infrastructure that could deliver personalized service can deliver personalized exploitation. The difference is what the system is optimizing for, and the system optimizes for whatever the institution deploying it has chosen.

When the institution is owned by a private equity firm with a five-year exit timeline, the metric the system optimizes for is short-term cash extraction. When the institution is owned by a family that plans to operate for generations, the metric is long-term customer retention. The technology is the same. The outcomes are different. The technology is not the variable. The ownership structure is.

This is why the algorithmic layer cannot be addressed independently of the financial layer. The algorithms reflect the priorities of the institutions that deploy them, and the institutions reflect the priorities of the people who own them. Reform requires addressing both. Better algorithms cannot fix worse ownership. Better ownership produces better algorithms because the underlying optimization changes.

Part II: Thirteen Industries in Decline

Airlines - From Glamour to Cattle Cars

Between 2008 and 2013, I flew Southwest Airlines almost every week. Renaissance festivals, if you can believe it. Ohio, Colorado, Arizona, New York, and dozens of other states. I was following the circuit, hauling costumes and gear to events where people spend their weekends pretending it's the 14th century. Southwest made that life possible. The fares were cheap enough that hopping a flight felt like a reasonable decision rather than a financial commitment. The open seating meant I could board, pick a spot near the front, stuff my bag in the overhead bin without anyone questioning its dimensions, and be reading before half the plane had sat down. No assigned seat fees. No carry-on extortion. No drama.

Now flying feels like paying premium prices to be processed through an industrial cattle operation designed by someone who actively hates customers. We shuffle through security theater, pack into seats designed for malnourished hobbits from the 1960s, and pay extra fees for privileges that used to be included in the ticket price. The magic died so gradually that we almost forgot it ever existed.

The numbers tell the story. In 1985, no major U.S. airline offered seats with less than 31 inches of legroom. Today, American, Delta, and United routinely cram passengers into 30-inch pitch configurations, with some budget carriers squeezing people into 28-inch spaces that would be illegal for transporting livestock. Seat width has shrunk from 18-19 inches in the 1980s to 17 inches today, while the average American has gained 15 pounds and grown taller.

But the real extraction happens in the fee structure. In 2024, airlines collected a record $148.4 billion in ancillary fees globally, representing nearly 15% of total airline revenue. Five airlines now earn more from fees than from ticket sales, with Frontier Airlines making 62% of its revenue from charges for seat selection, baggage, and overhead bin access.

This represents the complete financialization of human dignity. Airlines discovered they could advertise impossibly low base fares while extracting the real costs through dozens of mandatory add-ons. An $89 ticket becomes $280 after fees for checking a bag, selecting a seat that isn't in the bathroom, bringing a carry-on, getting something to eat, and accessing wifi that barely works. The practice is deliberately deceptive, designed to hook customers with bait-and-switch pricing that would be illegal in any other industry.

In 1978, before deregulation, a transcontinental flight cost about $1,400 in today's dollars. That sounds expensive until you consider what you got: real meals served on actual china, flight attendants who had four months of training instead of four weeks, seats with 34-35 inches of legroom, and service that treated passengers like valued customers instead of cargo that occasionally complains.

You could show up at the Pan Am terminal at JFK in 1970 and feel like the world was genuinely excited to take you somewhere. The Worldport, designed by Walther Prokosch and Tippetts-Abbett-McCarthy-Stratton, had a four-acre cantilevered roof that hovered out over the apron so passengers could walk to their plane without getting wet, the kind of detail an airline included when it wanted flying to feel like an event. They hired architects who built monuments because they wanted flying to feel like something worth doing. The counter agents knew the destinations they were selling. Ask someone at a Pan Am counter about Buenos Aires and you might get a ten-minute conversation. Ask the same question at an American Airlines kiosk today and you'll get a screen asking for your Advantage number.

Then deregulation happened in 1978, and everything went to hell in a handbasket with extra baggage fees.

Major airline consolidation sealed the deal. In 1985, ten major carriers controlled the domestic market. Today, four airlines control roughly 70% of all domestic capacity: American, Delta, United, and Southwest. Each merger reduced competition while increasing pricing power, creating regional monopolies that passengers can't avoid. The Department of Justice itself noted in 2013, when reviewing the American-US Airways merger, that industry consolidation had left fewer, more-similar airlines that found it easier to raise prices and impose new fees in lockstep. They approved the merger anyway.

Robert Crandall ran American Airlines from 1985 to 1998 and was sharp enough to see the future of aviation before anyone else did: the future was mathematical. Not engineering, not service, not hospitality. Math. He invented the AAdvantage frequent flyer program in 1981, pioneered the yield management system that repriced every seat on every flight dozens of times per day, and built the SABRE reservations system that American used as a competitive weapon against smaller rivals for two decades.

Crandall was legendarily precise about cost. The story that defines him best is small but perfect: he calculated that removing one olive from every salad served to passengers would save American Airlines $40,000 per year. Nobody would notice. The olive disappeared. That is the mind that built modern airline extraction, applying that same logic to everything from seat cushion thickness to the number of flight attendants per aircraft.

The four-carrier oligopoly didn't happen by accident. It was engineered through a series of mergers that regulators approved despite explicit warnings that consolidation would hurt consumers. Delta absorbed Northwest in 2008. United swallowed Continental in 2010. Southwest consumed AirTran in 2011. American merged with US Airways in 2013. Each deal came with promises of better service, lower fares, and expanded routes. Each deal delivered higher fees, fewer flights to smaller cities, and a narrowing of competitive options that left passengers with nowhere else to go.

The people who drove this consolidation weren't stupid. They understood precisely what fewer competitors meant for pricing power. Scott Kirby, who would later become United's CEO and collect $33.9 million in a single year, said at an industry conference in 2012 that as the industry consolidated, airlines would find it easier to coordinate on pricing. He wasn't describing a fear. He was describing a strategy.

Richard Anderson ran Delta from 2007 to 2016 and produced record profits by squeezing labor costs and consolidating routes. His successor Ed Bastian continued the profit extraction while adding a layer of premium segmentation. Delta divided its cabin into so many sub-categories that passengers needed a flowchart to understand what they'd purchased. Basic Economy meant no carry-on, no seat selection, no changes. Main Cabin meant all that plus the ability to board when your group was called. Comfort Plus meant a few extra inches of legroom at roughly twice the price. Premium Select, Delta One, First Class, Medallion status with its sub-tiers of Silver, Gold, Platinum, and Diamond. Every level existed to extract more money from the same seat while making passengers feel they were choosing rather than being squeezed.

The infamous incident where United security dragged Dr. David Dao off an oversold flight in 2017 wasn't an aberration. It was the logical conclusion of treating passengers like cargo that occasionally complains. The algorithm said the flight was oversold, crew scheduling demanded seats for deadheading employees, and corporate policy mandated passenger removal. That Dr. Dao was a paying customer with patients to see the next morning didn't register in the optimization equation.

Only after the video went viral, United's stock price tanked by $1.4 billion, and international media portrayed the airline as the face of American corporate brutality did the company discover empathy. The incident cost them hundreds of millions in market value, legal settlements, and lost business, proving that customer abuse eventually becomes expensive even for airlines with captive markets.

American's operational chaos during its years of financial stress produced its own catalogue of indignities. Flights canceled without explanation. Passengers stranded in airports for days while customer service lines stretched beyond the building. In 2022, American canceled thousands of flights during the summer travel peak because they had sold tickets without securing enough pilots to fly the routes. They knew about the shortage. They sold the tickets anyway and then blamed weather, air traffic control, and anything else that didn't implicate their own scheduling decisions.

A corporate culture so focused on cost extraction that basic maintenance was deferred, basic training was skipped, and basic human decency toward customers was optimized away. The airline that pioneered frequent flyer programs to create loyal customers spent the next decade systematically alienating them. By 2024, American ranked last among major carriers in customer satisfaction surveys for the third consecutive year. The response from leadership was to announce a renewed focus on the customer experience, which in airline terms means a press release rather than actual change.

But even Southwest couldn't resist the gravitational pull of extraction forever. The company that once prided itself on transparent pricing started adding fees in 2024, abandoning their iconic "Bags Fly Free" policy under investor pressure. The airline famous for reliable operations suffered a catastrophic system meltdown during the 2022 holidays that stranded hundreds of thousands of passengers and revealed that their technology infrastructure was held together with digital duct tape and executive delusion.

The Southwest meltdown wasn't just a technology failure. It was the predictable result of years of underinvestment in systems maintenance while extracting profits through share buybacks and executive compensation. From 2018 to 2021, Southwest reduced their technology workforce by 27% while overall employment declined by only 6%. They spent $8.5 billion on share buybacks and dividends while deferring critical infrastructure upgrades.

When Winter Storm Elliott hit in December 2022, Southwest's ancient crew scheduling system collapsed under stress that other airlines handled without major disruption. The airline couldn't locate pilots and flight attendants, couldn't track aircraft positions, and couldn't communicate with stranded passengers. Southwest canceled 16,900 flights over ten days, affecting nearly two million passengers during the peak holiday travel period. The Department of Transportation fined them a record $140 million.

Union leaders had warned for years that the technology systems were failing. The Southwest Airlines Pilots Association picketed the company in 2022 not for pay increases, but for basic technology upgrades to prevent exactly this kind of operational collapse. Management ignored the warnings because technology infrastructure doesn't show up in quarterly earnings reports until it fails catastrophically.

Elliott, run by billionaire Paul Singer, took a 16% stake in Southwest in 2024 when shares were trading around $30. Singer's firm is not known for patience or sentimentality. Elliott has forced changes at dozens of companies across multiple industries, and their playbook is consistent: accumulate a large stake, threaten a proxy fight, install friendly board members, demand operational changes that boost the stock price, then exit with their profits while the company deals with the consequences.

Southwest complied. In April 2025, the airline conducted its first ever mass layoffs, cutting around 1,750 employees, roughly 15% of its corporate workforce. Bags Fly Free became a slogan from a different era. Open seating, which Southwest had maintained as a genuine differentiator and customer benefit since 1971, disappeared. The airline that CEO Bob Jordan called "the most significant transformation in the company's history" became, in practice, a slightly worse version of every other domestic carrier, with lower fares replaced by fees that added up to the same thing.

Elliott's stock price target was achieved. Southwest shares rose more than 55% from their August 2024 lows.

By early 2026, with the transformation complete and profits briefly increased, Elliott began selling. They reduced their stake from 16% to 9% in early 2026, cashing in on the surge they'd engineered. Two Elliott-appointed directors resigned from the board. The activist investor that had forced the airline to gut its own identity quietly collected their profits and moved on to the next target.

Southwest stock went up. The airline that tens of millions of Americans had relied on as the humane, honest, budget-friendly option for decades became just another carrier charging for bags and fighting over armrests. Elliott made money. Paul Singer bought more art or whatever billionaires do after they've finished with a company. And the passengers who used to fly Southwest every week now have one fewer reason to think flying is anything but miserable.

The race to extract maximum revenue has systematically degraded working conditions for airline employees, creating a vicious cycle where overworked, underpaid staff deliver poor service to increasingly hostile customers. Flight attendants once earned middle-class wages with decent benefits and working conditions. Today, new flight attendants at major carriers start around $35,000 annually, barely above food stamp eligibility in many cities where airlines are based.

Scott Kirby, United's CEO, collected $33.9 million in compensation in 2024. His pay increased 83% that year. His flight attendants signed a contract that their union described as offering 40% in total economic improvements. Multiple flight attendants at United have publicly acknowledged needing second jobs to make ends meet. Some, according to industry reporting, have admitted to eating leftover passenger food on long-haul flights rather than buy their own meals.

Read that again. The CEO of a company with $57 billion in annual revenue made $34 million in a single year while his employees ate passengers' discarded dinner rolls.

Pilot wages tell an even more striking story. In 1978, a TWA captain earned about $85,000 annually, equivalent to $314,000 today. That salary supported a house in Newport Beach, a Porsche, and a personal aircraft at John Wayne Airport. Today, a first-year captain at a major airline earns around $200,000, representing a 35% decline in real wages despite requiring far more training and education than their 1970s predecessors.

Regional airline pilots face poverty-level wages that would be unacceptable for any other profession requiring equivalent training and responsibility. First officers at regional carriers often start below $40,000 annually while being responsible for multi-million-dollar aircraft and dozens of passenger lives. Many regional pilots qualify for food stamps and live in crew crashpads that resemble college dormitories.

The pilot shortage plaguing the industry isn't mysterious. Young people aren't willing to spend $200,000 on flight training to earn wages that barely cover student loan payments. Airlines created the shortage by systematically degrading compensation while increasing training requirements and work complexity.

Crandall's DINAMO yield management system, which he built in the 1980s, was genuinely elegant technology that helped American fill more seats and serve more passengers. Yield management meant that discount seats opened up on flights that would otherwise fly half-empty, making air travel accessible to people who couldn't have afforded it before. That technology had a service benefit and an extraction benefit at the same time. What airlines have done since is keep the extraction and eliminate the service.

The physical compression of airline seats represents extraction at its most literal. Airlines have systematically reduced seat pitch from 34-35 inches in the 1970s to 30-31 inches today, with budget carriers offering as little as 28 inches. They've shrunk seat width from 18-19 inches to 17 inches while Americans have grown larger and taller.

Modern airline seats are designed for able-bodied passengers up to 5'10" and under 180 pounds, reflecting body sizes from the early 1960s. Meanwhile, the average American male has gained 10% more weight since the 1970s introduction of the Boeing 747. Airlines have literally built their cabins for passengers who no longer exist.

The seat compression generates enormous revenue. Each inch of reduced pitch allows airlines to add another row of seats to most aircraft. On a Boeing 737 with 150 seats, reducing pitch from 32 to 30 inches enables adding 6-8 additional seats, generating $300,000-400,000 in additional annual revenue per aircraft.

In 2024, U.S. airlines collected $7.27 billion from checked baggage fees alone, with American, Delta, and United each surpassing $1 billion in baggage revenue. These fees generate nearly pure profit because baggage handling infrastructure already exists and marginal costs are minimal.

The Department of Transportation issued a rule in 2024 requiring pre-purchase disclosure of ancillary fees. Airlines immediately began exploring ways to redefine their fees to avoid the disclosure requirements. The extraction machine adapts.

The major U.S. carriers have created a system that treats customer satisfaction as an obstacle to profit maximization. They've discovered that customers will tolerate striking abuse when alternatives don't exist, and they've structured markets to eliminate meaningful alternatives through consolidation and regulatory capture. The four major carriers coordinate pricing so efficiently that the DOJ noted it in 2013 as a consequence of consolidation. Nothing has changed since except the fees have gotten higher.

Crandall himself, who built many of the extraction tools now running the industry, said in 2008 that the consequences of deregulation had been very adverse. "Our airlines, once world leaders, are now laggards in every category, including fleet age, service quality and international reputation." The man who removed the olive from the salad looked at what his inventions had wrought and found it wanting.

Real reform would require breaking up the oligopoly. Four carriers controlling 70% of domestic capacity cannot produce competitive pricing regardless of what any CEO says in a congressional hearing. It would require minimum seat standards, which the FAA has resisted for years under industry lobbying pressure. It would require making ancillary fees part of the advertised fare so that $89 tickets cost $89. The DOT's 2024 rule moved in that direction before industry lawyers began working on how to route around it.

Spirit Airlines died on May 2, 2026. Thirty-four years of yellow planes and stripped-down fares ended at three in the morning, when the last bailout gambit collapsed and the wind-down papers were filed. Seventeen thousand jobs gone. Tens of thousands of passengers woke up to canceled flights and worthless tickets. American, JetBlue,

Southwest, and United scrambled to rebook the stranded, then quickly added flights into the routes Spirit no longer flew. The big airlines had been waiting for this moment for years.

The Justice Department had blocked JetBlue's $3.8 billion offer for Spirit in 2024 on the theory that the merger would hurt budget-conscious consumers. By May 2026, the budget-conscious consumers had no Spirit to fly. They were free to fly American, Delta, United, or Southwest at whatever price the four-carrier oligopoly chose to charge them. The Trump administration had offered a $500 million bailout in exchange for what would have been up to a ninety-percent government stake. Spirit's bondholders rejected the deal, and within hours, the airline was gone. Spirit had not turned a profit since 2019. The mathematics had simply concluded.

The script went exactly as the consolidators had been writing it for forty years. Eliminate competitors. Capture pricing power. Wait for the discount carriers to fail under the cost structures the legacy carriers had successfully lobbied to make universal. The DOJ's 2024 attempt to preserve competition had been overtaken by economics. There was no Spirit to protect anymore. There was just American, Delta, United, and Southwest, dividing up what was left.

Restaurants - Gray Boxes Replace Character

For years, Panera Bread was my lunch. Every single day. I lived close enough that it became a ritual, walk in, get the soup and a sandwich, sit for a while, decompress in the middle of the workday. The soup was good. Real good. The bread was baked on-site and you could smell it when you walked through the door. It felt like a place that gave a damn about what it was serving.

Then the portions started shrinking. The menu shifted around in ways that felt random and joyless. The whole atmosphere changed, not dramatically, not all at once, but enough that it felt less like a lunch spot and more like a waiting room with food. I could have lived with all of that. What I couldn't live with was the soup.

One afternoon I watched a worker pull a plastic bag out of a box, drop it into a pot, and heat it. That was the soup. The broccoli cheddar that I'd been eating for years, that I'd assumed was made in that kitchen, it was a bag. A bag from a box from a warehouse somewhere that had nothing to do with bread or baking or anyone who cared about food. I paid my check, walked out, and never went back.

About a mile and a half from where I live, there used to be a Boston Market. And I mean a real one, whole turkeys, roast beef, actual rotisserie chickens turning in the window. You could smell the place from the parking lot. The sides were made there. The food had weight to it, the kind of weight that comes from something being cooked rather than reconstituted. I ate there regularly for years.

Then the same creeping rot set in. The food started arriving in bags. The store couldn't seem to open on time anymore because there wasn't enough staff to run the place. Some days you'd pull into the parking lot and the lights were off, no explanation, just closed. Then one day it was simply gone. Shuttered. The sign stayed up for a while, which felt like a small cruelty, the ghost of a restaurant still advertising itself to people who didn't know yet that it was dead.

Two restaurants. Years of loyalty. Both hollowed out and abandoned by the people who bought them for reasons that had nothing to do with food.

That's not bad luck. That's a business model.

Remember when restaurants had souls? When you could walk into a place and immediately know you weren't in Kansas anymore, or Cleveland, or any other interchangeable American strip mall? Those days feel as distant as rotary phones and reasonable airline legroom. We've traded neighborhood joints with personality for corporate gray boxes that serve reheated sadness with a side of algorithmic optimization.

The restaurant industry's descent into enshittification follows the same playbook we've seen everywhere else, but with a cruel twist: it destroyed the places where we gathered, celebrated, and created memories. Private equity didn't just ruin businesses. They erased the third spaces that made communities feel like home.

How Private Equity Guts Restaurants

The playbook starts with the leveraged buyout. When JAB acquired Panera for $7.5 billion, they didn't write a check for $7.5 billion. They put up roughly $2-3 billion in equity and borrowed the rest, using Panera's own assets as collateral. This immediately saddled the formerly debt-free company with massive interest payments that had to come from somewhere, the operations that once created value for customers.

Next comes the dividend recapitalization. Within months of acquisition, PE firms typically have their new subsidiary borrow additional money to pay special dividends back to the parent company. Sun Capital Partners perfected this technique across their restaurant portfolio, extracting dividends from Boston Market, Friendly's, and others while these companies struggled to maintain basic operations.

Then the sale-leaseback scheme. Companies sell their real estate to separate entities, often controlled by the same PE firm, then lease it back at inflated rates. This generates immediate cash while creating permanent rent obligations that drain the operating business for years.

Asset stripping comes next. Food distribution networks, recipes, brand licensing rights, customer databases, each sale generates cash while weakening the core business.

The final phase involves operational degradation designed to maximize short-term profits while destroying long-term value. This is where customers finally notice something's wrong, but by then the extraction is largely complete. The soup is already in bags. The whole turkeys are already gone. The staff has already been cut to the point where the place can't open on time. By the time you notice, the money is already out the door.

The Panera model

Panera Bread once marketed itself on a simple promise: fresh-baked bread, made in-store daily. The smell of rising dough greeted customers each morning. Bakers arrived before dawn, kneading and shaping loaves that would anchor sandwiches and comfort souls throughout the day. Then JAB Holding Company, a

Luxembourg-based investment firm, acquired Panera for $7.5 billion in July 2017.

JAB loaded the company with approximately $340 million in net debt as part of the deal. For a company that had been effectively debt-free, this represented a fundamental shift from growth investment to debt service. The bread wasn't the point anymore. The interest payments were.

What happened next became a masterclass in how to gut everything that made a restaurant special while keeping the marketing facade intact. JAB systematically replaced fresh dough operations with frozen, par-baked products. Panera's Fresh Dough Facilities had been the heart of their operation, centralized bakeries where skilled bakers mixed and shaped dough that was then delivered fresh to restaurants for final proofing and baking. In 2016, Panera operated 24 of these facilities across the country. By 2024, that number had been slashed as JAB replaced fresh dough with frozen, reheated substitutes.

One Panera baker described watching colleagues see their hours cut from full-time to just two to four hours per day, forcing many to quit. Cafes were remodeled with larger freezers to accommodate frozen products. The bakers who remained had been effectively demoted from craftspeople to heating technicians.

By April 2025, Panera announced plans to close all remaining nine Fresh Dough Facilities within two years, completing the transition to what they euphemistically called "on-demand baking." The name is a masterpiece of corporate euphemism. On-demand baking means a bag in a box in a walk-in freezer, heated to order. The demand is real. The baking is not.

The soups followed the same trajectory. The broccoli cheddar that customers had eaten for twenty years, that had been a genuine made-in-restaurant product, became a pre-portioned bag of product heated on demand. The mac and cheese: a bag. The chicken noodle: a bag. Customers noticed. Review sites filled with complaints about watery soups, half-empty bowls, and the specific hollow feeling of paying premium prices for something you could have heated at home yourself.

Panera's response to declining quality was to raise prices and reduce portions at the same time, a combination that requires some nerve to execute with a straight face. Customers who'd been eating there for years reported sandwiches with barely any meat, salads that barely filled the bowl, and soups that arrived lukewarm in cups smaller than the ones they remembered. On forums and social media, comparisons to hospital cafeteria food became common.

JAB didn't stop with Panera. The private equity giant controls Krispy Kreme (now publicly traded but majority JAB-owned), Peet's Coffee, Caribou Coffee, Einstein Bros. Bagels, Noah's New York Bagels, Manhattan Bagel, Bruegger's Bagels, and Pret A Manger. They specialize in acquiring businesses built on the promise of fresh, handmade food, then systematically industrializing them into hollow replicas of their former selves. The strategy is consistent because the goal is consistent. It's never been about the food.

Walk into a modern Panera and breathe deeply. You'll smell nothing. No yeast, no warmth, no life. Just the sterile air of a place optimized for efficiency over experience. The workers look as defeated as the bread tastes, because they know they're not bakers anymore, they're microwave operators in an elaborate theatrical production.

The irony cuts deep. Panera built its brand on being the anti-McDonald's, the place where food had integrity and preparation had soul. JAB turned it into McDonald's with better marketing and higher prices.

Boston Market: Financial Cannibalism

Boston Market tells an even grimmer tale. Once a legitimate rotisserie chicken concept with actual kitchens that roasted actual birds, it became a textbook example of how private equity can extract value while destroying everything that created it.

McDonald's bought Boston Market out of bankruptcy in 2000 for approximately $173 million, closed hundreds of underperforming stores, and ran it as a subsidiary for seven years without major changes. Then in August 2007, McDonald's sold Boston Market to Sun Capital Partners.

Sun Capital immediately implemented the standard playbook. They loaded Boston Market with debt, extracted immediate cash through dividend recapitalizations, and cut operational costs by eliminating skilled kitchen staff and replacing made-to-order preparation with reheating protocols.

Boston Market had built its brand on the theater of rotisserie cooking, whole chickens rotating visibly in front of customers, sides prepared fresh throughout the day, carving stations where skilled workers sliced meat to order. The whole turkey. The roast beef. The pot pie that had some heft to it. Sun Capital systematically eliminated these elements. The rotisserie chickens became sad, dried-out shadows spinning endlessly under lights that provided visual theater without actual freshness.

The staff evaporated. Not all at once, that would have been too obvious, but steadily, shift by shift, until locations couldn't consistently open on time because there weren't enough people to run them. Customers would arrive at the posted opening hour and find a dark restaurant with a handwritten note on the door. Then they'd try again a week later and find the same note. Then they'd arrive and find the sign still up but the restaurant permanently closed, no announcement, no explanation, just gone.

After 13 years, Sun Capital sold the struggling brand to Engage Brands in April 2020 at a fraction of the original asking price. The new ownership under Jignesh Pandya proved even more destructive. Pandya instructed employees not to pay suppliers unless they accepted discounts of 50-70%. When vendors refused, restaurants simply stopped carrying those products. US Foods sued for $11.3 million in unpaid bills, eventually winning a $15 million judgment in 2024. Pandya filed for personal bankruptcy in December 2023. The chain that started 2023 with about 300 locations had only 27 remaining by March 2024.

The Boston Market nearest to me didn't close dramatically. It just stopped opening reliably, then stopped opening at all, then one day the sign came down. The whole turkey was gone. The roast beef was gone. The smell from the parking lot was gone. What replaced it was nothing, an empty storefront, a ghost of a restaurant that had been good once, before the people who bought it figured out how to make more money killing it than running it.

The Applebee's Algorithm

Applebee's embodies the complete corporatization of casual dining. The transformation followed a careful sequence designed to maximize efficiency while minimizing customer awareness of the degradation, at least until the degradation became too obvious to miss.

First, centralizing food preparation in massive commissary kitchens operated by third-party contractors. Items that had once been prepared fresh, soups, sauces, marinades, side dishes, moved to industrial facilities where they could be manufactured at scale and distributed frozen.

Second, targeting the core menu items customers could see being prepared. The famous riblets became pre-cooked, pre-sauced products arriving in vacuum-sealed bags ready for reheating. The "grilled" chicken breast came pre-cooked with artificial grill marks, requiring only warming on a flattop.

The "Perfect Brownie" dessert became the perfect symbol of this transformation. It arrives frozen in individual portions. When ordered, servers place it in a microwave for exactly 45 seconds, add a scoop of ice cream, and present it as a freshly made dessert. The entire preparation process requires no skill, judgment, or culinary knowledge whatsoever. You could train a golden retriever to make it, assuming the retriever could work a microwave.

DineEquity executives didn't hide their strategy, they celebrated it in investor presentations. They boasted about "reducing complexity" in kitchens and "eliminating variables" in food preparation. What they meant was eliminating the human skill, judgment, and craft that once distinguished one restaurant from another. Variables, in this context, is another word for people who know what they're doing.

Former Applebee's cooks describe the psychological anguish of being reduced to microwave operators. One line cook who worked at an Applebee's in Phoenix for eight years watched the transformation firsthand: "I used to cook. I'd season the chicken, watch it on the grill, know when it was done by looking at it. Then they brought in these bags of pre-cooked stuff and told us to just heat it up. It wasn't cooking anymore. It was just following instructions like a robot."

Applebee's decline accelerated after 2016, when they closed over 100 restaurants in two years. The chain that had once felt like a neighborhood spot, louder than you'd like, sure, but warm and familiar, became a place people apologized for suggesting.

TGI Friday's: The Death of Flair

TGI Friday's pioneered the casual dining concept in 1965, creating the template for restaurants that felt like neighborhood bars where everyone could hang out. The original location in New York's Upper East Side became famous for its eclectic decor, creative bartenders, and servers with enough personality to make strangers feel like regulars. The flair wasn't just about juggling bottles, it represented a philosophy that restaurants should be fun, surprising, and human.

Private equity firm Sentinel Capital Partners acquired TGI Friday's in May 2014. Sentinel implemented the standard playbook: load the company with debt, extract immediate cash through dividends, cut operational costs to service debt payments.

The flair disappeared faster than you could say "loaded potato skins." The creative bartenders who had made each location unique got replaced with pour-count protocols and standardized drink recipes. Servers with personality got scripted interaction guidelines designed to maximize table turns and check averages. Point-of-sale systems tracked server performance metrics in real time. Managers received alerts when servers spent "too much" time at tables, when check averages fell below targets, or when alcohol sales lagged behind corporate projections.

One server who worked at a TGI Friday's in suburban Chicago during the transition remembered: "It used to be fun. We could talk to customers like human beings, recommend things we liked, have real conversations. After the buyout, everything became scripted. We had to hit certain talking points, suggest specific items, turn tables in specific time windows. It wasn't hospitality anymore. It was performance art, except nobody in the audience was entertained."

Walking into a modern TGI Friday's feels like visiting a museum exhibit titled "How Americans Used to Have Fun." The red-striped awnings and brass fixtures remain, but the energy is gone. In November 2024, TGI Friday's filed for bankruptcy and closed 86 locations in a single day. The chain that invented the American casual dining experience couldn't survive what private equity did to it. Sentinel Capital exited with their fees and returns. The bartenders who used to juggle bottles and know everyone's drink were left looking for work.

The broader casual dining category TGI Friday's helped invent has been in structural collapse for a decade. Denny's, Ruby Tuesday, Bob Evans, Friendly's, the mid-century idea of a restaurant that was nicer than fast food but approachable for a family on a regular Tuesday night is disappearing from the landscape. Private equity treated these chains as assets to strip rather than institutions to sustain, and the customers who depended on them as neighborhood gathering places have nowhere equivalent to go.

Red Lobster: When the Endless Shrimp Ends You

Red Lobster's collapse managed to be both tragic and farcical at the same time. The chain that had been a genuine treat for millions of middle-class families, the special occasion restaurant, the birthday dinner destination, the place where you got the Cheddar Bay Biscuits before you'd even ordered, got run into the ground by a combination of private equity extraction and a shrimp promotion that became a symbol of everything wrong with how these businesses get managed.

The ownership history alone tells the story. General Mills owned Red Lobster for decades, treating it as a steady cash generator within a diversified portfolio. Then in 2014, Darden Restaurants, feeling pressure from activist investors to unlock "shareholder value," sold Red Lobster to Golden Gate Capital for $2.1 billion. Golden Gate immediately executed the standard sale-leaseback scheme, selling Red Lobster's real estate to American Realty Capital Properties for $1.5 billion and then leasing it back, saddling the restaurant chain with rent obligations that would have been unthinkable the week before.

Thai Union, a Thai seafood conglomerate, became a major Red Lobster supplier and eventually took a significant ownership stake. This created a conflict of interest that would have been obvious to anyone who wasn't also trying to sell the chain as much shrimp as possible: Thai Union had every incentive to push shrimp-heavy promotions, regardless of whether Red Lobster could profit from them.

The endless shrimp promotion, which Red Lobster had run periodically for years as a limited-time offer, became a permanent menu item in 2023. The math didn't work.

Customers, correctly identifying a good deal when they saw one, ate far more shrimp than Red Lobster's pricing had accounted for. The chain lost $11 million in three months on the promotion alone. They had essentially sold dollar bills for fifty cents and then acted surprised when people kept buying.

Red Lobster filed for bankruptcy in May 2024. About 100 locations closed immediately. The Cheddar Bay Biscuits, warm, buttery, arriving before you'd even decided what to order, one of the genuinely beloved things about the place, became a punchline for how quickly a brand can collapse when the people running it care more about supplier relationships than customer ones.

What killed Red Lobster wasn't the shrimp. The shrimp was just the final absurdity in a long story of extraction. Golden Gate extracted cash through the sale-leaseback. Thai Union extracted favorable supplier terms. Activist investors extracted pressure for short-term returns. Nobody was asking what Red Lobster needed to be Red Lobster in twenty years. The question was always what could be pulled out of it today.

The families who'd been going there for birthdays for a generation didn't get a vote.

The Labor Behind the Bag

The workers who bore the cost of restaurant enshittification are rarely mentioned in financial press coverage of these transactions. They're treated as a line item, labor costs, to be optimized, rather than the actual humans who made the food and knew the customers by name.

When Applebee's replaced kitchen staff with bag-heating technicians, the experienced cooks who'd spent years developing skills in that kitchen didn't get transferred to better jobs. They got their hours cut and their roles redefined until most of them left. The institutional knowledge of a kitchen, how this particular grill runs hot, how to adjust seasoning for altitude, how to read the flow of a Friday night service, is irreplaceable and uncompensated when it walks out the door.

Restaurant work was never glamorous. But it used to have ladders. A dishwasher could become a prep cook could become a line cook could become a sous chef. A server could become a bartender could become a floor manager. These weren't paths to wealth, but they were genuine careers with skill accumulation and wage progression. Private equity's answer to kitchen complexity was to eliminate the complexity, which also eliminated the careers.

The Panera baker who went from four months of on-the-job training to two hours of shift work per day, heating frozen product, didn't just lose income. She lost a trade. The Boston Market carver who knew exactly how to portion a whole turkey for maximum yield and minimum waste, that person's skill became irrelevant the day the whole turkeys stopped coming in. Ghost kitchens hire workers at minimum wage with zero training requirements, because the job requires none. That's efficient for the spreadsheet. It's a catastrophe for the people.

Between 2020 and 2023, restaurant employment remained persistently below pre-pandemic levels not because people stopped wanting to work in restaurants, but because restaurants stopped being places where people wanted to work. The combination of low pay, reduced hours, and jobs stripped of any meaningful skill content made the industry less attractive than the warehouses and delivery companies competing for the same workers.

The irony is that the staffing crisis, the empty shifts, the locations that couldn't open on time, the "we're short-staffed" signs that became permanent fixtures, was a direct consequence of the choices that preceded it. Cut the staff, cut the hours, eliminate the skilled positions, hollow out the training, pay as little as possible. Then act surprised when nobody wants to work there.

Ghost Kitchens: Pure Extraction

The latest evolution might be the most dystopian yet: ghost kitchens that exist only in delivery apps, serving food with no physical location that customers can visit. These operations represent the complete separation of food from place, community from commerce, and human connection from dining.

A single ghost kitchen facility might operate as "Tony's Italian," "Seoul Kitchen," "Burger Palace," "Taco Express," and "Mama's Home Cooking" at the same time, using the same base ingredients, shared kitchen equipment, and identical preparation methods to create the illusion of choice and variety.

CloudKitchens, backed by former Uber CEO Travis Kalanick, represents this model taken to its logical extreme. The company leases warehouse space, divides it into kitchen pods, and rents those pods to operators who can run multiple virtual restaurant brands at the same time. Customers ordering from "Mama Rosa's Authentic Italian" receive food prepared in an industrial warehouse by workers following standardized procedures using ingredients that may bear no resemblance to Italian cuisine. The "family recipes" come from corporate food laboratories. The "local favorites" operate out of kitchens that serve dozens of ZIP codes at the same time.

Ghost kitchens eliminate the community functions that restaurants traditionally served. They provide no gathering places, no local character, no neighborhood employment of the kind that pays people to learn a trade. They provide a box of food dropped on your porch by a gig worker who gets paid by the delivery and has no stake in whether you enjoyed what was inside.

The delivery apps that made ghost kitchens viable are themselves extraction layers stacked on top of the restaurant business. DoorDash, Uber Eats, and Grubhub typically charge restaurants 15-30% commission on every order, leaving restaurants that already operate on thin margins with almost nothing. Many restaurants have calculated that delivery orders actively lose them money when commissions, packaging, and the labor of preparation are factored in. They accept delivery orders anyway because the alternative is invisibility, if you're not on the apps, a significant portion of potential customers can't find you.

The restaurant, at its best, was a third place. Not home, not work, but somewhere between the two where you could be among people without obligations. Ghost kitchens have no place. They have only logistics. You don't eat at a ghost kitchen. You receive a delivery from one, alone, in your home, which was always the point.

The Counter-Examples

Not every restaurant chain succumbed. The survivors offer essential lessons about what protects a business from being dismantled for value.

In-N-Out Burger remains family-owned. Current owner Lynsi Snyder has stated she could "never" see a time when she would franchise or go public. "The only reason you would do that is for the money and I wouldn't do it." Private family ownership enables long-term thinking that public companies can't match. In-N-Out pays starting wages of $19-22 per hour in most markets, well above industry standards. Store managers can make six-figure salaries, with the average manager having worked for the company over fourteen years.

In-N-Out sources never-frozen beef, cuts fries fresh from whole potatoes, and bakes buns daily using slow-rising dough. These practices cost more than industrial alternatives but create food quality that generates customer loyalty that weathers competitive pressure. You can't extract your way to a line out the door.

Trader Joe's, where I spent twenty years managing technology, offers another model. The stores are small by design. The private label products are developed with genuine care. The employees are paid well enough that turnover stays low and institutional knowledge accumulates. Customers become regulars because the experience is consistent and the people behind the counter know what they're selling. None of this is an accident. It's the consequence of an ownership structure that rewards long-term thinking over quarterly extraction.

The difference isn't secret. It's not exotic management philosophy or proprietary technology. It's simply who owns the business and what they're optimizing for. A family that plans to own a restaurant chain for fifty years makes different choices about ingredient sourcing, staff pay, and kitchen equipment than a private equity firm that plans to sell in five. Same economy. Same customers. Same supply chain. Completely different answers to the question of what the business is for.

Shake Shack built a loyal following by treating its burgers as food rather than a delivery mechanism for margin extraction. Chick-fil-A has maintained quality and service standards through a franchisee model that selects operators for long-term commitment rather than capital availability. Both companies operate in the same fast-food environment that produced the Applebee's algorithm. Neither looks like Applebee's.

The places that survived did so by remembering that restaurants serve people. Not shareholders. Not debt holders. Not activist investors who will be gone in eighteen months with their profits and no forwarding address. People who are hungry and want something good to eat in a place that feels like it was designed for humans.

Walking through any American suburb today, you can see the future that awaits restaurants that choose extraction over experience. Empty strip malls house the ghosts of chains that optimized themselves out of existence. Dead parking lots mark the spots where communities once gathered to share meals and create memories. Gray boxes sit vacant, waiting for the next corporate concept that promises efficiency over soul.

Boston Market was the first restaurant I ate at after moving to Florida. It was fantastic. Real food, not the kind that arrives in a bag. Panera Bread was the same era for me. I brought clients there because the food was good and the wi-fi was unlimited and they let you sit as long as you needed. I worked there for hours at a stretch when I needed to get out of the office. Both of those places felt like somewhere. Not a warehouse for eating. Somewhere.

Panera soup, for years, wasn't memorable food. It wasn't exceptional. But it was made there, by people who worked there, and when you walked in the bread smell hit you and the place felt like something. That's gone. What replaced it is a bag, heated to temperature, served in a smaller cup than the one you remember, at a higher price than the one you paid.

The Boston Market that used to smell like roasting turkey from the parking lot is now a vacant storefront with a faded sign someone hasn't gotten around to removing. The people who worked there, who knew how to carve a whole bird properly, are somewhere else now, doing something that isn't that.

Empty strip malls tell one story. The line out the door at In-N-Out tells another. Same economy, same customers, same technology available to both. The difference is what happens when the people signing the checks plan to stick around long enough to face the consequences of their decisions.

Department Stores - Palaces to Warehouses

My boss at Trader Joe's was John Shields, the CEO who grew the company from 27 stores to 174 and took sales from $132 million to over $2 billion during his tenure from 1988 to 2001. Before Trader Joe's, Shields had spent twenty years at Macy's California, eventually becoming Senior Vice President of Operations, and it showed. He ran things the way Macy's had been run when Macy's was genuinely great, with accountability at every level, with people who owned their areas rather than watching over them, and with a management philosophy that started by listening instead of dictating.

Shields used to walk into stores and ask employees one question: "What are we doing at the office to screw you up?" He'd fill notebooks with the answers. That philosophy, that corporate's job was to remove obstacles for the people doing the actual work, was baked into Macy's California when it was a great department store, and Shields brought it to Trader Joe's and made it great too. The connection between those two organizations, separated by decades, is one of the clearest examples I've seen of what good retail leadership looks like.

I watched what happened to Macy's after that era ended. It's a thin shell of itself now. Not a failure, it still exists, still operates, but diminished in ways that are hard to fully articulate unless you remember what it was. I watched the same thing happen to Sears, which is just tragic, and to JCPenney, which I used to shop at regularly. Good furniture. Decent prices. A store that felt like it was staffed by people who knew what they were selling.

All three are gone in different ways. Sears is dead. JCPenney is a ghost. Macy's is trying to remember what it was and finding the memory harder to access than expected.

There was a time when department stores were temples of possibility. You didn't just shop at Macy's or Marshall Field's, you made a pilgrimage. The escalators gleamed, the floors sparkled, and salespeople who knew your name guided you through wonderlands of carefully curated merchandise. These weren't just retail spaces; they were community anchors where families spent Saturday afternoons, where teenagers got their first jobs, where Christmas meant something magical.

Now they're mostly graveyards. Empty anchor stores haunt dead malls like monuments to a civilization that forgot what made shopping special. The survivors limp along as glorified warehouses, their once-proud sales floors converted into mazes of clearance racks watched over by skeleton crews who couldn't tell you where the bathroom is, let alone help you find the perfect dress for your daughter's wedding.

The department store apocalypse didn't happen overnight. It followed the same extraction playbook that's hollowed out every other industry in America, but with visible brutality. When private equity firms and corporate raiders got their hands on these retail giants, they didn't just destroy businesses, they demolished the physical spaces where communities gathered, shopped, and dreamed.

The Sears Autopsy

Sears once stood as America's everything store. For over a century, it equipped pioneers, housed suburbanites, and clothed generations of American families. The Sears catalog brought the world to rural doorsteps. The Sears Tower pierced the Chicago skyline as a monument to retail dominance. The company that had survived the Great Depression, two world wars, and the rise of Walmart seemed indestructible.

Then came Eddie Lampert.

Lampert's ESL Investments acquired Sears in 2005 through a complex merger with Kmart that valued the combined entity at $11 billion. Wall Street hailed the deal as visionary, a hedge fund genius who would revolutionize retail through balance-sheet wizardry. What happened was a masterclass in how to strip-mine a century-old institution while maintaining the pretense of trying to save it.

Lampert loaded Sears with debt from the acquisition, immediately diverting cash flow from operations to debt service. He sold valuable real estate assets to separate entities he controlled, forcing Sears to pay rent on properties it had previously owned outright. He spun off profitable divisions like Lands' End and Craftsman tools, extracting immediate cash while weakening the core business.

The real estate scheme was elegant in its cruelty. Lampert created Seritage Growth Properties, a real estate investment trust, and had Sears sell 235 of its most valuable properties to Seritage for $2.7 billion in July 2015. Sears then leased these same properties back from Seritage at above-market rents, creating permanent obligations that drained cash from operations while generating profits for Lampert's other investments.

When Sears struggled to pay these inflated rents, Lampert graciously allowed the company to pay with additional real estate instead of cash. A death spiral where Sears gave away its most valuable assets to pay rent on properties it had already given away. By the time this machine was done, there was nothing left to give.

Meanwhile, Lampert reorganized Sears into dozens of competing internal business units, each responsible for its own profitability. The idea, borrowed from Ayn Rand's objectivist philosophy, which Lampert had publicly praised, was that internal competition would produce efficiency. What it produced was a company where different divisions refused to cooperate, share resources, or support each other, because helping another division didn't improve your own unit's numbers.

The appliance department wouldn't share floor space with the clothing department. The tool section wouldn't cross-promote with the automotive center. Salespeople had no incentive to walk a customer to a different department because that customer's purchase would show up in someone else's metrics. Ayn Rand's philosophy, applied to retail, produced a store where nobody helped anybody with anything, which turns out to be a poor customer experience.

I shopped at all of them. I do not go inside department stores anymore. I get most of my shopping delivered from Walmart. The few times I have walked into a department store in recent years it feels unclean. The shelves are a mess. Instead of quality merchandise there is cheap product, most of it made in China, stacked in no particular order by people who do not know what they are selling. The staff that used to know the products is gone. What replaced them is not staff. It is a headcount.

The Sears that generations of Americans had relied on to buy their refrigerators, their Craftsman tools, their back-to-school clothes and their tires, that Sears was staffed by people who knew those products, who could troubleshoot a washing machine question or explain the difference between socket sets. That institutional knowledge doesn't survive when you fire the experienced staff and replace them with part-timers who are never there long enough to learn anything. It doesn't survive when departments are competitors rather than colleagues. It evaporates, and once it's gone there's no bringing it back.

The communities hit hardest were the ones where Sears was the only major retailer within reasonable distance, smaller cities, rural areas, the kinds of places that had watched Walmart arrive and the local hardware store close, and were now watching Sears close too. When a Sears shut down in a mid-sized Midwestern city, it didn't just eliminate shopping options. It eliminated jobs that paid living wages, anchor retail that kept adjacent businesses viable, and a gathering point that had served those communities for decades. The ripple effects in employment, commercial real estate values, and local tax bases outlasted the store's closure by years.

Sears eliminated over 250,000 jobs between 2005 and 2018. Entire communities lost their anchor retailers, transforming vibrant shopping centers into ghost towns. The company that had once employed skilled mechanics, knowledgeable appliance salespeople, and experienced tool specialists replaced them with part-time workers following computer scripts.

One appliance department employee who worked at a Sears in suburban Detroit for 22 years before the store closed in 2017: "People used to come to me because they knew I understood washers and dryers. I could explain the difference between models, help them pick the right size, arrange delivery and installation. By the end, they just wanted us to point people to the website. What's the point of coming to a store if nobody knows anything?"

The final insult came in 2018 when Lampert engineered Sears' bankruptcy sale to his own hedge fund for $5.2 billion. He bought the carcass of the company he had systematically destroyed, keeping a handful of stores operating while liquidating the rest. The man who had spent thirteen years extracting value from Sears then purchased its remains at a discount. It is among the most breathtaking conflicts of interest in American retail history, and it was entirely legal.

JCPenney: Death by Turnaround

JCPenney's destruction followed a different path but reached the same destination. Unlike Sears' slow-motion asset stripping, JCPenney died from a series of well-intentioned but catastrophically executed turnaround attempts that ignored everything customers valued about the chain.

I used to buy furniture there. Good furniture at honest prices. The store felt competent, staffed adequately, stocked properly, organized in a way that made sense. You could find what you were looking for, and usually there was someone nearby who could help if you couldn't. That basic retail competence sounds like a low bar, but it turns out to be rarer than you'd think and harder to maintain than anyone admits.

JCPenney had operated for over a century on a straightforward proposition: honest goods at fair prices, no tricks. James Cash Penney, who founded the company in 1902, called his first stores "The Golden Rule" stores, and the name was meant literally. The idea was that you treated customers the way you'd want to be treated yourself, clear prices, decent quality, no bait-and-switch.

That philosophy scaled surprisingly well. By the 1970s, JCPenney was one of the largest retailers in the country, anchoring malls from coast to coast and serving the working and middle classes who needed good clothes, reliable appliances, and decent furniture at prices they could pay.

The coupon circulars and sale events that later CEOs would try to eliminate weren't a cynical manipulation of customers. They were the continuation of that Golden Rule philosophy, here is how we can save you money, here is when to come in for the best prices, we are on your side in figuring out how to make your budget stretch. Customers who received the Sunday circular and planned their shopping around it weren't being tricked. They were being served by a retailer that had structured its promotions around their needs rather than its own convenience.

The most spectacular failure belonged to Ron Johnson, the former Apple retail executive who became CEO in 2011 with a mandate to transform JCPenney into an upscale lifestyle brand. Johnson's vision seemed logical on paper: eliminate the constant sales and coupons that trained customers to wait for discounts, create shops-within-shops featuring trendy brands, and modernize the shopping experience for younger customers.

The execution was breathtakingly arrogant. Johnson eliminated JCPenney's famous sales events without understanding that these weren't just pricing strategies, they were social rituals that brought families to the store. He removed clearance racks that budget-conscious customers relied on. He redesigned stores to appeal to affluent shoppers while alienating the working-class customers who had kept JCPenney profitable for decades.

Johnson never tested any of his ideas in a single store before rolling them out chainwide. When asked why not, he reportedly said that Apple didn't test. Apple also didn't have a hundred-year relationship with middle-America customers who came for the coupon book. The two situations had practically nothing in common, and the difference cost JCPenney $4.3 billion in revenue during Johnson's 17-month tenure.

The company laid off 43,000 employees and closed 33 stores. Customer traffic declined by 25% as longtime shoppers abandoned a chain that no longer seemed to want their business. By the time JCPenney fired Johnson and tried to restore the coupons and sales, the customers had found other places to shop and largely stayed there.

The COVID-19 pandemic provided the final push into bankruptcy in 2020. Simon Property Group and Brookfield Asset Management acquired the company for $1.75 billion, but the JCPenney that emerged bore little resemblance to the middle-America department store that had once anchored shopping malls across the country. The furniture sections, actual furniture, the kind you could sit on and decide about before buying, are largely gone. What remains is a smaller, less stocked, less staffed version of a store that used to be genuinely useful. James Cash Penney's Golden Rule stores became something he wouldn't recognize, run by people who had never heard of him and wouldn't have cared if they had.

Macy's: The Slow Bleed

Macy's presents the most painful case to watch, because I knew what it was before. John Shields spent twenty years there learning how retail was supposed to work, how accountability flowed from the people closest to the customer outward, not from corporate headquarters downward. How a well-run department meant a manager who owned that space, knew every product in it, and answered for the experience customers had there.

That operating philosophy built Macy's California into something worth working at and worth shopping at. Shields carried it to Trader Joe's and made that company into what it became. The tragedy is that somewhere between when Shields left in 1978 and what Macy's is now, that accountability culture got replaced by a balance-sheet logic that runs in exactly the opposite direction.

The decline began in earnest with the 2005 acquisition of May Department Stores for $11 billion. The merger eliminated beloved regional brands like Marshall Field's in Chicago, Foley's in Texas, and Hecht's in the mid-Atlantic, converting them all to Macy's stores. Customers who had shopped at Marshall Field's for generations, some of whose families had shopped there for generations, found themselves in Macy's stores that felt generic and impersonal. The local identity was gone. What replaced it was national brand homogeneity.

Chicago was particularly furious. Marshall Field's had been a civic institution since 1852. Its flagship on State Street was an architectural landmark with a Tiffany mosaic ceiling under a 40-foot dome. The clock on the corner was a meeting point for generations of Chicagoans. When Macy's converted it and removed the Marshall Field's name, the city held genuine public protests. Macy's converted the store anyway. You don't slow down a balance sheet for a Tiffany ceiling.

The cost-cutting that followed revealed management's fundamental misunderstanding of department store economics. Macy's eliminated commissioned sales positions, believing that hourly workers could provide the same level of service at lower cost. They reduced staffing levels until customers routinely waited twenty minutes for assistance. They cut inventory investment, ensuring that popular items were frequently out of stock. Each cut was justifiable in isolation. Together they destroyed the experience.

The real estate monetization accelerated the decline. Macy's sold its downtown flagship stores in major cities, often leasing back portions while converting the rest to office or residential use. These flagship closures weren't just real estate transactions, they were cultural amputations.

In late 2024, an internal accounting fraud came to light: a single Macy's employee had concealed approximately $154 million in delivery expenses over several years. The scandal revealed something the financial cuts had already suggested, that when you strip accountability from an organization at every level, you also strip the oversight systems that catch problems before they become disasters. The same culture that eliminated the commissioned salesperson who knew the cosmetics inventory cold also eliminated the redundant checks and cross-departmental communication that would have flagged a $154 million discrepancy earlier.

John Shields spent twenty years at a company that filled notebooks asking what they were doing wrong. The Macy's that emerged from two decades of cost-cutting and store closings apparently didn't know a $154 million problem was accumulating in its own books.

The current CEO, Tony Spring, is trying to reverse the decline with a program called "Bold New Chapter," a name that should make any skeptic reach for their wallet. The strategy involves prioritizing 125 stores for investment while allowing the rest of the fleet to wither. Higher staffing. Better merchandise. Faster inventory turnover. These are, notably, the exact things that a well-run department store had always done. The "Bold New Chapter" is a plan to return to basics that Macy's abandoned in pursuit of cost-cutting over two decades. Whether it works depends on whether the customer memory is long enough to give them another chance, and whether Wall Street will tolerate the investment required to do retail properly.

The answer from Wall Street, historically, has been no. Which is why Nordstrom went private.

The Death Spiral Mechanics

The destruction of American department stores followed a predictable pattern that repeated across every major chain.

Real estate extraction trumped customer experience. Department stores traditionally occupied prime real estate in city centers and suburban malls. This real estate became more valuable than the retail operations it housed, creating irresistible opportunities for sale-leasebacks and asset stripping. The sale-leaseback strategy generated immediate cash for investors while creating permanent rent obligations that constrained future operations. Once you've sold your building and started paying rent on it, every subsequent financial squeeze means cutting the store, not the rent. The building's new owners collect regardless of whether the retailer inside can pay its other bills.

The inventory death spiral destroyed browsing experiences. Department stores required massive inventory investments to create the sense of discovery that differentiated them from specialty retailers. Financial pressure forced inventory reductions that destroyed that browsing experience. Stores that had once been treasure troves became picked-over clearance centers. Customers stopped coming in to browse because there was nothing worth browsing. Less traffic meant less justification for inventory investment. Less inventory meant fewer customers. The spiral had one direction.

This is the mechanism that confounds people who say "Amazon killed department stores." Amazon didn't cause JCPenney to cut its inventory. JCPenney's debt load caused JCPenney to cut its inventory. Amazon then offered a more convenient shopping experience to customers who were already disappointed by JCPenney's empty shelves. The sequence matters. You can't blame the competition for winning a race that you deliberately ran backward.

Service elimination proved a false economy. Commissioned salespeople had incentives to learn about products, build customer relationships, and generate higher transaction values through knowledgeable recommendations. Hourly workers following computer scripts couldn't provide the same value. They couldn't justify the premium prices that department stores needed to cover their high overhead costs. The cosmetics counter that used to employ someone who knew your skin type and remembered what you'd bought last time became a self-service display with a bored minimum-wage worker nearby whose job was to restock, not advise.

When you eliminate the expertise that justified the price, you also eliminate the reason to shop there rather than online. Department stores made the case for their own irrelevance with every service cut, every staffing reduction, every commission structure they converted to hourly. They spent a decade answering the question "why shop here instead of Amazon?" by removing every honest answer they had.

Technology as the Wrong Answer

Department stores responded to the Amazon threat with technology investments that mostly made things worse. Self-checkout kiosks replaced cashiers who knew the merchandise. Mobile apps replaced salespeople who knew the floor. Endless aisle ordering systems replaced buyers who knew what customers in that specific community wanted.

The technology wasn't wrong in principle. The question was what problem it was solving. The right problem was: how do we use technology to help our salespeople serve customers better? The problem most department stores solved was: how do we use technology to justify cutting more salespeople?

Macy's invested heavily in its website and mobile app while at the same time cutting floor staff. The result was a store where you could order online and pick up in store, but once you were in the store, nobody could help you find anything, there wasn't enough stock on the floor to browse effectively, and the experience of shopping there in person had deteriorated to the point where picking up your online order and leaving seemed like the best option. The technology investment validated its own premise: if the in-store experience is bad enough, people will shift to online shopping, which proves you needed to invest in digital rather than stores. The circular logic is complete.

The department stores that deployed technology well used it to augment rather than replace human expertise. Nordstrom's salespeople use inventory systems that let them check stock across all locations, arrange ship-from-store for items not available locally, and maintain customer preference records that make relationships continuous rather than transactional. The technology extends the salesperson's capability rather than replacing them. The difference in how it feels to shop there is not subtle.

Counter-Examples

Not every department store chain succumbed. Nordstrom's resistance to enshittification stems from its continued family influence and cultural commitment to customer service excellence. While the company went public in 1971, the Nordstrom family maintained significant ownership and operational influence across generations. In 2024, they took the company private again in a $6.25 billion deal, explicitly to escape the short-term pressure of public markets. The family decided they'd rather own the whole thing than keep explaining to quarterly earnings calls why they were investing in salespeople and inventory.

Nordstrom's service culture requires continuous investment in employee training, inventory selection, and store experience that publicly traded competitors struggle to justify to analysts. Salespeople receive extensive product education. Return policies favor customer satisfaction over loss prevention. The famous story of a Nordstrom employee accepting a tire return, despite Nordstrom not selling tires, is probably apocryphal, but the fact that it circulates at all says something real about what the company's values are.

The contrast with Sears is direct and instructive. Lampert's internal competition structure pitted departments against each other and eliminated any reason for cooperation. Nordstrom's structure aligns everyone toward the same outcome: a customer who leaves satisfied and comes back. One system produces a store where nobody helps anybody. The other produces a store where helping is the job. The accountability culture John Shields learned at Macy's California and brought to Trader Joe's is recognizable in how Nordstrom operates. It's also recognizable in its complete absence from everything Sears became under Lampert.

Costco offers a different model that solves the same problem. Rather than competing with traditional department stores on selection and service, Costco built a warehouse membership model that aligned its incentives with customers in a fundamentally different way. The membership fee means Costco makes its money before you buy anything. That removes the pressure to sell you things you don't want and creates the unusual incentive of making sure what they stock is worth buying. Costco's buyers are relentless about quality because their customers are paying for the promise that Costco has already done the work of sorting good from bad.

Costco pays its employees wages that produce genuine careers rather than temporary jobs. The turnover rate at Costco is a fraction of the retail industry average, which means the person at the membership desk has likely been there for years and knows the store cold. That institutional knowledge, knowing where everything is, knowing what's seasonal, knowing which items are genuinely good versus which are just prominently displayed, is the thing that the cost-cutting playbook systematically destroys everywhere else and that Costco systematically preserves.

What Dies When Department Stores Die

The destruction of American department stores represents more than retail market evolution. It's the elimination of cultural institutions that had served multiple community functions for over a century.

Department stores had pioneered retail as entertainment. The elaborate window displays at Christmas, the fashion shows that introduced new seasons, the personal shopping services that made ordinary customers feel special, these weren't just marketing gimmicks. They were cultural productions that made shopping a social activity rather than a transaction. Lord & Taylor's Fifth Avenue windows New York newspapers reviewed them the way they reviewed theater productions. Macy's Thanksgiving Day Parade was a national television event that started as a marketing promotion and became a cultural institution that outlasted any particular product it ever advertised.

The seasonal transformations marked community calendars. Back-to-school shopping meant family expeditions where you outfitted three kids in one trip and the salespeople helped track what went in which bag. Prom dress selection involved mothers and daughters spending entire afternoons trying on gowns, with someone on the floor who knew the stock and could suggest what they hadn't thought to look for. Christmas shopping meant wandering through decorated floors while holiday music played overhead and the windows outside told stories. Online retail can ship you a dress in two days. It cannot do any of the rest of that.

The bridal registry that Macy's or JCPenney maintained for a couple in 1985 was more than a shopping convenience. It was a community coordination system, three hundred people, one couple's household, handled by staff who knew the inventory and could talk guests through options over the phone. The couples who built households from those registries are in their sixties now. Their children are getting married by posting a link to a website. Something was lost in that transition, and it wasn't just inefficiency.

Department stores provided structured career advancement for workers without college degrees.

Salespeople could advance to department managers, then store managers, then regional leadership based on performance and customer relationships rather than educational credentials. The cosmetics counter career, the housewares buyer who started as a stock clerk, the store manager who had walked every department for twenty years, these trajectories existed at scale. When department stores replaced commissioned salespeople with hourly workers, they eliminated one of the few remaining industries where interpersonal skills and product knowledge could generate middle-class incomes without a four-year degree.

The closure of downtown department stores in smaller cities triggered the abandonment of entire commercial districts. When the anchor store closes, foot traffic disappears. Other businesses become economically unviable. Commercial real estate values collapse. The tax base erodes. Cities that had maintained vibrant downtowns anchored by a Sears or a JCPenney watched those downtowns hollow out over the decade following the store's closure, a slow-motion disaster that showed up in municipal budgets and local employment figures long after anyone was paying attention to the retail story.

Amazon and other online retailers succeeded by focusing on efficiency, selection, and convenience, the aspects of retail that could be digitized. But they couldn't replicate the social, cultural, and employment functions that department stores had provided for over a century. Algorithms can suggest products based on purchase history, but they can't replicate the serendipity of finding unexpected items while browsing through curated displays, or the experience of having someone help you dress well for an occasion you'd described to them in a dressing room while they pulled options from the floor.

Walking through another dead mall today, past the empty anchor stores and boarded-up shop fronts, you can still feel the ghost of what American retail used to be. The echoes of families browsing together on Saturday afternoons. The memory of a salesperson who remembered what you bought last time and asked how it worked out.

John Shields asked employees what the office was doing to screw them up. That question implies that the people in the store matter, that their obstacles matter, that the goal is to make the work go well rather than to extract maximum value from a captive workforce before moving on. The department stores that forgot that question, or never asked it in the first place, are the ones we're walking through empty now.

The grand escalators have stopped. The Christmas displays are memories. But the question those empty anchor stores pose isn't whether department stores can survive. Nordstrom answers that daily. The question is whether we'll keep pretending their destruction was inevitable when the evidence says it wasn't.

Automotive - Engineering Pride to Planned Obsolescence

I drive a Kia Soul. Bought it because it was reasonably priced, does exactly what a car is supposed to do, and doesn't require a monthly subscription to unlock the heated seats. The heating elements are in the seat. The heat works. Nobody charges me extra for it. This should not be a radical position in 2026, but here we are.

Every time someone at a dinner party starts explaining why I should get a Tesla, I ask one question: what happens when the battery dies out of warranty? The answer, depending on the model, is somewhere between $10,000 and $22,000. For a battery. In a car you already own. A car that worked fine yesterday and will cost you more to fix than some people pay for their entire vehicle.

My Kia will not do that to me. When something breaks on a Kia Soul, I can take it to any mechanic within driving distance, buy parts from multiple suppliers, and pay a reasonable rate for labor. The diagnostic codes are standardized. The parts are available. The repair costs money but not a life-altering amount of money. This is how cars used to work, and it is how most cars still work, except for the ones that have been deliberately engineered to prevent it.

The automotive industry's transformation from mechanical engineering to software-gated subscription extraction is not an accident of technology. It is a choice. The same engineering teams that build a great powertrain also choose whether to lock it behind proprietary diagnostics, whether to require a dealer visit for a software update, whether to tie features you already paid for to a monthly fee. The complexity is not inevitable. It is profitable.

Once upon a time, American cars meant something. They weren't just transportation, they were statements of purpose, crafted by engineers who took pride in solving problems and building machines that would outlast their creators. A 1960s Mustang wasn't just fast; it was a declaration that someone had spent sleepless nights perfecting the curve of the hood and the growl of the exhaust. A Chevy truck from the 1980s didn't just haul your stuff; it hauled your stuff for thirty years while you cursed at it, kicked it, and secretly admired its stubborn refusal to die.

I noticed this firsthand with repair shops. They would pad the estimate with things I did not need. I started bringing a mechanic friend with me. He would look at the estimate and tell them, item by item, what I needed. One shop cut the CV boots on my car deliberately. Happened more than once, several hundred dollars each time. Same mechanic spotted it, confronted them, and I got refunded. These were not honest mistakes. They were fraud dressed up as service.

Those days are gone. Modern American automobiles are financial instruments wrapped in sheet metal, designed around financial models that reward planned obsolescence: shortened product lifespans, subscription-locked features, and complexity engineered to prevent independent repair. The soul of automotive engineering has been extracted and replaced with the logic of the extraction economy, which has discovered that a car you can only service at one place, running features you pay monthly to access, is more profitable than a car that simply works.

The enshittification of the American auto industry didn't happen because foreign competitors built better cars, though they did. It happened because financial engineers replaced mechanical engineers, quarterly profits replaced long-term reputation, and shareholders replaced customers as the primary constituency.

General Motors: Financial Engineering Replaces Actual Engineering

General Motors once stood as the pinnacle of American industrial might. The company that had built tanks to win World War II, pioneered modern manufacturing techniques, and employed entire cities worth of skilled workers represented everything impressive about American capitalism.

Then came the MBA invasion.

The transformation began in the 1970s when GM's leadership decided that the company's real business wasn't building cars, it was managing financial portfolios. Roger Smith, who became CEO in 1981, epitomized this shift from engineering excellence to financial optimization. He spent over $40 billion on factory automation and acquisitions while systematically eliminating the institutional knowledge that had made GM's engineering divisions world-class. The company acquired Electronic Data Systems for $2.55 billion and Hughes Aircraft for $5.1 billion, diversifying into businesses that management understood even less than automobile manufacturing.

GM eliminated over 600,000 jobs between 1979 and 1992, destroying entire communities built around automotive manufacturing as well as individual livelihoods. The skilled machinists, tool and die makers, and assembly line workers who understood how to build reliable cars got replaced with computer-controlled systems that could produce cars faster but couldn't adapt when things went wrong.

The quality decline was predictable and catastrophic. The 1981 Oldsmobile diesel engine became a symbol of GM's engineering decline, failing so consistently that the company faced class-action lawsuits and had to buy back thousands of vehicles. The engine had been rushed into production to meet federal fuel economy standards without adequate testing, a decision driven by regulatory compliance deadlines rather than engineering readiness. It was the first major sign that GM's financial engineers had taken control from its mechanical ones.

The ignition switch scandal of the 2000s revealed how deeply the rot had penetrated. GM had known for over a decade that faulty ignition switches in Chevrolet Cobalts could cause engines to shut off while driving, disabling power steering, brakes, and airbags. Instead of fixing the problem immediately, GM conducted cost-benefit analyses that determined it was cheaper to pay lawsuit settlements than to recall and repair the vehicles.

The switches cost 57 cents each. The replacement switches that fixed the problem cost 57 cents each. GM's financial engineers calculated that recalling millions of vehicles would cost more than occasionally paying wrongful death settlements. At least 124 people died. The people who made that calculation received their bonuses and moved on.

One powertrain engineer who worked at GM for 23 years before retiring in 2019: "We used to argue about how to make engines run better, last longer, use less fuel. By the end, every meeting was about hitting cost targets. The bean counters would tell us we needed to cut fifty cents from a part, and we'd have to figure out how to make it cheaper without making it so bad that warranty claims would cost more than the savings. It wasn't engineering anymore, it was cost accounting with technical constraints."

Chrysler: The Private Equity Pinball Machine

Chrysler's destruction followed an even more chaotic path as the company bounced between different owners, each extracting value while leaving the core business weaker. The company that had pioneered the minivan became a financial pinball, passed from one extraction specialist to another until almost nothing remained of its engineering capabilities.

The beginning of the end came in 1998 when Chrysler merged with Daimler-Benz in what was marketed as a "merger of equals" but quickly revealed itself as a German acquisition of American assets. Daimler paid $36 billion for Chrysler, then spent nine years stripping valuable technology and market positions while underinvesting in new product development.

When Daimler finally tired of subsidizing Chrysler's losses, they sold 80% of the company to Cerberus Capital Management for $7.4 billion in 2007. Cerberus, a private equity firm with no automotive experience whatsoever, brought in managers from consulting companies and investment banks who understood spreadsheets but not automobiles. They eliminated research and development spending, closed engineering facilities, and laid off the experienced workers who still remembered how to design reliable vehicles.

The private equity approach to a car company is particularly destructive because automotive engineering runs on institutional knowledge that takes decades to accumulate and years to destroy. When Cerberus cut Chrysler's engineering staff, they weren't just eliminating headcount, they were eliminating the accumulated understanding of why certain parts fail under certain conditions, why specific tolerances matter, why a suspension geometry that looks fine on paper doesn't survive Michigan winters. That knowledge walks out with the people who carried it, and no spreadsheet gets it back.

The 2008 financial crisis forced Chrysler into bankruptcy and sale to Italian automaker Fiat. Under CEO Sergio Marchionne, the company adopted a strategy of maximizing short-term profits from existing models while minimizing investment in new technology. The Jeep brand became a cash cow to subsidize Fiat's European operations. Chrysler's other brands were slowly starved until Stellantis, the merger entity that absorbed both Fiat Chrysler and Peugeot, emerged as a conglomerate optimizing across a portfolio rather than building great cars under any particular nameplate.

One powertrain engineer who worked at Chrysler for 28 years, surviving multiple ownership changes before being laid off in 2017: "Each new owner came in promising to restore Chrysler's engineering excellence. But they all did the same thing, cut costs, eliminate people, and focus on next quarter's numbers. By the end, we had maybe a quarter of the engineering staff we'd had in the 1990s, and most of the institutional knowledge was gone."

The Planned Obsolescence Algorithm

Modern automotive enshittification extends beyond traditional quality problems into deliberate design strategies that maximize long-term revenue extraction. Contemporary vehicles incorporate planned obsolescence techniques that ensure failure at predetermined intervals, subscription services for basic functionality, and complexity that prevents independent repair.

Electronic systems fail at rates that conveniently accelerate once warranty coverage expires, a pattern consistent enough across manufacturers that consumer advocates and right-to-repair litigants have argued it is structural rather than coincidental. Modern cars contain dozens of computer modules that control everything from engine management to door locks. When a $15 sensor fails, it can disable entire vehicle systems and require hundreds of dollars in diagnostic fees before any repairs begin, fees that flow exclusively to authorized service centers because the diagnostic tools required are proprietary.

BMW pioneered the subscription model for automotive features when it began charging customers monthly fees for heated seats, even in vehicles where the heating elements were already installed. The hardware exists in every vehicle. The software lock preventing its use is the product being sold. This is not an innovation. It is a toll booth erected on a road you already paid to build.

Other manufacturers adopted similar models for remote start, navigation updates, advanced safety features, and performance upgrades that unlock horsepower already available in the engine. General Motors charges a monthly fee for OnStar services that customers discover are required for features they assumed were included in the purchase price. Ford charges for connected services. The subscription layer has been inserted between the customer and the car they bought.

Tesla has taken this model to its logical extreme with "over-the-air updates" that can remotely enable or disable vehicle features based on payment status. Tesla owners have reported losing functionality when their vehicles were sold to new owners who hadn't paid for specific software packages. The company can literally reach into your garage and turn off parts of your car. The machine in your driveway that you paid $50,000 for contains features you don't own.

And then there's the battery. A Tesla Model 3 battery replacement outside warranty runs $13,000 to $15,000 through Tesla service centers, with Model S replacements reaching $20,000 to $22,000. The eight-year warranty protects you for eight years. After that, you own a car with a potential five-figure bill waiting for you. The car that was sold as the future of transportation comes with a liability that a 2005 Kia would never impose on its owner.

The Right to Repair Battle

The complexity that enables subscription services also prevents independent repair, and the automotive industry has spent years and millions of lobbying dollars ensuring that's not an accident.

Modern vehicles generate thousands of diagnostic codes that require proprietary software to interpret. Service manuals that were once freely available now cost thousands of dollars and require ongoing subscription fees. Diagnostic software is licensed rather than sold, ensuring that manufacturers can revoke access if independent shops become too competitive. The tools required to service a modern vehicle from certain manufacturers cost more than many independent shops earn in a year.

The economics are straightforward from the manufacturer's perspective. Every repair at an independent shop is a repair that didn't happen at a dealer. Dealers pay the manufacturer for parts at wholesale and charge retail. Independent shops buy parts from suppliers at prices that compete with dealers and charge less for labor. Every dollar that flows through a dealer service department generates revenue for the manufacturer's ecosystem. Every dollar that flows through an independent shop does not. The complexity that makes independent repair impossible is not a side effect of modern technology. It is a deliberate design choice with a clear financial rationale.

When the Massachusetts Right to Repair law passed in 2020, requiring manufacturers to provide independent shops with access to the same diagnostic data they share with their dealer networks, the automotive industry spent over $25 million fighting it. They lost the vote but immediately challenged the implementation in federal court, arguing that sharing diagnostic data with independent shops would create cybersecurity vulnerabilities. The cybersecurity argument is creative but not credible, the same data that independent mechanics need to diagnose your car is the same data dealers already access routinely. The security concern appeared primarily when independent repair threatened dealer revenue.

The right to repair movement has made this battle visible. When John Deere locked farmers out of repairing their own tractors using proprietary software, equipment they owned outright, on their own land, for their own crops, the absurdity of software-gated ownership became undeniable. The automotive version of the same battle is less visible because most people live close enough to a dealer to have an alternative, but the principle is identical. You bought the machine. You can't fix the machine. You can only pay the people the manufacturer authorizes to fix it, at the rates they set, using the parts they approve.

One independent repair shop owner who ran his business in suburban Phoenix for 22 years before closing in 2023: "The last few years, we couldn't fix anything newer than about 2015. The diagnostic equipment cost more than we made in a year, and even if you bought it, the manufacturers would change the software requirements every few months. They wanted to force everyone to use their dealers, and they succeeded. I had customers who'd been coming to me for twenty years. I couldn't help them anymore. I referred them to the dealer and closed."

The dealer markup on parts and labor is not a coincidence of the market. It is the point. When independent repair is made economically impossible, dealers become the only option, and dealer rates are set by the manufacturers who benefit from them. The complexity of modern vehicles is partly genuine technological advancement and partly an engineered barrier to competition.

The Death of Mechanical Sympathy

The transformation from mechanical systems to electronic control represents more than technological evolution, it's the systematic elimination of the connection between drivers and their vehicles.

Mechanical sympathy, the intuitive understanding of how machines work, once defined the relationship between Americans and their automobiles. Drivers could hear when their engines needed attention, feel when their transmissions were struggling, smell when brakes were overheating, and understand which maintenance tasks required immediate attention. That knowledge was ownership in the truest sense, understanding the machine you depended on well enough to participate in its care.

Electronic control systems eliminate this connection by design. Computer modules monitor hundreds of parameters and make adjustments without driver input or awareness. When problems develop, they're communicated through cryptic warning lights and diagnostic codes instead of mechanical symptoms that drivers can recognize and respond to. The "check engine" light has become a symbol of customer helplessness, a vague warning that something is wrong with no useful information about what, why, or how urgently it requires attention.

The complexity gap between modern vehicles and driver understanding creates opportunities for systematic overcharging. Service advisors can justify expensive repairs with diagnostic printouts that customers can't interpret. The authority of the printed code is absolute because the customer has no independent way to evaluate it. A shop that tells you your oxygen sensor threw a P0420 code has told you nothing you can verify or challenge without several hundred dollars of equipment.

One Toyota mechanic who worked for 35 years before retiring in 2020: "The old cars would tell you what was wrong. You could hear a bad bearing, feel a worn clutch, see when belts were fraying. The new cars don't communicate with drivers anymore, they communicate with computers. When something breaks, the computer just throws a code and disables the system. Customers have to trust us to interpret the codes, and a lot of shops take advantage of that trust."

The Dealer Network Scam

The automotive dealer network represents one of the most successful rent-seeking operations in American commerce, inserting expensive middlemen between manufacturers and customers while providing minimal value and extracting maximum profit from both parties.

State franchise laws in most jurisdictions prohibit manufacturers from selling directly to customers, forcing all transactions through dealer networks that add substantial markups without corresponding value. These laws were written in the mid-twentieth century to protect small business dealerships from manufacturer pressure. They now primarily protect large dealer groups, AutoNation, Penske Automotive, Lithia Motors, that operate hundreds of locations and capture legal protection designed for small operators without any of the small-business character that justified it.

Dealers generate revenue through vehicle sales markups, service departments that charge two to three times what independent shops charge for identical work, and financing products that represent the most profitable aspect of automotive retail. Dealers routinely mark up interest rates by one to three percentage points above what customers qualify for. A customer who qualifies for 5% financing might pay 8% through dealer arrangement, generating thousands in additional interest payments that flow directly to the dealer. The customer often doesn't know this is possible, because dealers present the financing as the result of their negotiation with the lender rather than a markup they applied to a rate they could have passed along.

The average American spends more time negotiating a vehicle purchase than in any other consumer transaction, hours of back-and-forth on price, then the finance office, then the extended warranty pitch, then the paint protection sealant, then the gap insurance. Each product in that sequence carries a profit margin that makes the vehicle itself look like a loss leader. The process is designed to wear customers down until they agree to things they didn't plan to buy when they walked in.

Extended warranties sold by dealers typically cost more than the average repair expenses they cover while excluding most problems customers encounter. Service contracts, paint protection packages, gap insurance, and nitrogen tire inflation are profit centers sold to customers who don't understand what they're buying or how to evaluate whether it's worth the price.

One service advisor who worked at a Ford dealership for six years before quitting in 2022: "The pressure to upsell was constant. We had monthly quotas for service revenue, extended warranties, and additional work recommendations. Management would monitor our sales performance and pressure us to find ways to increase customer bills. A lot of the additional work we recommended wasn't necessary, but customers trusted us because we were the authorized dealer." That trust, the assumption that an authorized dealer's recommendation must be legitimate, is what the franchise protection system preserves and what the upselling depends on.

Tesla, ironically, built its sales model around selling directly to consumers and bypassing the dealer network entirely, and promptly faced legislation in dozens of states prohibiting the practice. The dealer lobby is powerful enough to make it illegal for a manufacturer to cut out the middlemen, even when customers explicitly prefer the direct model. Arizona, Texas, Michigan, and other states prohibit or severely restrict direct Tesla sales. The franchise law that was supposed to protect small dealers from manufacturer bullying has been weaponized to protect large dealer groups from competition and customers from choice.

Counter-Examples: What Honest Engineering Looks Like

Toyota built the world's most successful automotive company on a philosophy that is almost radical in the current environment: make something reliable and people will keep buying it. The Toyota Production System, developed in the decades following World War II, embedded continuous improvement and defect elimination into every stage of manufacturing. The goal was not to build cars that would last until the warranty expired. The goal was to build cars that would last.

Toyota's quality philosophy, called kaizen, continuous improvement, runs directly counter to the planned obsolescence model. Where GM calculated that a 57-cent switch failure was acceptable because the warranty cost analysis favored inaction, Toyota built a system where any defect at any stage is cause for line stoppage until understood and corrected. Where Chrysler cut engineering staff to hit quarterly numbers, Toyota has maintained engineering investment across generations and economic downturns. The results are visible in any parking lot in America, the proportion of Toyotas still running past 200,000 miles is not an accident.

A 2005 Camry at 250,000 miles is not an anomaly. It is evidence of a design philosophy that prioritized longevity over replacement cycles, engineering excellence over cost minimization, and the customer's long-term interest over the manufacturer's short-term extraction. Toyota dealerships are not a great experience, no dealership is, but a Toyota owner is not the captive audience that a manufacturer dependent on service revenue needs. The car is too reliable. When your product works so well that customers don't need to come back for expensive repairs, you have to sell them a new car on its merits rather than on its failure.

Kia and Hyundai have found their own version of this model. The Kia Soul is not a prestigious vehicle. Nobody buys one to impress their neighbors. It is transportation, honest, reliable, reasonably priced, and serviceable by any competent mechanic who isn't required to pay for proprietary diagnostic software first. The ten-year, 100,000-mile powertrain warranty that Kia introduced in the 1990s was not a marketing gimmick. It was a statement about what the company was willing to stand behind, and it was a competitive necessity, Kia came to the American market as an unknown brand and needed a reason for skeptical customers to take a chance. The reason was: we'll pay for it if it breaks. Manufacturers who build things that fail don't offer that warranty. Manufacturers who know their engineering is solid can afford to.

The contrast between a Kia Soul owner's relationship with their car and a Tesla owner's relationship with their car tells you everything about which ownership model treats the customer as a person and which treats them as a revenue stream. The Kia needs an oil change and occasionally a brake job. The mechanic charges a fair rate, uses parts from multiple suppliers, and hands you the keys without asking for a monthly subscription. The Tesla offers a striking driving experience and then presents you with a potential $15,000 battery bill after the warranty expires, locks features behind monthly fees, and periodically sends software updates that change how things work without asking your permission. One of these is a car. The other is a product designed to maintain its manufacturer's access to your wallet indefinitely.

Subaru built customer loyalty through a different approach, targeting specific communities (outdoor enthusiasts, environmentally conscious buyers, dog owners, for reasons that remain somewhat mysterious) and building vehicles that matched their values reliably over time. Subaru owners are not typical car buyers. They replace their Outbacks with other Outbacks. They are the anti-enshittification customer: loyal because the product earned the loyalty rather than because switching costs make leaving painful.

Honda has largely maintained engineering integrity through a corporate culture that still considers itself primarily a company that makes engines rather than a company that manages a financial portfolio. Their motorcycles, generators, and outboard motors share DNA with their automobiles because the company has resisted the pressure to separate engineering from the financial operation. The result is cars that work, are relatively straightforward to maintain, and don't require a software subscription to access their full functionality.

The Subscription Car

The automotive industry's ultimate enshittification goal is transforming vehicle ownership from a one-time purchase into a permanent subscription relationship. General Motors has publicly discussed transitioning to subscription-based revenue models for connected features, and every major manufacturer has built connected services infrastructure designed to generate ongoing revenue long after the sale. The car you buy becomes a platform that continues extracting money from you for as long as you drive it.

Tesla's Full Self-Driving capability, which costs $15,000 but can be revoked if the vehicle is sold, demonstrates how manufacturers can extract multiple payments for the same functionality. The software remains with Tesla's servers instead of the vehicle. What you bought was access, not ownership. When the car changes hands, Tesla can reach in and strip out the capability. The buyer pays again, or does without.

Connected vehicles monitor driving behavior, location patterns, and vehicle usage for analysis and sale to third parties. Insurance companies pay for driver behavior data. Retailers pay for location data. Government agencies pay for traffic pattern data. Vehicle owners have no meaningful way to opt out of data collection as a condition of using features they paid for, because the data collection is built into the connected services infrastructure that also delivers the features they want.

General Motors' OnStar system, originally marketed as emergency assistance and turn-by-turn navigation, has evolved into a comprehensive data collection and subscription management platform. The emergency call button that gave elderly drivers peace of mind is now bundled with subscription tiers that determine which vehicle features are accessible. Customers who cancel their OnStar subscription discover that their remote start, their keyless entry app, and their vehicle diagnostics are also gone. The emergency button remains, because removing it would create liability. Everything else is behind the paywall.

BMW's decision to charge monthly fees for heated seats, hardware already installed in every vehicle, requiring only a software unlock, received significant public ridicule when it was announced. BMW walked back the policy in some markets after the backlash. But the intent was clear: features that customers paid for at purchase would become recurring revenue streams. The heated seat subscription failed because it was too obvious. The same logic, applied more subtly, is already standard practice across the industry.

The 1970 Chevelle being rebuilt in someone's garage right now will never be remotely disabled. It will never require a subscription to start in cold weather. Its owner will never receive a bill for unlocking the horsepower that was always in the engine. The engineers who built it would be disgusted by what their industry has become, and they'd be right.

Somewhere between the 57-cent ignition switch and the $22,000 battery replacement and the monthly fee for heated seats sits the answer to why people like me keep their Kia Souls and ignore the people who tell them they should upgrade. We upgraded. We upgraded to a car that works, that we can fix, that we own outright, and that doesn't charge us a monthly fee for the features we already paid for.

That's not a failure of imagination. That's the only rational response to an industry that decided its customers were a subscription waiting to happen.

Newspapers and Media - Community Pillars to Clickbait

On July 20, 1969, I watched Walter Cronkite cover the Apollo 11 moon landing. I was a kid, and I remember Cronkite going speechless, literally unable to speak for a moment, when Neil Armstrong stepped onto the lunar surface. He'd covered wars, assassinations, political upheaval. He'd stared down death as a correspondent in World War II. And when Armstrong put his boot in the dust of the Sea of Tranquility, the toughest reporter in America sat there rubbing his hands together and said, "Wally, say something. I'm speechless."

I do not read newspapers anymore. The major ones are either left or right and all of them are, to varying degrees, fake news. What I read now is focused publications like Geopolitical Futures, no advertising, minimal bias, mostly data and analysis. When I want to understand what is happening in the world I go to sources that are not trying to make me angry. The newspapers abandoned that contract with readers. So I stopped reading them.

That was journalism at its highest. CBS had mobilized over a thousand staff members. They had remote feeds from 31 locations inside the United States and 13 countries overseas. They ran 46 straight hours of live coverage. They spent millions on the broadcast and made essentially no money doing it. Nobody asked whether it would generate enough clicks to justify the cost. Nobody optimized the headline for engagement. The news division of CBS treated the biggest story of the century as a sacred obligation and covered it like one.

David Brinkley was the same kind of journalist at NBC, calm, dry, precise, allergic to sensationalism. The Huntley-Brinkley Report was appointment television for a generation not because it was entertaining but because it was true. "Good night, Chet. Good night, David." Two men who had earned the public's trust by refusing to abuse it, signing off every night with the confidence that they'd done their jobs honestly.

Both of them are gone now, and so is the journalism they practiced. What replaced it is something different in every important way: biased, loud, built around outrage, staffed by freelancers paid by the piece, optimized for engagement rather than accuracy, and owned by companies that view news as a content product rather than a civic function.

I watched every newspaper I read become obviously biased, some left, some right, all of them agenda-first. It was not subtle after a while. It was the story selection, the framing, what they left out as much as what they put in. I stopped trusting them one by one. Now I pay for specific publications that take no advertising, like Geopolitical Futures, where the business model is not to keep me angry enough to click. When you remove the advertiser from the equation, you get a different product. Most people have not figured out yet that the free news is what costs them.

I don't watch cable news anymore. I don't know many people who do, who then describe feeling informed rather than inflamed. Something that looks like news and functions like a rage generator has replaced the machine Cronkite, Brinkley, and Murrow built.

There was a time when newspapers mattered. Not just as sources of information, but as the beating hearts of their communities. The local paper didn't just tell you what happened at the city council meeting, it told you who was there, who wasn't, who said what they really meant, and who was probably lying through their teeth. The editor knew your mayor's golf handicap, your police chief's drinking problem, and which city councilman was sleeping with whose wife. This wasn't gossip; it was governance. Democracy depended on people who showed up, asked questions, and refused to let the powerful operate in darkness.

Now we have Facebook posts and TikTok videos and AI-generated content farms that produce seventeen different versions of the same press release while calling it "local news." The newsrooms that once employed armies of reporters, editors, and photographers have been strip-mined down to skeleton crews of overworked twenty-somethings who cover five beats each and fact-check stories between Uber shifts.

The death of local journalism wasn't a natural evolution. It was a systematic extraction operation that turned community watchdogs into corporate content mills.

What Real Journalism Required

The Apollo 11 coverage was not typical even for 1969, but it illustrated the scale of resources that serious broadcast journalism maintained. CBS had correspondents physically present at every relevant location. Cape Canaveral, Mission Control in Houston, the recovery ship in the Pacific, the homes of the astronauts' families, and remote feeds from observatories and space agencies on multiple continents. They had science correspondents who had spent years developing the expertise to explain what was happening. They had editors who could filter information in real time. They had the infrastructure to do this because they considered it their mission, not their content strategy.

The CBS Evening News under Cronkite maintained bureaus in every major American city and in dozens of foreign capitals. If something happened anywhere in the world, CBS had someone nearby who understood the context, knew the local players, and could get on camera in time to explain it. This wasn't efficiency, it was enormously expensive. It was also what journalism required to do its job.

Network news divisions in the Cronkite era operated at a structural loss. The entertainment divisions of CBS, NBC, and ABC subsidized the news divisions because the networks believed, or at minimum were required by their broadcast licenses to believe, that public information was a civic obligation that went beyond the profit motive. The fairness doctrine required broadcast licensees to air contrasting viewpoints on controversial matters. The public interest standard embedded in broadcast licensing meant that news divisions had obligations to the public that existed independently of advertiser revenue.

When the fairness doctrine was repealed in 1987 under the Reagan administration, the regulatory foundation that had treated journalism as a civic obligation disappeared. What followed was not a sudden collapse but a gradual transformation, as the economic logic of news shifted from public service to audience capture. The same broadcasters who had run news divisions at a loss because the law required public interest programming now ran news divisions according to the same profit calculus as their entertainment divisions.

The result was predictable. Content that generated audience engagement, conflict, outrage, fear, attracted more advertising revenue than content that informed citizens about complex matters that required sustained attention. The news division that covered Apollo 11 for 46 hours because it was the most important story in human history gave way to the news division that covered missing white women for weeks because the demographic data said it held the right audience.

Alden Global Capital: The Destroyer of Democracy's Infrastructure

If you want to understand how financial vampires drain the lifeblood from an entire industry while maintaining the pretense of trying to save it, study Alden Global Capital. This hedge fund has perfected the art of buying local newspapers, gutting their newsrooms, selling their real estate, and extracting maximum profit while the communities they once served descend into informational darkness.

The real estate always goes first. Local newspapers typically owned their buildings in prime downtown locations, accumulated over decades when the paper was the anchor institution of its community. Alden sells these buildings to separate entities, forcing the newspapers to pay rent on properties they previously owned outright. This generates immediate cash while creating permanent overhead that drains resources from journalism. The newspaper that spent a century earning its building now pays monthly tribute to the fund that stripped it away.

The Denver Post provides a textbook example. When Alden acquired the paper's parent company in 2010, The Denver Post employed over 300 newsroom staff. By 2018, the newsroom had been reduced to fewer than 70 people. The paper that had covered Colorado's growth, politics, and community life for over a century was reduced to a skeleton operation unable to cover the state capitol adequately, let alone the dozens of local communities that had depended on it.

The editorial philosophy under Alden shifted from community service to cost minimization. Investigative reporting, which requires months of research and produces uncertain revenue returns, was eliminated first. Beat reporting, the daily presence of a reporter who knew the school board or the police department well enough to notice when something was wrong, was replaced with generic assignment desk journalism that covered events rather than understanding institutions.

The Denver Post's own editorial board published a brutal assessment in 2018, writing that the hedge fund was "strip-mining" the newspaper and calling for new ownership. The editorial, titled "As Vultures Circle, The Denver Post Must Be Saved," represented an almost unprecedented public condemnation of ownership by the newspaper's own staff. The people who remained were being asked to produce journalism with resources insufficient to do it honestly, and they knew it.

Alden's response was predictable: more layoffs and deeper cuts. The editorial board that spoke up had made a public relations problem. The solution was to make the problem smaller.

Gannett: Death by Homogenization

Gannett represents a different model of newspaper destruction, death by corporate consolidation and algorithmic optimization. While Alden strips individual papers for parts, Gannett absorbs local newspapers into a homogenized content machine that eliminates local character while maximizing operational efficiency.

The company that once promoted itself as "A World of Different Voices Where Freedom Speaks" became a factory for generic content that could be produced anywhere and published everywhere. After Gannett's 2019 merger with

GateHouse Media, creating a company controlling over 260 daily papers, the combined entity immediately began "combination" programs that destroyed what made individual newspapers unique. Combination, in this context, meant firing the people who know the community and replacing them with centralized content that could go anywhere.

Gannett newspapers now share sports writers who cover multiple teams in different states, business reporters who write about companies they've never visited, and lifestyle writers who create "local" content about communities they've never seen. A high school football story in Iowa might be written by someone in Ohio using statistics provided by a stringer paid $50 to attend the game. The byline says local. The knowledge does not.

The advertising and circulation departments that once understood local markets have been replaced with national call centers. The personal relationships that sustained local newspaper economics, the banker who advertised because he knew the editor, the car dealer who bought space because the sports writer covered his son's basketball team, disappear when human connections get replaced with algorithmic optimization. The system is more efficient. The product is worse. The community is poorer.

One community editor who worked for a Gannett paper in Ohio for eight years before being "restructured" in 2020: "We used to know our readers personally. After the merger, everything became metrics and algorithms. We had to write headlines that would get clicks instead of accurately describing local issues. It wasn't local journalism anymore, it was content creation with local branding."

The Freelancer Economy

The staffing structure of modern journalism has completed what the ownership structure began. Where Cronkite's CBS maintained permanent bureaus staffed by salaried correspondents with benefits, institutional knowledge, and long-term investment in their beats, modern digital media operations run on freelancers paid by the piece.

A freelancer covering city hall doesn't develop a relationship with the city attorney over three years of regular contact and therefore doesn't know when the city attorney starts being evasive about something. A freelancer covering a police department doesn't notice when the overtime statistics change in a way that suggests something is being hidden. A freelancer paid $200 for a story doesn't have the economic incentive to spend three weeks developing a source who might eventually confirm something important. They find the story available today, write it, and move to the next assignment.

The institutional knowledge that made beat reporting valuable is accumulated over years and cannot be recreated by a rotating cast of temporary workers producing content on demand. The city editor who spent twenty years covering the same municipality knew which department heads were competent and which were covering things up. The police reporter who had been on the beat for a decade understood the department's culture well enough to recognize when something was wrong. That knowledge is not transferable. When the experienced reporter leaves and the freelancer arrives, the community loses a watchdog that cannot simply be replaced.

The economics of this shift are designed to sound like progress. Freelancers are more flexible. They don't require benefits. They can be paid only for work produced rather than for time spent developing expertise. The cost per story drops. The cost per piece of actual accountability journalism, the kind that prevents corruption, exposes waste, protects vulnerable people, is not measured and therefore does not appear in the analysis.

The Facebook Apocalypse

Facebook didn't just compete with traditional media for audience attention, it systematically destroyed the economic foundation that had supported local journalism for over a century.

Facebook's advertising model created a massive sucking sound that pulled revenue away from local media toward a centralized platform that provided no local content in return. A restaurant owner who once advertised in the local paper could now target Facebook ads to people within a five-mile radius who had shown interest in dining out. When local businesses advertised in newspapers, they were paying for journalism. When they advertised on Facebook, they were paying for access to attention captured by content created elsewhere. The revenue migrated. The journalism did not follow.

The "pivot to video" trend that Facebook promoted in the mid-2010s illustrates how the platform manipulated media companies into destructive decisions based on false metrics. Facebook told publishers that video content was generating massive engagement and encouraged them to hire video producers and pivot away from text-based journalism.

Hundreds of media companies fired experienced reporters to hire video producers. Then Facebook admitted it had been inflating video engagement metrics by up to 900%. The "massive engagement" was largely fictional, but the journalism jobs that had been eliminated were permanently gone. The reporters who were fired to make room for the video team didn't come back when the video strategy failed.

The algorithm changes that Facebook subsequently implemented to prioritize "meaningful social interactions" over news content delivered the final blow to outlets that had restructured themselves around the platform's stated priorities. Local newspapers that had invested in Facebook strategies found themselves at the mercy of algorithmic decisions made by engineers in Menlo Park who had never considered how their optimization choices might affect democratic governance in small American towns.

The Information Desert

The elimination of local journalism creates information deserts where citizens lose access to the news they need to participate in democratic governance.

Local government accountability suffers immediately when newspapers eliminate beat reporters. City councils, school boards, and county commissions that once operated under journalistic scrutiny find they can make decisions without public attention. Academic research has documented how municipal bond costs increase when local newspapers close, reflecting investor concerns about reduced government accountability. Communities without local news coverage experience increases in government spending and municipal debt that suggest reduced oversight enables fiscal irresponsibility.

This is not theoretical. In communities where the local paper has closed or been gutted, documented increases in corruption prosecutions, not decreases, appear in the years following closure, because the misconduct that was being deterred by scrutiny now runs to completion before being discovered. The absence of journalism doesn't prevent bad things from happening. It just means nobody finds out until much later, when the damage is deeper.

Voter turnout in local elections drops significantly when newspapers close or reduce coverage. Citizens become less likely to attend public meetings or participate in community organizations. The social capital that democracy requires erodes when people lack shared sources of information about their communities. The town meeting where fifty people showed up because they'd all read the same story in the morning paper becomes a meeting where six people show up and twenty others argue on Facebook about things they read from sources in other states.

The Bias Problem

Cronkite ended every CBS Evening News broadcast with "And that's the way it is." He omitted the phrase on nights when he was giving opinion or commentary, because he considered it dishonest to use his objectivity signature on content that wasn't objective. That distinction, the deliberate, institutionalized separation of fact from opinion, was not universal in his era, but it was the operating standard of the organizations that claimed to practice journalism.

Cable news obliterated that distinction and replaced it with the opposite principle: opinion is the product, and it is most profitably sold as fact. The business model of partisan cable news requires a permanent state of outrage among its audience, because outrage is what drives viewership and viewership is what drives advertising revenue. A calm, accurately informed citizen makes a poor cable news viewer. An enraged, frightened citizen who needs to know what the enemy is doing today is the ideal customer.

The "both sides" problem that emerged as broadcast journalism tried to respond to partisan criticism produced its own distortions. If every story required a representative of each "side" to be given equal time regardless of what the evidence showed, then climate science and climate denial occupied equal airtime, vaccine efficacy and vaccine skepticism received equivalent treatment, and demonstrably false claims were regularly presented alongside accurate ones in the name of balance. The journalist's job shifted from determining what was true to presenting what both sides said, which is a fundamentally different activity.

Neither Cronkite nor Brinkley was above having opinions. Cronkite's editorial on Vietnam, his on-air conclusion in 1968 that the war was a stalemate and America should negotiate, reportedly led President Johnson to say "If I've lost Cronkite, I've lost Middle America." The power of that moment came precisely from its rarity. Cronkite had spent years demonstrating that he distinguished between what he knew and what he believed. When he blurred that line for one broadcast, it meant something. When the line is permanently blurred, it means nothing.

The Chain Newspaper Collapse

McClatchy, once one of the largest newspaper chains in America, provides a case study in how corporate ownership and the LBO model destroyed newspapers that had served their communities for generations. The company's 2006 acquisition of Knight Ridder for $4.5 billion loaded McClatchy with massive debt at exactly the moment when newspaper revenues were beginning their permanent decline. It was the airline playbook applied to journalism: borrow the money to buy the asset, then watch the asset's revenue decline while the debt payments stay fixed.

Knight Ridder, before its sale, had been one of the better-run newspaper chains in the country. Its papers included the Miami Herald, the Philadelphia Inquirer, the San Jose Mercury News, and dozens of regional papers that served their communities with serious resources. The Knight Ridder Washington bureau had broken major stories. The Miami Herald had won multiple Pulitzer Prizes covering Latin America with a full bureau of correspondents who spoke the languages, knew the governments, and understood the histories. When McClatchy acquired Knight Ridder and immediately began debt service, those bureaus started closing.

The Miami Herald that had maintained bureaus throughout Latin America could no longer afford to send reporters to Tallahassee for legislative sessions. The paper that had once been the institutional authority on South Florida, Cuba, and Caribbean affairs became dependent on wire service reports about the region it had covered as its primary mission. McClatchy in the end filed for bankruptcy in 2020. The papers it had acquired emerged leaner, less staffed, and less capable than when they were purchased.

Digital First Media, which became part of Alden's empire, exemplified the worst aspects of chain ownership combined with hedge fund extraction. The company operated newspapers using a centralized management system that treated journalism as a commodity to be produced at minimum cost. High school sports stories followed identical formats regardless of whether they were published in Colorado or California. City council coverage used standardized approaches that missed local political dynamics visible only to reporters who had spent years in those rooms.

The Economics of Outrage

Cronkite's CBS invested millions in moon landing coverage and made essentially no money. That is not a business model that survives in an industry where the primary metric is quarterly earnings per share.

The transformation of journalism into an engagement-optimization business did not happen because the people who owned news organizations were uniquely evil. It happened because the economic signals pointed clearly in one direction. Stories that generated outrage got more clicks. More clicks meant more advertising revenue. More advertising revenue meant better financial performance. Better financial performance meant higher stock prices and satisfied shareholders. The logic was internally consistent. The consequence was that the news product optimized itself toward content that made people angry, afraid, or contemptuous of their fellow citizens, not because journalists wanted to produce that content, but because the market rewarded it.

The 24-hour news cycle that CNN pioneered when Robert Wussler, who had been Cronkite's executive producer at CBS, left to help found the network, was supposed to mean more news, more thoroughly covered. What it meant was more hours to fill with less staff, which meant more repetition, more speculation, more commentary, and eventually more partisan content that could fill air time without requiring the expensive infrastructure of actual reporting.

By the time Fox News launched in 1996 with an explicitly partisan framework, and MSNBC followed with its own version of the same product aimed at the opposite audience, the transformation was complete. News as civic function had become news as entertainment product, differentiated by which audience's political preferences it validated. The audience was not being informed. The audience was being served content that confirmed what it already believed, charged per eyeball to advertisers who wanted access to it.

Cronkite ended his broadcasts by saying "And that's the way it is." His modern successors end their broadcasts by implicitly saying "And here is why you should be furious about it." Both are journalism. Only one is honest about what it is.

The AI Content Farm

The latest evolution has made the freelancer economy look almost artisanal. AI-generated content farms can now produce hundreds of local news articles per day using algorithms trained on wire service reports, press releases, and public data. A single company can operate hundreds of "local news" websites at the same time, each publishing dozens of daily articles that appear local but contain no local knowledge, no local sourcing, and no accountability to the communities they claim to serve.

These operations are sometimes called "pink slime" journalism, the news equivalent of processed meat, something that has the shape and texture of the real thing without the substance. They scrape public records databases for meeting agendas, police blotter items, and sports scores. They publish press releases as news. They hire no reporters, maintain no sources, and take no risks. They generate advertising revenue by appearing in local search results for people looking for community news, capturing the advertising dollars that once supported real journalism.

The FCC's local ownership rules, which were designed to prevent a single company from dominating a community's information environment, have not kept up with the digital reality that a company with no physical presence in a community can dominate its information environment completely. The hedge fund that owns the only remaining local newspaper and the algorithm that generates fake local news for a hundred websites at the same time are both extracting value from the community's need for information without providing the civic function that need represents.

What they are taking, beyond advertising revenue, is something harder to quantify: the shared informational foundation that makes community possible. Cronkite and Brinkley were watching the same things and telling the same audience about them. That shared attention, however imperfect, however limited to the people who could access network television, was a civic infrastructure. When algorithmic content personalized to confirm each person's existing beliefs replaces it, the common ground disappears.

The moon landing was watched by an estimated 125 to 150 million Americans at the same time, nearly two-thirds of the country, through a broadcast infrastructure that had been built on the premise that the public had a right to share important information. Walter Cronkite sat at an anchor desk with over a thousand people behind him, drawing on thirty years of experience, and told America what was happening on the moon.

Who does that now? Who has earned that trust, commands that audience, and maintains that infrastructure?

The question answers itself.

While corporate chains collapsed under financial pressure, family-owned community newspapers that maintained close connections between publishers, advertisers, and readers continued doing the job.

The Storm Lake Times in rural Iowa represents the kind of community journalism that corporate media abandoned as unprofitable. The paper, owned and operated by the Cullen family for over three decades, has won two Pulitzer Prizes for editorial writing while serving a town of fewer than 11,000 people. The model works because the owners live in the community they serve. The paper covers city council meetings, school board decisions, agricultural policy, and local business developments with the detailed attention that residents need to participate in community governance.

Art Cullen, who has served as editor for over 20 years: "We live here. Our kids go to school here. We shop at the businesses we cover and vote for the officials we report on. We can't just extract value and move on to the next market, we have to live with the consequences of our journalism. That creates accountability that corporate ownership can't match."

That accountability is exactly what Cronkite had in 1969. He was going to have to face his colleagues, his sources, his audience, and his own conscience every time he went on air. The check on his journalism was not algorithmic; it was human. It was the accumulated reputation of a person who had decided, early in his career, that accuracy mattered more than popularity and had spent decades proving he meant it.

Art Cullen still covers the Storm Lake city council. His paper still wins Pulitzers. The model works because the people running it live with the consequences of their journalism. Walter Cronkite lived with the consequences of his. The algorithm does not.

The "most trusted man in America" was trusted because he earned it, one broadcast at a time, by telling the truth even when it was complicated, by saying "I'm speechless" when he was speechless instead of filling the silence with confident-sounding noise.

That's not a technology problem. That's not a business model problem. That's a values problem, and no amount of innovation in content delivery solves it.

Banking - Relationships to Fee Extraction

I banked at Security Pacific for years. When I needed something, a loan, a question answered, anything that mattered, I walked into the branch and talked to the manager. He knew me. Not in the corporate-script sense of reading my account number off a screen while pretending to remember me, but knew me. My situation, my history, what I was trying to accomplish. When you know someone, you can help them. That's what banking was.

In April 1992, BankAmerica acquired Security Pacific in what was then the largest bank merger in American history. Richard Rosenberg, the BankAmerica chairman, promised customers they would "notice few changes except for the name change." He said this while announcing $1.2 billion in annual savings to be achieved through branch closings and layoffs. Both statements were true. Both could not coexist. The name changed. So did everything else.

Bank of America is a decent enough bank. The app works. The online tools are functional. If you need to move money or pay a bill or check a balance at 2 a.m., it does the job without complaint. What it cannot do is what the Security Pacific manager could do: look at your specific situation, apply judgment, and help you. The algorithm doesn't help. The algorithm processes. The difference between those two things is the difference between a bank and a financial utility, and American banking spent the last thirty years becoming a utility.

Your grandfather's banker knew his name, his business, and probably his wife's birthday. When drought hit the farm or the factory laid off half its workers, the banker understood what that meant for the community and adjusted payment schedules accordingly. The bank president lived three blocks away, sent his kids to the same schools, and had a genuine stake in whether local businesses succeeded or failed. Banking was boring, profitable, and at its core about relationships, moving money from people who had it to people who needed it while keeping enough spread to pay the bills and fund community growth.

Now your bank is a sprawling financial conglomerate that sees you as a walking bundle of fee-generation opportunities. The friendly neighborhood branch has been converted into a sterile customer-harvesting operation where undertrained staff push credit cards and investment products while algorithms in distant data centers analyze your spending patterns to identify maximum extraction potential.

The Consolidation Wave

In 1984, there were 14,469 commercial banks serving communities of all sizes across America. By 2022, that number had fallen to 4,135, with the largest institutions controlling an ever-increasing share of deposits and lending. The community banks that once provided personalized service were either acquired or driven out of business by larger competitors who could absorb regulatory compliance costs that smaller institutions couldn't.

The Security Pacific acquisition was a preview of what the entire industry was about to become. The two largest banks in California merged into an institution with nearly $190 billion in assets. The economies of scale that justified the merger, $1.2 billion in annual savings by eliminating redundant branches and staff, were achieved exactly as promised. The people who had worked at those branches, who had known the customers by name and understood their situations, were part of the savings.

What the merger economics never measured was what those relationships were worth. The Security Pacific manager who knew a small business owner's seasonal cash flow patterns and had extended credit accordingly was a risk management asset. His replacement, an algorithm trained on credit scores and debt-to-income ratios, couldn't distinguish between a landscaper with predictable seasonal income variation and a genuinely unstable borrower. Both looked the same to the model. Only one of them was a credit risk.

The consolidation accelerated through the 1990s and 2000s as deregulation removed the geographic barriers that had kept banks local. The Riegle-Neal Interstate Banking Act of 1994 allowed banks to operate across state lines for the first time since the Depression. Within a decade, regional banks that had anchored communities for generations were absorbed into national institutions whose executives had never visited the communities they were now serving.

NationsBank absorbed MNC Financial, Boatmen's Bancshares, Barnett Banks, and then merged with BankAmerica in 1998 to create what became the modern Bank of America. JPMorgan swallowed Bank One, then Washington Mutual. Wells Fargo absorbed Wachovia. Each merger extracted savings through staff reductions and branch closings. Each merger left fewer people in the surviving institution who understood the communities it was supposed to serve.

The community banks that disappeared in this process were not failing institutions. Many were profitable, well-run, and deeply connected to their communities. They were acquired because the consolidating institutions needed their deposits and their branch locations, and because their owners received attractive offers in an era of cheap money and loose regulation. The customers had no vote. The communities had no vote. The shareholders received their premium and moved on.

By 2010, the five largest banks in America controlled over half of all banking assets, up from about a quarter in the early 1990s. The local banker who knew your name had not become more efficient. He had been replaced by a national institution that treated every customer in every community identically, according to policies written by people who had never visited most of the places those policies affected.

Wells Fargo: The Fake Account Factory

Wells Fargo's descent from respected community bank to criminal enterprise provides the perfect case study in how corporate incentive structures can transform banking from customer service into customer exploitation.

The fake account scandal that exploded in 2016 wasn't an aberration or the result of a few rogue employees. It was the inevitable outcome of a corporate culture that prioritized revenue generation over customer service. The "Eight Is Great" program established sales quotas requiring each customer to maintain eight different Wells Fargo products. Branch employees faced termination if they couldn't convince enough customers to sign up for products they didn't need, couldn't afford, or didn't understand.

The quota system put employees in an impossible position. The customers who walked into a Wells Fargo branch in a working-class neighborhood often needed basic services, checking accounts, small loans, bill payment. They didn't need eight products. They couldn't afford eight products. But the employee who failed to sell eight products would lose their job.

When customers resisted, Wells Fargo employees began creating accounts without permission, forging signatures, and generating fake email addresses. The bank's own investigation eventually identified 3.5 million unauthorized accounts. Customers discovered the fraud when they applied for mortgages and found their credit damaged by accounts they'd never opened. Small business owners faced overdraft fees because unauthorized account openings had redirected their direct deposits. Elderly customers on fixed incomes found themselves paying monthly fees for services they never requested.

Despite systematically defrauding millions of customers over several years, the bank faced minimal consequences. The $185 million combined fine represented less than three weeks of Wells Fargo's normal profit. CEO John Stumpf testified that employees had caused the fraud. He claimed they "did not honor our vision and values," deflecting responsibility from the corporate policies that had made fraud inevitable. The people who had implemented those policies kept their bonuses. The tellers and branch employees who had been trapped between impossible quotas and customer service ethics were the ones terminated.

The "Eight Is Great" philosophy had turned every bank employee into a salesperson and every customer into a sales target. The branch manager who once helped you was replaced with a quota-driven sales associate who needed to sell you something before you left. The relationship was gone. The extraction machine was running.

Bank Consolidation and Predatory Practices

When Bank of America acquired FleetBoston Financial in 2004 for $47 billion, Fleet's customers in New England suddenly found themselves subject to Bank of America's national fee schedule regardless of regional economic conditions. The bank that had understood the specific character of the New England economy, the fishing industry, the university towns, the seasonal rhythms, was replaced by a national institution applying uniform rules across fifty states.

Bank of America closed over 1,000 branches between 2019 and 2022, typically targeting lower-income communities where the revenue per customer was lower but where the alternative financial options were also worse. The communities that most needed accessible banking got fewer branches. The communities where wealthy customers could easily access financial services kept theirs. This is not incidental to the business model. It is the business model.

When a bank branch closes in a lower-income neighborhood, it does not simply inconvenience customers. It creates a financial services desert where people are pushed toward check-cashing services and payday lenders that charge dramatically more for equivalent services. A payday loan that costs $15 per $100 borrowed for two weeks carries an annual interest rate of nearly 400%. The customers who end up there are not people who chose high-cost credit. They are people whose bank branch closed.

The overdraft fee policies that national banks implemented after consolidation provide clear examples of how monopoly power enables predatory practices. Community banks typically worked with customers experiencing temporary financial difficulties because those customers were their neighbors. National banks implemented automated systems that maximized overdraft fee generation by processing transactions in orders designed to trigger multiple penalties.

JPMorgan Chase's systems analyze transaction patterns to determine optimal processing sequences that generate the highest fee revenue. A customer who overdraws their account by $5 might face $175 in penalties because the bank processes transactions in an order designed to trigger multiple overdraft fees. This is not a software glitch. It is a deliberate design choice that generates billions in annual revenue from the customers least able to pay it.

One auto repair shop owner in Cleveland who operated successfully for fifteen years before his community bank was acquired: "My original banker knew my business, my customers, my seasonal patterns. After the merger, everything became forms and credit scores that didn't account for the relationships and reputation I'd built. They offered me a credit card with a 23% interest rate instead of the business line of credit I needed."

The Rise of Junk Fees

Banks discovered they could generate enormous profits by charging fees for services that were once considered basic customer service. ATM fees that didn't exist in 1990 now cost $5 or more per transaction, and they stack: the foreign ATM charges you a fee, and then your own bank charges you a separate fee for using a foreign ATM. Two fees for one transaction you had no alternative to completing.

Monthly maintenance fees for checking accounts transformed banking from a service into a subscription. The minimum balance requirements that trigger fee waivers ensure that lower-income customers pay monthly charges while wealthy customers receive free banking. A customer who maintains a $10,000 balance receives free service, while someone living paycheck to paycheck pays $12 per month for the same account. The fee structure is a regressive tax levied by private institutions on the people least equipped to avoid it.

Banks collect over $12 billion annually from overdraft fees, with the majority coming from customers who overdraw more than ten times per year. These frequent overdraft customers are typically living paycheck to paycheck, making overdraft fees a regressive tax on poverty disguised as a customer choice. The choice is illusory. When you have $23 in your account and need to buy groceries, you don't have meaningful options.

One college student in Phoenix discovered how overdraft fees create debt spirals when her account was overdrawn by $8 for a coffee purchase. "They charged me $35 for the overdraft, then $35 more for each of the next three small purchases before I realized what was happening. A $4 coffee turned into $148 in fees because I didn't check my balance that morning."

The overdraft fee trap is not a bug. It is a feature. Banks know which customers overdraft regularly. The data on who will trigger fees and when is precisely the kind of information that algorithmic systems excel at collecting and analyzing. That analysis is not used to help customers avoid fees. It is used to maximize fee generation. The same technology that could send a customer a warning notification before an overdraft is instead used to sequence transactions to produce the maximum number of overdraft events.

Wire transfer fees, safe deposit box fees, paper statement fees, inactivity fees for accounts that aren't used enough, returned payment fees, stop payment fees, the modern bank account is surrounded by a minefield of charges that extract money from customers for doing ordinary things that used to be free. The Security Pacific manager never handed you a fee schedule and suggested you memorize it to avoid accidental penalties. That was not a bank. That was an ambush wearing a bank's logo.

The Algorithmic Replacement of Judgment

The replacement of human underwriters with algorithmic decision-making systems eliminated the local knowledge that once made banking a service rather than a processing operation.

Credit scores reduce complex financial situations to three-digit numbers that may not accurately reflect creditworthiness. Medical debt, which affects millions of Americans through no fault of their own, can severely damage credit scores and prevent access to affordable loans for years. Meanwhile, having multiple credit cards and high credit limits improves scores regardless of actual financial responsibility. The algorithm measures what it measures. What it cannot measure is what the Security Pacific branch manager knew: who you are, what your situation is, and what you're trying to accomplish.

Traditional community banks understood local economic patterns. Farmers and small business owners who managed seasonal cash flow through community relationships could qualify for loans that algorithmic systems automatically reject. The landscaper in rural Oregon whose revenue varies with the weather and the season is not a bad credit risk. He is a credit risk that requires judgment to evaluate, and judgment has been optimized out of the banking system.

One landscaping business owner in rural Oregon who was rejected for equipment financing by three different banks: "My revenue varies seasonally because landscaping work depends on weather. The old bank president understood my business and knew I always paid my bills. Now they just run my information through computers that see income volatility and automatically decline. The algorithm doesn't know that landscape contractors always have irregular income or that I've never missed a payment in eight years."

The algorithm also doesn't know it doesn't know. It produces a decision with algorithmic confidence, and the bank employee who presents that decision to the customer has no authority to override it and often no understanding of why it was made.

The Deregulation Engine

The consolidation wave didn't happen in a regulatory vacuum. A series of legislative and regulatory changes engineered it, systematically dismantling the protections that had kept banking relatively boring and relatively honest since the Depression.

The Glass-Steagall Act of 1933 had separated commercial banking, taking deposits, making loans, serving customers, from investment banking, underwriting securities, trading, speculating. The separation was not accidental. Congress had watched commercial banks take depositor money and gamble it in the markets during the 1920s, and had decided that the people's savings should not be subject to the risks of speculation. For sixty years, the wall held.

In 1999, the Gramm-Leach-Bliley Act repealed the Glass-Steagall separation. The same institutions that held your checking account and your mortgage could now also trade mortgage-backed securities, underwrite stock offerings, and speculate in derivatives. The people who had lobbied for the repeal argued that the separation was outdated, that modern risk management made it unnecessary, that combining the two would create efficiencies that would benefit customers.

The 2008 financial crisis provided the definitive rebuttal. Banks had taken the depositor funds that Glass-Steagall had protected and used them to fund mortgage-backed securities that they knew were failing. When the securities collapsed, the banks required a taxpayer bailout to survive. The deposits that ordinary Americans thought were being held safely were connected, through chains of derivatives that most customers could not have traced, to the speculative instruments that nearly destroyed the global financial system.

The banks that were too big to fail in 2008 were bigger after the crisis than before it. Bear Stearns was absorbed by JPMorgan. Washington Mutual was seized and sold to JPMorgan. Merrill Lynch was acquired by Bank of America. Wachovia was absorbed by Wells Fargo. The consolidation that had spent two decades concentrating banking power in a small number of massive institutions now used the crisis to concentrate it further. The institutions that had caused the crash were rewarded with their competitors' assets.

The executives who had presided over this catastrophe largely kept their jobs and their bonuses. The homeowners whose mortgages had been turned into securities and then defaulted were foreclosed upon. Over eight million Americans lost their jobs. Several million lost their homes. The banks got bailouts. The customers got nothing.

Wells Fargo's Aftermath

The Wells Fargo fake account scandal seemed like it might produce meaningful accountability. It didn't.

CEO John Stumpf was forced to resign in 2016 and was eventually barred from the banking industry by the OCC, a meaningful punishment that nonetheless came six years after the fraud began and affected only him personally. The bank paid $3 billion in fines in 2020 to resolve criminal and civil charges, the largest penalty in Wells Fargo's history. It represented roughly six weeks of the bank's normal profit.

The Federal Reserve imposed an asset cap on Wells Fargo in 2018, preventing the bank from growing beyond the $1.95 trillion in assets it held at that time until it had demonstrated adequate reforms. That cap remained in place into 2025, making it one of the longest and most significant regulatory consequences any major bank had faced in recent memory.

But the customers whose credit had been damaged by unauthorized account openings, who had paid fees for services they never requested, who had suffered consequences they didn't understand for years before the scandal became public, most of them received minimal compensation. The $142 million class action settlement worked out to approximately $40 per affected customer. The overdraft fees, the credit score damage, the stress of discovering accounts in your name that you never opened, $40.

The bankers who built the incentive structures that made fraud inevitable received their compensation. The tellers and branch employees who had been trapped between impossible quotas and ethical obligations got fired. The customers got $40.

The pattern is consistent across banking's modern history. When the banks win, the profits go to shareholders and executives. When the banks cause harm, the costs go to customers and taxpayers. The system is not broken. It is working as designed.

Credit Unions: What Member Ownership Can Achieve

Credit unions, which operate as member-owned cooperatives instead of shareholder-owned corporations, demonstrate how different ownership structures can transform banking from extraction to service. Credit unions typically charge lower fees, pay higher interest on deposits, and provide better customer service because their obligation is to members instead of shareholders.

The credit union model is the Security Pacific model in cooperative form: people who know the community, serving the community, with their own financial wellbeing tied to the community's wellbeing. When a credit union serves teachers in a school district, the people running it understand what teachers earn, what their financial pressures are, and what products help them. When a national bank serves the same teachers as one of forty million customers, none of that understanding is present.

Navy Federal Credit Union, the largest in the country with over 13 million members, consistently outperforms national banks on customer satisfaction because its incentive structure is fundamentally different. Every fee it doesn't charge is money that stays with its members. Every service it provides efficiently is a benefit to the people it exists to serve.

The community banks that survived consolidation demonstrate the same principle at smaller scale. The banker who lent to small businesses based on character and local knowledge, and who was held accountable by living in the community where those businesses operated, outperformed the algorithmic lending systems on long-term loan performance. Relationships contain information that credit scores cannot capture. Judgment adds value that an algorithm cannot replicate. The local knowledge that looks like an inefficiency from a distance is a risk management asset that the spreadsheet cannot see.

The Personal Touch That Isn't Coming Back

The Security Pacific manager who knew my situation cannot be replicated by a chatbot. He cannot be replaced by an app that processes my requests efficiently. The Bank of America app works well because it is a tool for executing transactions I've already decided to make. It cannot help me figure out what I should do, whether a particular financial choice makes sense for my specific situation, or whether there's an option I haven't considered.

Banks used to provide that service as part of the relationship. The relationship has been replaced by a transaction volume and revenue per customer metric. The manager's job now is not to help customers make good financial decisions. It is to ensure that customers are enrolled in the maximum number of products and generating the maximum revenue per relationship.

The choice between extraction and service in banking isn't determined by technology or market forces. It's a decision about what kind of financial system we want. Your grandfather's banker knew that banking was at its core about relationships and community trust. That wisdom didn't become obsolete when the computers arrived. It was abandoned because extracting fees from millions of faceless account numbers generates better short-term returns than building relationships with the people those numbers represent.

The Security Pacific manager is retired now, or gone. The bank he worked for ceased to exist in April 1992, folded into something larger and more efficient that had no interest in knowing who I was. The branch I walked into is probably something else now, or closed. The relationship is gone. What replaced it processes transactions reliably and charges fees automatically and generates revenue efficiently.

That's not banking. That's a utility that used to be a bank, wearing a bank's name.

The Housing Crisis Connection

The deregulated banking system didn't just charge fees. It engineered a financial catastrophe that cost millions of Americans their homes and their savings, and then paid no meaningful price for it.

The subprime mortgage crisis that destroyed the economy in 2008 was not a natural disaster. It was the product of deliberate choices by banks freed from Glass-Steagall's constraints. Banks originated mortgages they knew were likely to fail, packaged them into securities their own analysts privately described as toxic, sold those securities to pension funds and institutional investors who trusted the banks' ratings, and collected fees at every stage. The homeowners who were sold adjustable-rate mortgages with teaser rates designed to become unpayable were not financially sophisticated enough to understand what they were signing. The banks that sold those mortgages were.

The mortgage brokers who originated the loans were paid by volume, not quality, so they had no incentive to warn borrowers. The banks that securitized the loans immediately sold the risk to someone else, so they had no incentive to ensure soundness. The rating agencies that blessed the securities were paid by the banks creating them. Every party in the chain had aligned incentives pointing toward originating as many mortgages as possible with no regard for whether they would be repaid.

When the structure collapsed in 2008, the federal government provided emergency bailouts totaling over $700 billion. Exactly zero major bank executives were criminally prosecuted. The banks that caused the crisis emerged from it larger, more concentrated, and more explicitly "too big to fail", providing an implicit government guarantee that made the next round of excessive risk more likely, not less.

Over eight million Americans lost their jobs. Several million lost their homes. The banks got bailed out. The customers got a HAMP modification process that worked for almost nobody and a $25 billion settlement with the five largest servicers that worked out to roughly $2,000 per affected homeowner.

The Security Pacific manager who knew his customers would not have originated a mortgage he knew would fail. He had to face those people afterward. He lived in that community. He carried the consequences of his decisions. That accountability is precisely what the consolidation wave eliminated. And the housing crisis is what that elimination produced, at scale, across the country, in a way that took a decade to fully unwind.

That's not a banking story. That's a story about what happens when you remove the human being from the transaction, automate the judgment, and allow the people making the decisions to escape the consequences.

The personal touch that Security Pacific provided is not coming back. The industry has been structured against it for thirty years. But the costs of its absence are real, and they are distributed unevenly, mostly to the people who needed a banker who knew their name and are now dealing with a bank that doesn't.

Who hasn't dealt with this. I have lost several doctors to private equity acquisitions. Doctors I trusted, who knew my history, absorbed into a system that immediately changed how they practiced and in some cases drove them out entirely. I have had prescriptions denied outright or repriced so high they were effectively denied. I have had procedures denied. The appeals process is designed to exhaust you. Most people give up. That is not a bug in the system. It is the business model. I say this not to congratulate myself but to make a point: the people for whom healthcare works reasonably well are largely invisible to each other, while the people for whom it is a grinding nightmare of denials and bills and prior authorizations and surprise charges are often too exhausted and financially destroyed to speak loudly about it.

The enshittification of American healthcare is not evenly distributed. It falls hardest on people who get seriously ill, people with chronic conditions, people without employer coverage, people in communities where hospital consolidation has eliminated competition, and people who make the mistake of getting sick near an out-of-network provider. For the people it works for, people like me, at least right now, the system is easy to defend because we're not seeing what it does to everyone else.

What it does to everyone else is brutal.

There was a time when your family doctor knew your name, your history, and your grandmother's tendency toward high blood pressure. Dr. Morrison made house calls during blizzards, delivered babies in farmhouse kitchens, and sent bills that people could pay. He understood that healing meant more than prescribing pills, it meant knowing the whole person, the family struggles, the community context that shaped health and sickness. Medicine was still a calling, not a business model.

Now healthcare is a labyrinthine corporate machine designed to extract maximum revenue from human suffering while providing minimum actual care. Your "doctor" is whoever the scheduling algorithm assigns you, and they've got seven minutes to diagnose, prescribe, and move on to the next billing opportunity. Insurance companies employ more people to deny claims than hospitals employ doctors. Medical bills arrive written in incomprehensible code, demanding payment for services you can't remember receiving at prices no human being could have negotiated in advance.

Insurance Companies: The Middleman Monopoly

Health insurance companies represent the purest expression of capitalist parasitism in American healthcare. They produce no medical care, cure no diseases, and heal no patients. Instead, they position themselves between sick people and doctors, collecting billions in premiums while employing armies of bureaucrats whose job is finding reasons to deny payment for care that patients have already purchased.

The business model is elegant in its cruelty: collect premiums when people are healthy, deny claims when they get sick.

UnitedHealthcare, the largest health insurer in America, employs over 400,000 people, but only a tiny fraction provide any medical services. The vast majority work in claims processing, utilization review, and other bureaucratic functions designed to minimize medical expenses while maximizing premium collections. The company reported $22 billion in profit in 2023. Every dollar of that profit is a dollar that did not go toward medical care for someone who needed it.

The prior authorization system demonstrates how bureaucratic friction can be weaponized against sick patients. Doctors must spend hours calling insurance companies to get permission for treatments they know their patients need, often waiting on hold with representatives who have no medical training but have been given scripts to deny requests. The American Medical Association found that 93% of physicians reported that prior authorization delays led to negative clinical outcomes for their patients. The system is not a quality control mechanism. It is a delay tactic designed to make care so difficult to obtain that some patients give up.

One oncologist in Denver: "I have patients dying of cancer, and I have to spend two hours on the phone convincing some twenty-two-year-old in a call center that chemotherapy is medically necessary. They'll approve the cheapest drug first, make us wait for it to fail, then approve the second-cheapest option. Meanwhile, the cancer is growing."

The claims denial algorithms scan medical claims for any excuse to reject payment, flagging treatments as "experimental," "not medically necessary," or "not covered under plan terms" based on keyword searches calibrated to maximize denial rates. A 2023 class action lawsuit, supported by a STAT News investigation, alleged that UnitedHealthcare pressured employees to follow an AI tool called nH Predict to issue denials for post-acute care, with managers setting goals to keep patient rehabilitation stays within one percent of what the algorithm predicted. The lawsuit further alleged the tool carried a 90% error rate, meaning nine of ten appealed denials were in the end reversed. UnitedHealth denies using nH Predict to make coverage determinations, calling it a care guidance tool rather than a decision-making system. The lawsuit, as of this writing, is proceeding toward discovery.

The algorithm does not have a conscience. It does not feel awkward telling a cancer patient that her treatment is not medically necessary. It processes and denies, at scale, without the friction of human discomfort.

In December 2024, UnitedHealthcare CEO Brian Thompson was shot and killed outside a Manhattan hotel where he was attending the company's investor conference. The suspect, Luigi Mangione, had inscribed the words "delay," "deny," and "depose" on the shell casings he left behind, an explicit reference to the insurance industry's claim denial practices. The public reaction was striking, and revealing. Alongside the expected horror at the violence, a significant portion of Americans expressed, with uncomfortable candor, that they understood the rage that drove it. Thousands of people shared their own stories of insurance denials, of family members who had died while fighting for coverage, of medical debt that had destroyed their finances. The grief and fury that poured out was not manufactured. It was the accumulated experience of millions of people dealing with a system that had, at some point, treated them or someone they loved as a billing problem rather than a human being.

None of which is a defense of what happened that morning. Murder is murder. Mangione is presumed innocent until a court says otherwise, and if convicted he should answer for it. The point of recounting the public reaction is not to justify the act. The point is that a country in which strangers respond to an executive's killing not with universal horror but with detailed catalogs of their own grievances against the industry he ran is a country where something has broken that public relations cannot fix. The reaction was the diagnostic, not the prescription.

The assassination did not improve insurance denial rates. Nothing in the weeks and months following the killing suggested that UnitedHealthcare or its competitors were reconsidering their practices. The machine continued processing. What the event made visible, uncomfortably, violently visible, was how much rage had been quietly accumulating under the surface of a system that many people interact with only as an abstraction until the moment it becomes catastrophically personal.

The surprise billing epidemic illustrates how insurance company network games create opportunities for price gouging. A patient can go to an in-network hospital for surgery, only to receive separate bills from out-of-network anesthesiologists or radiologists who work at the same facility. One woman whose appendix burst during a family vacation woke up from surgery owing $47,000 because doctors who worked at her insurance company's preferred hospital weren't covered under her plan. "The insurance company told me I should have asked about network status before having emergency surgery. I was unconscious and dying, but apparently that's not their problem."

The No Surprises Act of 2022 addressed some of the most egregious surprise billing practices, but the insurance industry's response was to increase the frequency of prior authorization denials and develop new categories of coverage exclusions. When one avenue for denying care becomes legally constrained, another opens.

Hospital Consolidation: When Healing Becomes Private Equity

Private equity firms discovered that hospitals provide perfect opportunities for leveraged extraction because patients can't shop around when they're having heart attacks. This captive market dynamic makes healthcare ideal for aggressive cost-cutting and price optimization. The person in the ambulance does not comparison shop.

Steward Health Care, owned by Cerberus Capital Management, provides a textbook example. Cerberus loaded Steward with debt, sold the hospital real estate to separate companies, and forced the hospitals to pay rent on buildings they previously owned. The private equity owners extracted hundreds of millions in dividends and fees while cutting staff, reducing services, and deferring maintenance on critical medical equipment.

Patients started dying from preventable causes. Nurses reported using broken equipment, rationing medical supplies, and watching patients suffer because the hospitals couldn't afford adequate staffing. Several Steward hospitals closed entirely in 2024, leaving communities without emergency services while private equity investors counted their returns. Eight hospitals in Massachusetts, Texas, and other states simply shut their doors. The communities they had served for generations had no emergency room, no labor and delivery unit, no ICU. The investors had extracted what they needed and moved on.

One doctor who worked at a Steward hospital before it closed: "They cut nursing staff to dangerous levels, eliminated departments that weren't profitable enough, and deferred maintenance on everything from elevators to heart monitors. I watched patients die because we didn't have enough staff or working equipment to provide basic care. The executives who made these decisions never set foot in the hospital."

Private equity's involvement in healthcare has expanded beyond hospitals to nursing homes, physician practices, emergency medicine staffing, and hospice care. Ensign Group, Apollo Global Management's involvement in nursing home chains, and TeamHealth's control of emergency medicine staffing at hundreds of hospitals represent the same playbook applied to every corner of medicine that can be monetized. Emergency rooms staffed by private equity-owned physician management companies have been documented billing at rates dramatically higher than hospital-employed physicians for identical services, because the extraction opportunity is there and the patient in the emergency room cannot negotiate.

The nursing staffing crisis that follows private equity hospital management is one of the most consequential and least visible healthcare stories. When these firms cut nursing staff to maximize margins, they don't simply inconvenience patients with longer wait times. They create conditions where medication errors increase, where post-surgical complications go undetected, where patients fall because nobody is available to assist them, where sepsis progresses because the nurse who would have caught it is covering too many rooms. The California nurse staffing ratios law, fought bitterly by hospital industry groups when it passed in 1999, has been consistently associated with better patient outcomes and lower mortality. The industry fought it because mandated ratios constrain the margin extraction available through understaffing.

The hospital consolidation wave has reduced competition across most American markets. When one health system controls the hospitals in a region, it controls prices. Prices at hospitals in markets with one dominant system are dramatically higher than identical services in competitive markets. The consumer protections that apply to most industries fail here because most people do not choose their hospital. They go where the ambulance takes them, or where their insurance is accepted, or where the only labor and delivery unit within an hour operates.

When a hospital closes its obstetrics unit because it's not profitable enough, a pattern that has eliminated labor and delivery services from hundreds of rural hospitals over the past decade, the women in those communities have no market-based alternative. They drive longer to deliver, increasing the risk of complications that develop en route.

The market has spoken: their babies are not profitable enough to deliver.

Pharmaceutical Price Gouging

The pharmaceutical industry has perfected the art of extracting maximum profits from human desperation by obtaining monopoly control over essential medications and defending that control through a patent system that was designed to encourage innovation and has been adapted to prevent it.

The insulin pricing scandal illustrates how pharmaceutical companies extract wealth from captive patients. Three companies, Eli Lilly, Novo Nordisk, and Sanofi, control over 90% of the global insulin market, and they've coordinated price increases that have made this century-old medication unaffordable for millions of diabetics. Insulin was discovered in 1921 and its inventors sold the patent for $1 to ensure it would remain affordable. A century later, it costs less than $10 per vial to manufacture but sells for over $300 in American pharmacies. People have died rationing insulin they could not afford. The companies that manufacture it report billions in annual profits.

The evergreening strategy that pharmaceutical companies use to extend patents beyond their original term has turned the patent system into a perpetual monopoly machine. When a patent is about to expire, the manufacturer makes minor modifications, a new formulation, a new delivery mechanism, a new dosage schedule, and files for a new patent. The generic that would have provided affordable competition gets delayed for years or decades. The company collects premium prices far longer than the original innovation warranted.

Humira, AbbVie's blockbuster anti-inflammatory drug, generated over $200 billion in sales over its patent life and remained the best-selling drug in the world for years partly because AbbVie filed over 200 patents related to the drug, effectively preventing biosimilar competition in the United States until 2023. The drug had been available in Europe with biosimilar competition, and dramatically lower prices, for years before American patients gained access to alternatives. AbbVie spent heavily on lobbying and patent litigation to maintain its monopoly while patients paid $80,000 per year for a drug that cost a fraction of that in other developed countries.

Valeant Pharmaceuticals under CEO Michael Pearson built an entire business model on buying drugs rather than discovering them, eliminating research and development, and raising prices as high as the market would bear. When Valeant acquired the rights to Daraprim, a drug used to treat a potentially fatal parasitic infection, it raised the price from $13.50 per pill to $750 overnight. The drug had been on the market since 1953. No new research had been done. The only change was ownership and the associated freedom to charge whatever a monopoly could command.

The international price discrimination reveals how artificial American pricing is. The same companies that charge Americans $300 for insulin sell identical products in Canada for $30 and in Germany for less than $10. American patients subsidize lower prices worldwide while their own government was prevented by law from negotiating drug prices on their behalf, a provision inserted into the Medicare Modernization Act of 2003 by pharmaceutical industry lobbyists that cost Americans hundreds of billions over two decades. The Inflation Reduction Act of 2022 finally allowed Medicare to negotiate a limited number of drug prices, a modest reform the pharmaceutical industry fought for years and is still challenging in court.

The Electronic Health Records Scam

Electronic Health Records systems represent one of the most successful frauds perpetrated on American healthcare, extracting billions from hospitals and doctors while making medical care less efficient, more expensive, and in some documented cases more dangerous.

Epic Systems has built a near-monopoly through a business model centered on vendor lock-in. Hospitals pay tens of millions to implement Epic systems, then find themselves trapped by proprietary technology that communicates poorly with competitors and requires constant expensive upgrades. Epic's architecture is deliberately incompatible with rivals, ensuring hospitals cannot easily switch and cannot share patient data with facilities using different systems. The interoperability that should be the central purpose of electronic health records, ensuring any doctor treating any patient can see that patient's complete history, is exactly what the current system prevents.

Doctors who once spent most of their time with patients now spend hours clicking through electronic forms, documenting symptoms for billing purposes rather than medical care. Studies have found that physicians spend more than half their working hours on electronic documentation. One family physician in Seattle: "I used to see thirty patients a day and spend real time with each one. Now I see twenty because I spend so much time on documentation. I became a doctor to help people, not to be a data entry clerk for a software company."

Physician burnout has reached epidemic levels, with multiple studies finding that more than half of American physicians report symptoms of burnout. The electronic health record is consistently cited as a primary driver. The administrative burden that these systems impose, click here to confirm you've reviewed this, document this separately for billing purposes, complete this quality metric form, respond to this message in the patient portal, has made the practice of medicine progressively less about medicine. Experienced physicians leave the profession early. Medical students choose specialties based partly on which offer the least administrative burden. The system that was supposed to make healthcare better has made it worse for the people providing it and the people receiving it, while making the software companies that build it extremely profitable.

The federal government spent over $35 billion incentivizing adoption of electronic health records through the HITECH Act of 2009. The intent was a nationwide interoperable health information infrastructure. What the money produced was a profitable industry building incompatible systems that serve billing needs more effectively than patient care needs. The government paid for the infrastructure of extraction.

Medical Debt: Weaponizing Sickness

Medical debt collection represents the cruelest intersection of healthcare dysfunction and financial predation. Hospitals employ debt collectors who garnish wages, place liens on homes, and sue patients for emergency care they couldn't have refused while unconscious.

Medical expenses contribute to over 60% of personal bankruptcies, and most medical bankruptcy victims had health insurance when they got sick. Insurance coverage provides the illusion of protection while leaving patients vulnerable to deductibles, copays, and coverage denials that can reach hundreds of thousands of dollars. The average deductible for an employer-sponsored health plan has tripled since 2010. A family with insurance and a $6,000 deductible is effectively uninsured for the first $6,000 of medical expenses every year, enough to cover most routine care and the beginning of most catastrophic care. You are insured against the catastrophe as long as you can survive the ordinary.

Nonprofit hospitals that receive tax exemptions for providing charitable care sue patients for unpaid bills and garnish wages from minimum-wage workers. Johns Hopkins Hospital, one of the most prestigious medical institutions in the world, was sued by the Maryland attorney general for aggressive debt collection practices against low-income patients. One teacher in Virginia whose daughter was treated for leukemia: "The hospital saved my daughter's life. But then they came after us like we were criminals. They sued us, garnished my husband's wages, and put a lien on our house. We had insurance, but the copays and out-of-network charges added up to over

$200,000. They literally saved our daughter and then tried to make us homeless."

The nonprofit status that exempts hospitals from billions in taxes annually is supposed to be exchanged for charity care and community benefit. Research has consistently found that many nonprofit hospitals spend less on charity care than they receive in tax exemptions. The community benefit that justifies the exemption exists largely in creative accounting, hospital executives' salaries, research overhead, and services that break even are all counted alongside actual free care to patients who cannot pay.

The CFPB's 2023 rule change removing most medical debt from credit reports was a meaningful reform, but it addressed the symptom rather than the disease. The debt itself remains. The garnishments continue. The liens are still filed. Removing medical debt from credit scores makes it harder for hospitals to use financial ruin as a collection tool, but it does not prevent the hospitals from filing the suits that create the debt in the first place.

The Direct Care Alternative

The path back from healthcare as extraction runs through models that remove the insurance company from the transaction and restore the direct relationship between doctor and patient that once made medicine a calling.

Direct primary care practices charge patients a monthly membership fee, typically $50 to $150, for unlimited access to a primary care physician. Without insurance billing, the practice eliminates the administrative overhead that consumes roughly a third of every healthcare dollar in the traditional system. Doctors in direct primary care practices typically see 600 to 800 patients instead of the 2,000 to 3,000 required to sustain a fee-for-service practice. They have time to know their patients. They can give out their cell phone numbers. They make house calls sometimes. They can spend twenty minutes on a visit instead of seven.

The model doesn't solve every healthcare problem, it doesn't cover hospitalization, surgery, or specialty care, but it demonstrates what medicine looks like when the insurance intermediary is removed. The doctor who knows you, who has time for you, who can call in a prescription without requiring an office visit, who understands your history well enough to notice when something has changed. That is what the system once provided to everyone and now provides mainly to people wealthy enough to pay out of pocket for it.

Some countries manage to provide this kind of care universally. The United Kingdom's National Health Service, for all its genuine problems and waiting lists, maintains a model of general practitioner care that keeps a doctor assigned to each patient for continuity. Germany's system of social insurance provides broad coverage with cost controls that limit the extraction opportunities available to pharmaceutical companies and hospital conglomerates. These systems are not perfect. They are not free. They are, by most measures, better than what Americans receive at dramatically higher cost.

The United States spends more on healthcare per person than any other developed country, roughly twice what countries with universal coverage spend. Americans are sicker, die younger, and experience worse outcomes on most measures of population health than residents of countries that spend far less. The money is in the system. The care is not. The difference between what Americans pay and what they receive is the extraction, the insurance company premiums that pay for denial teams, the pharmaceutical company profits that fund lobbying instead of research, the private equity returns that come from hospital real estate sales and nursing staff cuts.

For me, healthcare works. For now. I am one serious illness away from discovering the difference between the system I think I have and the system that exists. The person who reads about healthcare enshittification with detachment, as something that happens to other people, is usually someone who hasn't been seriously ill yet, or whose employer coverage is good, or whose income is high enough that even the gaps don't threaten financial ruin.

The system reserves its worst behavior for the moments when people are least equipped to fight it, when they are sick, frightened, in pain, and focused on survival rather than appeals processes. That's not an accident. It's an optimization. The algorithm that denies claims knows that most denials will not be appealed. The hospital that sues for medical debt knows that most patients will not navigate the legal system effectively. The pharmaceutical company that raises insulin prices knows that diabetics will pay rather than die.

The family doctor who made house calls understood something the algorithm doesn't: that the person in front of you is a person, not a billing event. We built a system that has largely forgotten that. We can build one that remembers it again. But only if we're willing to name what the current one is doing and to whom.

The Administrative Burden

The administrative overhead of American healthcare is not an unfortunate side effect of a complex system. It is, for many parties in the system, the product. Insurance companies employ entire departments whose function is denying care and creating friction. Hospitals employ billing specialists, prior authorization coordinators, denial management teams, and coding experts whose sole purpose is navigating the insurance bureaucracy. The doctors who once practiced medicine now practice documentation.

American healthcare administrative costs consume roughly 34% of total healthcare spending, more than twice the administrative overhead of single-payer systems. That percentage represents hundreds of billions of dollars annually that flow to insurance company overhead, hospital billing departments, and healthcare consulting firms rather than to actual medical care. Every prior authorization that takes two hours of physician time represents a physician not seeing patients. Every billing dispute that occupies a hospital administrator for weeks represents resources not devoted to patient care. The administrative system is not waste in the traditional sense, it is profitable for the people running it. The waste exists for everyone else.

The doctor who made house calls in 1965 had an administrative burden that consisted of writing up a bill and mailing it. The doctor practicing today in an insurance-dependent system spends more time on administrative tasks than on direct patient care, has a staff member dedicated to billing and insurance coordination, faces prior authorization requirements for treatments that were standard of care a decade ago, and generates documentation primarily calibrated to billing codes rather than clinical accuracy. The system has turned medicine into paperwork with occasional patient interaction.

Medicine is still practiced, in this system, by people who chose it as a calling. The physicians who stay are doing so despite the administrative machinery, not because of it. The physicians who burn out and leave represent an enormous hidden cost, the expertise and dedication that walked out the door is not captured in any insurance company's financial statement. It shows up in access problems, in communities without enough doctors, in patients who can't get appointments for months, in emergency rooms overflowing with people who have no other way in.

The family doctor who made house calls understood that healing required relationship, trust, and community knowledge that no algorithm could replace. That wisdom didn't become obsolete when healthcare became corporate. It just got buried under layers of bureaucracy and extraction, waiting for a system willing to dig it back out.

Telecommunications - Innovation to Rent-Seeking

My telecom works fine. Internet comes in, calls go out, the bill arrives monthly with only the predictable surprises rather than the catastrophic ones. I am not one of the 21 million Americans who lack access to broadband at all, or one of the millions more who have access to exactly one provider and pay whatever that provider decides to charge because the alternative is nothing. I am not the rural family whose kids do homework in a McDonald's parking lot because the house has no internet. I am not the small business owner who discovered that the only provider in his building raised rates 40% because there is no other building.

The telecommunications enshittification story is mostly invisible to people like me, because the people it hits hardest are the people with the least visibility and the least power to do anything about it. Monopoly geography and regulatory capture have produced a system that extracts maximum revenue from captive customers while investing minimally in the infrastructure that makes any of it work. The people who can leave generally don't experience the worst of it. The people who can't leave experience all of it, all the time, with no recourse.

Remember when getting a phone installed was an event? The Bell System technician would arrive in a crisp uniform, tool belt properly organized, and spend however long it took to make sure your phone worked perfectly. He'd test the line, adjust the connections, and explain how everything worked before leaving you with a device that would function flawlessly for decades. The phone itself was built like a tank, designed to survive family fights, teenage tantrums, and the occasional hurling across the room. Most importantly, it worked every single time you picked it up.

That phone came with something revolutionary: unlimited local calling for a flat monthly rate. No surprise charges, no hidden fees, no anxiety about talking too long. The Bell System had figured out that communications infrastructure worked best when people could use it without fear of bankruptcy. The network effects of universal service made everyone on it more valuable, which made the whole system more valuable, which justified the investment in making it work for everyone.

That logic, build it for everyone, make it work for everyone, and watch the economics follow, has been replaced by its exact opposite. Build it where it's profitable, charge what the market will bear, invest only what's necessary to avoid regulatory intervention, and let the people without options pay whatever you decide they owe.

The Cable Monopoly Playbook

Comcast has turned customer service into an art form of deliberate torture. The company operates as a geographic monopoly in most of its markets. When you live in a Comcast territory, Comcast is your only option for cable television and frequently for broadband internet. The company's customer satisfaction scores have ranked at or near the bottom of all American industries in surveys conducted by the American Customer Satisfaction Index for years running. These aren't mediocre scores. They are the scores of a company that has calculated, correctly, that customer satisfaction doesn't matter when customers have nowhere else to go.

The infamous 2014 recording of a Comcast retention specialist browbeating a customer for eighteen minutes revealed the systematic nature of this abuse. The representative refused to process a simple cancellation request, bombarding the customer with aggressive sales pitches. When the customer remained calm and polite while repeatedly requesting cancellation, the representative became increasingly hostile. This wasn't a rogue employee. It was trained corporate strategy, implemented at scale.

The maze of phone menus, the deliberately understaffed call centers, the hold times measured in hours, the "retention specialists" authorized to offer discounts only after customers threaten to leave. Every element serves the same purpose: keeping customers paying while minimizing the cost of serving them. The company's own internal documents, revealed in lawsuits and regulatory proceedings, have shown that customer service staffing is deliberately calibrated to the minimum necessary to prevent customers from leaving rather than the level necessary to serve them adequately.

Comcast's CEO Brian Roberts collected $32.5 million in compensation in 2023. The company's engineers could build a system that works reliably and a customer service operation that helps people efficiently. The company chooses not to because it doesn't have to. That's not a technology problem. It's a monopoly power problem.

The Reassembly of the Bell System

The 1984 breakup of AT&T was supposed to produce competition. The Department of Justice spent a decade litigating the antitrust case, won, and broke the regional Bell companies apart from AT&T's long-distance business. The intent was a competitive telecommunications market. The result, over the following two decades, was a methodical reassembly of most of what had been broken up.

SBC Communications acquired Pacific Telesis, then Ameritech, then in 2005 bought AT&T Corp itself (the long-distance company the government had separated from it in 1984) and renamed itself AT&T. Bell Atlantic merged with NYNEX, then merged with GTE to form Verizon. By 2007, roughly two-thirds of the original Bell System had been reconstructed under two names. The government had spent ten years breaking something apart, and the industry spent twenty years quietly putting it back together with regulators waving each merger through.

The argument for each merger was always the same: the combined entity would invest more in infrastructure and serve customers better. The evidence across thirty years is that prices rose, investment as a percentage of revenue declined, and the companies consistently chose buybacks and dividends over network buildout. AT&T spent over $60 billion on buybacks in the decade following the 2017 tax cuts. The networks they were supposed to build with that money went instead to shareholders.

The wireless industry consolidated on the same schedule. Four national carriers became three when T-Mobile acquired Sprint in 2020. The conditions the Justice Department attached to approval were supposed to promote competition. They produced a Dish Network wireless business that struggled from birth and eventually merged away. The comfortable oligopoly of Verizon, AT&T, and T-Mobile has mastered a pricing coordination so efficient that when one raises rates, the others follow within weeks. The "unlimited" plans all three market contain so many limitations that the word requires a legal definition the size of a footnote.

Infrastructure Decay by Design

Network infrastructure gets deliberately under-maintained to create artificial scarcity. Comcast and its competitors could upgrade their networks to handle peak demand, but doing so would eliminate their ability to charge premium prices for priority service tiers. The technology exists to provide consistent high-speed internet to every customer. The business model depends on maintaining bottlenecks.

The data cap does not reflect a genuine scarcity of network capacity. It reflects a pricing mechanism designed to extract additional revenue from heavy users who have no alternative. When ISPs market data caps as necessary network management, they are describing a problem they have deliberately created and are charging customers to solve.

The build-out promises that telecommunications companies make when seeking regulatory approval or public subsidies have a consistent track record: promises made, subsidies collected, buildout doesn't happen, consequences minimal. CenturyLink and Frontier received millions in federal subsidies to extend broadband to underserved areas and subsequently informed the FCC they had failed to meet their deployment milestones. The penalty for failing to deploy broadband to communities that had waited years for it amounted to a fraction of the subsidy they'd collected. The subsidy-and-fail model is not an accident. It is a business strategy.

American taxpayers provided hundreds of billions to telecommunications companies for network upgrades that were promised and never delivered. The American Rescue Plan and Infrastructure Investment and Jobs Act provided additional tens of billions in broadband funding to reach unserved areas. Whether this round of funding produces different results depends entirely on whether the oversight mechanisms are strong enough to enforce the commitments, which the industry's track record of capturing those oversight mechanisms does not encourage.

The Municipal Broadband Threat

When cities build their own fiber networks, they consistently deliver faster speeds at lower prices with better customer service than the private monopolies they compete with. This experiment has been run enough times to have a clear result, which is why the telecommunications industry fights it with such consistency.

EPB in Chattanooga, Tennessee, provides gigabit internet for $68 per month while Comcast charges significantly more for much slower speeds in the same region. The municipal utility serves 116,000 customers, has never raised its prices, and generated an estimated $2.69 billion in economic benefits for the community. EPB didn't just compete with Comcast. It demonstrated that Comcast's limitations are choices, not necessities.

Longmont, Colorado. Wilson, North Carolina. Ammon, Idaho. Everywhere communities have built their own networks, the private monopolies suddenly discover they can offer competitive pricing that was impossible the week before. The corporate response to these successes is not to compete honestly. It is to sue municipalities, lobby state legislatures for restrictions, and fund campaigns against ballot measures. Twenty-three states have laws restricting municipal broadband, nearly all written by telecommunications industry lobbyists. Tennessee passed laws preventing EPB from expanding beyond its electric service territory, so that the rural neighbors of Chattanooga's gigabit network rely on DSL delivering speeds one thousand times slower than what the city ten miles away has available.

Google Fiber launched in Kansas City in 2012 and offered gigabit internet for $70 per month. Within months, AT&T and Time Warner Cable both announced fiber expansion plans that had been economically impossible the week before. The limitations ISPs cite as reasons for not providing better service disappear the moment a competitor appears. The problem was never technical or economic. It was the absence of competitive pressure.

What the Monopoly Costs

The gap between what Americans pay for telecommunications and what they receive ripples through every sector of the economy. Remote work capability, telehealth access, educational technology, small business viability: all depend on reliable, affordable broadband that tens of millions of Americans cannot access at any price, and that tens of millions more access only through monopoly providers charging what they can get away with.

South Korean consumers enjoy internet speeds that make average American broadband look backward, at prices that would be considered impossibly low by U.S. standards. Japanese customers pay about $30 per month for fiber connections delivering gigabit speeds reliably. European mobile customers pay roughly half what Americans pay for comparable service. These are not countries with fundamentally different infrastructure challenges. The difference is regulation, competition policy, and whether governments have treated broadband as essential infrastructure rather than a private market commodity.

The student doing homework in a parking lot because the house has no internet is not a vivid exception. She is a data point in a systematic failure. The rural hospital that cannot implement telemedicine because the local internet is too slow is not an edge case. It is the predictable result of allowing telecommunications companies to build where they choose and ignore everywhere else.

Every American paying a telecommunications bill is paying a hidden tax on a system designed to minimize what they receive while maximizing what they pay. Installation fees not disclosed in the advertised price. Equipment rental fees for hardware that pays for itself within a year. Broadcast TV fees and regional sports network fees that are functionally part of the cable price but excluded from the advertised rate. Early termination fees making switching expensive even when a better option appears. The practice of advertising one price and billing another is so universal in telecommunications it has a common name: bill shock. The FCC has issued guidelines about transparent billing. The industry responded by making bills more complex.

What the Bell System technician understood, and what the modern telecommunications executive has forgotten, is that the infrastructure is worth more than any individual company's ability to extract revenue from it. Universal service made the telephone network what it was: the connective tissue of American commerce and community. What replaced it is extractive where it should be connective, exclusionary where it should be universal, and optimized for quarterly returns where it should be optimized for the long term.

My telecom works fine. The question worth asking is why that should feel like luck.

Retail Pharmacies - From Neighborhood Chemists to Corporate Mills

I switched to mail order for most of my prescriptions. The retail pharmacies have gotten slower and the understaffing is obvious every time you walk in. One pharmacist covering the counter, the drive-through, and the phone at the same time. You can see it on their faces. Mail order works. But I should not have to route around a broken system to get my medications reliably.

Which means I'm not in the retail pharmacy system that millions of Americans depend on for their medications, and which has been systematically destroyed by the same balance-sheet logic that hollowed out every other industry in this book. The mail order option that works for me works because I have stable prescriptions, reliable mail delivery, and enough advance planning to not need a medication in the next four hours. A lot of people don't have all three of those things, and those are the people standing in the CVS line.

The neighborhood pharmacy, the one where somebody knew your name and your medication history and your family, is largely gone. What replaced it is a corporate processing operation that is understaffed by design, priced through conflicts of interest so elaborate they require their own section of this chapter to explain, and closing at a rate of roughly eight locations per day.

There was a time when the corner pharmacy was a healthcare institution in its own right. The pharmacist knew everyone by name and their medical histories. When a customer needed a special compound, he mixed it himself. When money was tight, he quietly noted "pay when you can" on the receipt. The pharmacy was an extension of the neighborhood doctor's office, a place where healthcare happened with a human touch.

Today that place is mostly a CVS or a Walgreens where a single frazzled pharmacist juggles drive-through orders, phone calls, vaccination appointments, and a growing queue of increasingly irritated customers. The prescription called in three days ago isn't ready. The pharmacist, who looks like she hasn't slept adequately in weeks, apologizes while frantically typing at her computer terminal. Behind her, dozens of prescription bags sit unfilled, representing medications that people need and cannot get.

The Pharmacy Benefit Manager Scam

To understand how retail pharmacy got this bad, you have to understand pharmacy benefit managers, the middlemen that nobody outside the industry knows about and that have extracted billions from both pharmacies and patients while providing no medical value whatsoever.

Pharmacy benefit managers, or PBMs, position themselves between insurance companies and pharmacies, negotiating drug prices and processing pharmacy claims. The three largest, CVS Caremark, Express Scripts (owned by Cigna), and OptumRx (owned by UnitedHealth Group), control roughly 80% of prescription drug transactions in the United States.

The conflicts of interest embedded in this structure are staggering. CVS Caremark is both a PBM that processes claims for insurance companies and a pharmacy chain that fills those prescriptions. It sets reimbursement rates for competitor pharmacies through its PBM arm while steering patients toward its own pharmacies through insurance plan design. The company negotiating on behalf of your insurance company is the same company collecting your prescription at retail. It is playing both sides of the transaction at the same time.

When CVS completed its merger with Caremark in 2007, creating this vertically integrated operation, independent pharmacies found themselves in an impossible position: accept below-cost reimbursements set by a competitor, or lose access to patients covered by that competitor's PBM clients. It was playing poker against someone who owned the casino, dealt the cards, and set the rules.

PBMs also practice "spread pricing", charging insurance plans more for a drug than they pay the pharmacy that dispensed it, and pocketing the difference. An insulin prescription might cost the PBM $20 to reimburse the pharmacy while the PBM charges the insurance plan $50. The $30 spread goes to the PBM. The patient sees none of it. The pharmacy gets less than cost. The PBM profits from the gap without providing any service.

Between 2010 and 2021, nearly one-third of all retail pharmacies closed. Independent pharmacies were more than twice as likely to close as chain stores, and the closures disproportionately affected Black and Latino neighborhoods where independent pharmacies were more common. The PBM reimbursement structure was a primary driver, independent pharmacies couldn't absorb the below-cost reimbursements that chains could partially offset through their own PBM operations.

The Extraction Machine

By the time the PBM consolidation had reshaped the market, the surviving pharmacy chains had their own extraction strategies well developed.

Walgreens pursued aggressive geographic expansion, often opening stores directly across from successful independent pharmacies. Once the independent closed, Walgreens would often close its competing location, leaving the neighborhood with reduced pharmacy access overall. The strategy wasn't to serve customers better. It was to eliminate competition and then reduce costs by closing the locations the competition-elimination had required.

CVS perfected the upsell model, transforming pharmacies into retail stores where the prescription counter was one department among many, and not the most profitable one. The CVS front end, with its cosmetics and seasonal merchandise and snack food, generates higher margins than the pharmacy counter. The company had effectively used the pharmacy's customer base to build a general merchandise retailer, then used the revenue from that retailer to subsidize the pharmacy operations that drew customers in.

The ExtraCare loyalty program collected customer data that could be sold and used for marketing. The minute clinic attached to many CVS locations added healthcare service revenue while generating additional pharmacy prescriptions. The business model layered extraction on extraction, each component designed to capture more revenue from the customer who had walked in needing medication.

The Understaffing Catastrophe

By 2020, the pharmacy industry reached a breaking point when pharmacists began walking off the job. The immediate trigger was COVID-19, which dramatically increased demand while chains refused to hire adequate staff. But the crisis had been building for years through systematic understaffing designed to maximize profits.

The Ohio Board of Pharmacy's investigation into CVS revealed the scope. At one Canton, Ohio location, inspectors found a pharmacy running over a month behind on prescription fills. Staff had repeatedly asked management to temporarily close the store to catch up, but the request was denied. When investigators arrived, they found overwhelmed workers who didn't even notice the inspection team's presence.

The human cost was staggering. According to federal prosecutors, one pharmacist developed a urinary tract infection after being unable to take a bathroom break during a 13-hour shift. Another vomited on the side of the road after their shift because they had no time to eat all day. Pharmacy employees filed hundreds of complaints through CVS's ethics line about dangerously insufficient staffing, but management ignored them. The ethics line existed to document that concerns had been raised, not to address them.

The patient safety implications were equally serious. At one CVS in Virginia Beach, a state inspector reviewed 200 prescriptions and found 74 mistakes, an error rate of roughly 37%. In at least two cases, pharmacists dispensed medications at multiple times the prescribed dosage. A pharmacy error is not an inconvenience. It can kill the person taking the wrong medication or the wrong dose.

One former CVS pharmacist in Indianapolis: "It would just be me running everything: pick up, drop off, walk-in vaccines, filling, verifying, everything. We had thousands of prescriptions behind." She told investigators: "There's no shortage at all. We have enough technicians. We have enough pharmacists. They're not allowing us the hours."

The staffing decisions were made by people who calculated that the labor cost savings exceeded the legal and reputational costs of the errors and the walkouts. The calculation held until regulatory investigations and pharmacist strikes made the understaffing undeniable enough to require a response. Even then, the response was incremental.

The Great Die-Off

Nearly 2,300 pharmacies shut their doors in 2024 alone, at a pace of around eight locations per day.

Rite Aid's collapse illustrated how quickly a major chain could disintegrate. After filing for bankruptcy twice in less than two years, Rite Aid sold pharmacy assets from more than 1,000 stores to competitors. The chain that had once been America's third-largest pharmacy retailer simply evaporated, leaving behind pharmacy deserts and unemployed workers. Rite Aid had been profitable until it wasn't, the transition accelerated by the PBM reimbursement squeeze, the debt from an acquisition strategy that made sense when borrowing was cheap, and the COVID disruptions that stressed every part of its operations at the same time.

But Rite Aid's demise didn't create more pharmacy access. It consolidated the market further into the hands of CVS and Walgreens, the same chains whose staffing and reimbursement practices had contributed to the crisis. CVS workers told state inspectors that the company didn't add staff to handle the extra business from closed competitors. More prescriptions, same number of people. The error rate didn't improve. The wait times got longer.

The closures created pharmacy deserts, communities where residents had to travel significant distances to fill prescriptions. Closure rates were higher in predominantly Black and Latino neighborhoods than in predominantly white ones. The pattern is consistent across enshittified industries: the communities with the least political power and the fewest alternatives experience the worst of what extraction produces.

Nearly a third of independent pharmacies are now at risk of going out of business due to PBM reimbursement rates set below their actual costs. The National Community Pharmacists Association has warned that if a third of all community pharmacies close, it will be a catastrophe for seniors, a hardship for most other patients, and a devastating blow to the healthcare system. The warning has been consistent for years. The trend has continued.

The Pharmacist as Casualty

The profession of pharmacy has been degraded by the same forces that degraded the industry. Pharmacists spend six to eight years in training to earn their doctorate degrees, longer than most physicians require. They are among the most accessible healthcare providers in America, available without appointments in most communities. They can identify drug interactions, counsel patients on medication management, administer vaccines, and perform basic health screenings.

In the corporate pharmacy model, these capabilities are largely unused. The pharmacist whose training enables complex medication therapy management spends most of their time processing prescription queues as fast as possible to hit the fill-rate metrics that determine their performance review. The clinical knowledge exists but the system doesn't create space for it.

Pharmacist burnout rates have climbed to match those of physicians. Young pharmacists are leaving retail pharmacy for hospital positions, specialty pharmacy, or other careers entirely. The pipeline into retail pharmacy suffers from the reputation of the working conditions, which are well known to pharmacy students before they graduate. The same dynamics that produce pilot shortages in aviation, the training is expensive, the compensation doesn't match, the conditions are degrading, apply to retail pharmacy.

What Good Still Looks Like

H-E-B Pharmacy in Texas demonstrates that pharmacy doesn't have to work this way. The chain has ranked first among supermarket pharmacies in customer satisfaction studies for multiple consecutive years. What made H-E-B different wasn't revolutionary technology, it was adequate staffing and a commitment to service. Pharmacists have more support staff, which means they have time to talk to patients, answer questions, and apply the clinical knowledge their training provides.

Independent pharmacies that survived the consolidation wave did so by focusing on services chains couldn't replicate. Compounding pharmacies providing custom medications, pharmacies in underserved areas that became essential community health centers offering blood pressure monitoring and diabetes education, specialty pharmacies serving patients with complex medication regimens. These pharmacies survived by doing what the corporate model had abandoned: treating the patient as a person with a healthcare need rather than a transaction to be processed.

The mail order pharmacy that works for me works because I have stable, predictable prescriptions and the patience to plan three months ahead. It is efficient and convenient and removes me from the retail pharmacy system's worst dysfunction. That's not a solution to the retail pharmacy crisis. It's an escape from it available to people with the right circumstances. The person who needs an antibiotic today, the elderly patient who can't manage a complex mail order process, the person who needs to ask a pharmacist a question, they're still standing in that CVS line.

The neighborhood pharmacist who knew your name and your history, who would mix a custom compound when needed and note "pay when you can" on the receipt, that person provided something the algorithm cannot replace. He is mostly gone now, replaced by an undertrained technician processing a queue that never shortens, in a store optimized for cosmetic sales with a pharmacy counter attached.

American pharmacy was once a respected profession focused on community health and patient care. The choice between pharmacies that extract value from sick people and pharmacies that help communities stay healthy was made decades ago, by companies that never set foot in the neighborhoods they were dismantling.

Mr. Kowalski would have known which one to choose. He'd have chosen wrong by Wall Street's standards and right by every other standard that matters.

The Opioid Connection

The retail pharmacy's role in the opioid crisis illustrates how thoroughly the industry had abandoned its clinical mission in pursuit of revenue. CVS, Walgreens, and Rite Aid all paid billions in settlements related to their dispensing practices during the opioid epidemic, settlements that acknowledged their pharmacies had filled prescriptions for opioids that showed clear signs of being fraudulent or problematic.

Pharmacists at these chains have testified that they were pressured to fill prescriptions without adequate time to review them, that concerns about suspicious prescribing patterns were ignored or actively discouraged, and that the metrics they were evaluated on emphasized volume and speed rather than clinical judgment. A pharmacist who slowed the queue to consult with a prescriber about a suspicious prescription was a pharmacist who was falling behind on fills. The system created incentives to keep filling and penalties for slowing down.

The result was that pharmacies that were supposed to be the last line of defense against dangerous prescribing became willing participants in dispensing medications they should have questioned. The communities hardest hit by the opioid crisis, rural communities, post-industrial communities, communities with few healthcare alternatives, were also communities where the pharmacy was often the only accessible healthcare touchpoint. When that touchpoint failed its clinical mission, the consequences were catastrophic.

Walgreens agreed to pay $5.7 billion to settle opioid-related claims in 2022. CVS agreed to pay $5 billion. Rite Aid faced opioid-related claims that contributed to its bankruptcy. These were enormous settlements, and they represented a fraction of the profits the chains had made during the years they were overfilling opioid prescriptions.

The people who made the decisions that led to these settlements, the executives who set the metrics, who ignored the pharmacist concerns, who pressured for higher fill rates, were not personally liable for the settlements. The shareholders paid. The executives kept their compensation. The communities dealing with the consequences of the opioid epidemic continued dealing with them.

The PBM Reform Battle

The pharmacy benefit manager problem has attracted legislative attention across the political spectrum, because few healthcare issues are more obviously parasitic than a middleman that profits from both sides of a transaction while making the medication more expensive for patients and less profitable for pharmacies.

The Federal Trade Commission launched an investigation into PBM practices in 2022, issuing reports in 2024 documenting how the three major PBMs had used their market power to squeeze independent pharmacies, steer patients toward their affiliated pharmacies, and inflate drug prices. The reports confirmed what pharmacists and patient advocates had been saying for years: the PBM model is designed around extraction, not service.

Congress has debated PBM reform legislation across multiple sessions without producing comprehensive reform. The insurance industry, which benefits from having PBMs manage the complexity of pharmacy benefits, and the pharmacy chains with their own PBM operations, both lobby against reforms that would constrain their market power. The result is that the system continues producing the outcomes it was designed to produce: higher costs for patients, lower reimbursements for independent pharmacies, and larger profits for the vertically integrated giants.

State-level PBM regulation has produced some results. Arkansas passed legislation requiring PBMs to reimburse pharmacies at rates at or above the cost of the drug, the simplest possible protection against below-cost reimbursement. The law was challenged in court and its fate traced through the federal judiciary for years, eventually surviving in modified form. That protecting pharmacies from being required to sell medications at a loss required years of litigation illustrates how thoroughly the system had been captured by the interests that benefit from it.

Technology as the Right Answer and the Wrong One

Mail order pharmacy, the system that works for me, is a legitimate use of technology to improve medication access for patients with stable, chronic conditions. Centralized dispensing with sophisticated automation reduces error rates, allows pharmacist review of larger prescription volumes with fewer interruptions, and provides 90-day supplies that reduce the burden of monthly refills. When I say my pharmacy works great, I'm describing a system where technology is doing what technology is supposed to do: making a routine process more efficient and reliable.

The retail pharmacy chains have deployed technology in ways that serve the corporation rather than the patient. Automated dispensing systems can handle high-volume fills, freeing pharmacist time for clinical consultation, or they can be used to justify further staffing cuts, creating the same volume with fewer people. Predictive analytics can identify patients at high risk for medication non-adherence and prompt clinical intervention, or they can identify patients most likely to respond to upselling of premium services. The technology is neutral. The purpose it serves is not.

CVS's MinuteClinic model embedded basic healthcare services inside pharmacies, making clinical consultations accessible without appointments. The model has genuine value for the patient who needs a strep test or a blood pressure check and can't get a same-day appointment with their physician. It also generates additional prescription revenue for the attached pharmacy, extends CVS's relationship with the customer, and collects clinical data that feeds back into the company's broader healthcare strategy. The service and the extraction happen at the same time.

The pharmacy app that allows refill requests, provides medication reminders, and facilitates communication with the pharmacy team can be a genuine clinical tool or a loyalty program that increases CVS's share of the customer's prescription spending. Most pharmacy apps are both, because the companies building them have mixed motives and the patient is both a healthcare recipient and a revenue source.

The technology that would serve patients, interoperable medication histories that any pharmacist could access, real-time drug interaction checking across all of a patient's prescriptions and providers, automated identification of patients who might benefit from medication therapy management, exists and is used in some settings. It is not the priority of the major chains, because it doesn't directly generate revenue and requires infrastructure investment.

What the Loss Costs

The independent pharmacist who knew your name knew something the algorithm doesn't: that medication adherence is partly a relationship issue. Patients who trust their pharmacist take their medications more reliably. They mention the side effect they've been experiencing because they know it will be taken seriously. They ask about the drug interaction they read about because they feel comfortable asking. They come in for a blood pressure check because the pharmacist suggested it last month and they like the pharmacist.

These interactions have documented clinical value. Patients with strong pharmacist relationships have better chronic disease management, lower hospitalization rates, and better outcomes on the measures that determine healthcare costs. The independent pharmacist was not just a dispenser. He was a healthcare provider embedded in the community, providing low-cost, high-access clinical touchpoints that prevented more expensive interventions downstream.

When the independent pharmacy closes and the patient transfers to CVS, they lose that relationship. They gain a phone tree and a queue. The CVS pharmacist would like to provide the same service but cannot, because the staffing model and the metrics don't create space for it. The system is efficient at filling prescriptions. It is not efficient at keeping people healthy, because keeping people healthy doesn't generate the same quarterly revenue as filling prescriptions.

The pharmacy deserts created by closures, the communities where the nearest pharmacy is now 30 minutes away, produce measurable health effects. Medication adherence drops when access is difficult. Chronic conditions worsen when patients miss doses because refilling prescriptions requires a car trip and half a day. Emergency room visits increase when preventable conditions aren't managed. The healthcare system pays more, downstream, for the savings the pharmacy chains generated upstream by closing locations.

My mail order pharmacy is great. It exists because I'm the easy customer, stable conditions, reliable mail delivery, enough margin in my schedule to manage the process. The people who most need accessible, relationship-based pharmacy care are the least likely to be served by it, and the most likely to be standing in a CVS line watching a single overwhelmed pharmacist try to do the work of three.

That's not a technology problem. That's a choice about what pharmacy is for.

The Compound Pharmacy Exception

One corner of pharmacy that has survived the extraction wave is compounding, the preparation of customized medications for patients whose needs can't be met by commercially available products. A patient who needs a specific dosage not available commercially, or who needs a medication in a form they can take (a liquid rather than a pill, for instance), or who has an allergy to an ingredient in a commercial product, relies on compounding pharmacies.

Compounding pharmacies are disproportionately independent. The business model rewards expertise, relationship, and customization, exactly the things that corporate chains have optimized away. A compounding pharmacist who knows that Mrs. Hendricks needs her hormone therapy in a specific formulation and that Mr. Okafor's arthritis compound works better at a slightly different concentration than the standard formula is providing a clinical service that CVS's automated systems are fundamentally incapable of offering.

The compounding pharmacy sector has faced its own regulatory challenges, particularly following contamination incidents at large-scale outsourcing facilities, but the core independent compounding model has survived because it provides something genuinely irreplaceable. You cannot automate personalization. You cannot scale individualized medication preparation through a drive-through window.

The compounding pharmacist is the closest living relative to Mr. Kowalski mixing his compounds in the back room. He survived because the corporate model couldn't do what he does, not because the corporate model didn't try to displace him.

Specialty Pharmacy: The Growing Exception

Specialty pharmacy, the dispensing of high-cost, complex medications for conditions like cancer, rheumatoid arthritis, and HIV, is one area where genuine clinical expertise has maintained value against the extraction pressure. Specialty pharmacies typically employ pharmacists with clinical training in specific disease states, provide patient counseling and monitoring services, and maintain relationships with both prescribers and patients that affect treatment outcomes.

The irony is that specialty pharmacy's clinical value model is what all pharmacy was supposed to be. The neighborhood pharmacist who knew your history and could identify a dangerous interaction was doing a version of what specialty pharmacists now do at scale for specific disease populations. The difference is that specialty medications cost enough to make the clinical service economically viable, while routine medications have been stripped to the point where the only sustainable model is volume processing.

The lessons from specialty pharmacy, that pharmacist expertise and patient relationships produce measurable health and economic value, could inform the redesign of retail pharmacy toward something more like what it used to be. They haven't been applied because applying them requires staffing investment that reduces short-term margins, and the companies running retail pharmacy are focused on short-term margins.

The mail order pharmacy that serves me well, the specialty pharmacy that serves patients with complex conditions, and the surviving independent pharmacies serving their communities all share one characteristic: they've found models where the pharmacist's clinical value is recognized and resourced. The retail pharmacy that's closing at eight locations a day hasn't found that model because it hasn't been looking. It's been looking at throughput metrics and cost per fill and square footage per employee, and optimizing accordingly.

The neighborhood pharmacist knew which numbers mattered. The corporate model chose different numbers. The communities living with pharmacy deserts and medication errors are paying for that choice.

Hotels and Hospitality - Service Excellence to Upcharge Everything

Hotels are all the same now. There is no real differentiation between them. Pay more, get more. That is true at all of them. The brands used to mean something different from each other. Now they are variations on the same beige box with the same amenities at different price points. I traveled constantly for years and stayed at hundreds of them. At some point I stopped noticing which chain I was in.

Route 66 used to be a museum of American hospitality ambition. Not grand hospitality, nobody was staying at the Ritz in Tucumcari, New Mexico, but genuine hospitality, the kind where the owner met you at the door and the place had a personality because somebody had put real thought into making it theirs. Holbrook, Arizona had the Wigwam Motel, where you slept inside concrete tepees built in 1950 because Chester Lewis thought travelers deserved something memorable. The Blue Swallow Motel in Tucumcari with its neon sign that had been running since 1941, operated by innkeepers who knew the road and the travelers on it. The Route 66 Motor Inn in Oklahoma where the owner's wife made breakfast and you could hear her in the kitchen before you'd even fully woken up.

These places had identities. You could tell, from the moment you pulled into the parking lot, that a human being with opinions had made decisions about what this place would be. The curtains were a specific color because someone chose that color. The sign had a particular font because someone hand-lettered it. The breakfast menu had three items because three items was what the kitchen could do well and the owner knew it.

I've been in a lot of hotels since then. The good ones, the ones with character, with quirk, with a sense that someone cares about the place, are rarer than they used to be and harder to find. What replaced the Blue Swallow and the Wigwam and the hundreds of other roadside originals is the Hampton Inn and the Marriott Courtyard and the Holiday Inn Express, laid out on identical floor plans, furnished from the same catalog, operating from the same corporate handbook, staffed by people who would be equally at home in the identical property three states over because the properties are identical.

The boxes aren't bad. They're clean and functional and reliably mediocre in ways you can predict before you arrive. That predictability is the point. The modern hotel chain optimized away the surprise, which also optimized away the delight, the personality, the sense that you've arrived somewhere rather than merely stopped.

Remember when checking into a hotel felt like stepping into a pocket of civilization? The lobby had actual humans at the front desk who knew which restaurants served the best late-night tacos and could personally guarantee your room would be perfect. Room service arrived on real china. Staff acted like hosts welcoming you home, not extraction specialists calculating how much they could squeeze from your wallet.

Those days got buried under an avalanche of resort fees, upcharges, and algorithmic pricing that makes airline executives look bashful. The modern hotel industry perfected death by a thousand cuts, each one small enough to avoid open rebellion, but collectively transforming hospitality into financial extraction.

The Franchise Machine

To understand how Route 66's motels became Hampton Inns, you have to understand the franchise model that replaced individual ownership with corporate standardization at enormous scale.

The brand franchise model works like this: a hotel owner licenses a brand name, operating system, and reservation platform from Marriott or Hilton or IHG in exchange for fees and adherence to brand standards. The brand doesn't own the property. It licenses the name and provides the system. The owner pays a percentage of revenue in royalties, contributes to the brand's marketing fund, and agrees to maintain the brand's physical and service standards.

The benefits are real: instant recognition, access to loyalty program customers, corporate reservations infrastructure. The costs are equally real: brand standards that mandate identical physical appearance across thousands of properties, guest experience requirements that prioritize consistency over personality, and fees that typically total 10-15% of gross revenue before the mortgage payment.

An independent motel owner in 1965 could paint his building whatever color struck him, serve whatever breakfast he could make well, and greet guests however his personality inclined. A Hampton Inn franchise owner in 2025 gets a contract that specifies the exact shade of beige, the exact contents of the complimentary breakfast, and the exact script for the check-in greeting. The resulting product is consistent enough to book without hesitation and boring enough to forget immediately.

The franchise system also created a powerful incentive against anything distinctive. A Hampton Inn that tried to offer something unusual, a local artist's paintings in the lobby, regional food at breakfast, individually decorated rooms, would risk non-compliance with brand standards and the loss of the franchise license. The system punishes personality. Consistency is not a side effect of the franchise model. It is its primary product.

The Resort Fee Virus

The transformation started innocently with resort fees at actual resorts. A small charge covering WiFi, fitness center access, pool usage at properties where guests genuinely used those amenities. What began as $10 daily at vacation properties metastasized into $45-per-night mandatory fees at urban business hotels offering little more than a tiny fitness room and internet speeds that would have embarrassed 1995 dial-up.

Marriott turned fee extraction into performance art. Their resort fees now appear at properties that bear zero resemblance to resorts, including business hotels in downtown areas where the only pool is metaphorical, filled with guest tears. These fees hide from initial booking prices, appearing at checkout like surprise parties thrown by your least favorite accountant.

The resort fee model spread because it worked: hotels could advertise lower room rates, attract price-sensitive bookers, and then recapture the revenue at checkout when cancellation was no longer practical. The customer who books a $99 room and discovers at checkout that the mandatory resort fee brings the total to $144 has already arrived. Returning home is not free. The complaint is noted, the fee stands.

Parking fees exceeding the most expensive urban garages. Internet charges treating WiFi as a luxury amenity. Early check-in fees for accessing rooms that sat empty since the previous guest left. Late checkout fees charging you for sleeping past 11 AM. Some hotels charge "facilities fees" for using the lobby you're standing in. Each fee is individually small enough to swallow. Collectively they represent a systematic deception in which the advertised price has no real relationship to the amount you will pay.

MGM Grand in Las Vegas charges a $45 daily resort fee supposedly covering WiFi, fitness center access, and local phone calls. The WiFi works intermittently, the fitness center stays perpetually overcrowded, and nobody has made local calls from a hotel room since the Clinton administration. The fee exists not because it represents value delivered but because guests will pay it, are already there when they find out about it, and have no leverage.

The FTC has investigated resort fee practices. The Biden administration made junk fee elimination a policy priority. Congress held hearings. The resort fees remain, because the regulatory and political will to enforce transparency requirements against an industry that donates substantially to political campaigns has been insufficient to match the industry's will to keep collecting them.

The Staffing Devastation

Modern hotels discovered the best margin improvement: eliminate employees. Route 66's motel owner greeted you personally because he was the owner, the manager, and often the maintenance staff. That's not efficiency, it's economics. What happened in branded hotels is different: systematic removal of people who provided service, replaced by technology that provides the appearance of service while eliminating its substance.

Housekeeping staff once given reasonable time to clean rooms now operate under productivity quotas that produce rooms looking clean at first glance but revealing shortcuts upon inspection. Bathrooms with mysteriously sticky floors. Beds made with sheets not quite changed. Carpets "vacuumed" with minimal enthusiasm. Many housekeepers work for subcontracting agencies rather than the hotel directly, receiving minimum wage without benefits, with no institutional connection to the property or its guests.

The pandemic gave hotels the excuse to eliminate daily housekeeping entirely, an "opt-in" model that turned out to be permanent at many properties. The service that was standard returned as a premium, at additional cost. Guests who had paid for rooms and expected rooms to be cleaned discovered that what they had paid for and what they received were different things, and the hotel's response was that pandemic-era policy changes had simply become the new normal.

Front desk staff routinely work alone during busy check-in periods, creating 45-minute lobby waits while the property projects the appearance of efficiency through digital check-in options that mostly don't work. Bell staff elimination means guests haul their own luggage while paying rates that once included this service. Room service quietly disappeared at many properties, replaced by delivery app partnerships that charge additional fees and serve cold, soggy food because the elevator ride from the lobby takes twelve minutes.

The Blue Swallow Motel's innkeeper knew which room had the best view and could tell you without checking a computer. She knew because she lived there and paid attention. The night audit clerk at the Hampton Inn is following a checklist. Both can check you in. Only one can make you feel welcome.

Technology as Hospitality Destroyer

The hotel industry embraced self-service technology with the enthusiasm of an industry that had calculated exactly how much it could save by replacing humans with screens.

Mobile check-in sounds convenient until you realize it eliminates the human interaction that once served as the baseline of hospitality. The person at the desk who noticed you looked exhausted and upgraded you to a quieter room, who warned you about the construction noise on the east side of the building, who connected you with the restaurant they personally liked, that interaction has been replaced by a notification that your room is ready and a digital key that may or may not work.

Keyless entry through smartphone apps fails with sufficient regularity that it has produced a well-documented category of hotel complaint: the guest who stands in a hallway at 11 PM, phone battery at 3%, frantically attempting to get a door to recognize their existence. When the app fails and the guest trudges back to the front desk, they often discover that the one remaining human employee cannot override the system because the system is "cloud-based" and the cloud is having a bad day.

The Wigwam Motel's door had a physical key. It worked every time. Chester Lewis could have given you a spare without involving a call center in another time zone.

Algorithmic Price Manipulation

Hotels embraced dynamic pricing with the fervor of an industry discovering that computers could do what front desk managers used to do intuitively, but at a scale and speed that removed any human judgment from the process.

Room rates fluctuate hour by hour now, not just season by season, based on browsing history, booking platform, device type, and algorithms that detect signals of urgency and adjust prices accordingly. The same room viewed at $149 in the morning costs $247 by afternoon, not because demand changed materially but because the algorithm detected that you'd looked at the room three times and concluded you were likely to book regardless of price.

Airlines pioneered this model. Hotels observed that it worked and adopted it with fewer constraints, because unlike airlines, hotels don't have to put their prices on public searchable databases with regulatory oversight. The price discrimination is more granular and less visible than airline pricing, because the mechanisms are more opaque.

The consequences reach beyond individual bill shock. When hotels price algorithmically, they systematically extract maximum revenue from business travelers on expense accounts (who are price-insensitive) and leisure travelers who have already committed to a destination (who are captive). The families who can only afford to travel once a year, who planned their trip months in advance only to find that prices have doubled by the time they need to book, discover that algorithmic hospitality doesn't care about their vacation.

The Boutique Bait and Switch

"Boutique" hotels promised personalized service and unique character as a response to the homogenization that franchise brands had produced. Corporate groups quickly discovered they could charge premium rates while delivering standardized mediocrity with trendier lighting.

These properties feature Instagram-worthy lobbies filled with expensive, uncomfortable furniture, the kind that looks good in photographs and hurts after twenty minutes of sitting, surrounding rooms that prioritize aesthetics over the fundamental question of whether you can sleep in them comfortably. The mattress may be genuinely good. The lighting will be deliberately too dim to read by. The shower will feature a confusing array of controls and no instructions.

Many "boutique" properties are management contracts operated by companies that also run Hampton Inns and Holiday Inn Express locations, using different branding to justify charging three times as much for service levels that differ primarily in the font used for the in-room stationery. The personality is curated rather than authentic, sourced from a design firm rather than an owner with opinions. The local art on the walls was selected by a corporate art consultant. The "locally inspired" menu items in the restaurant were developed in a corporate test kitchen.

The Route 66 motel that had personality had it because the owner lived there and cared. The boutique hotel that projects personality has it because a brand consultant decided it would appeal to the target demographic. Both experiences are available at higher prices now than the original. Only one of them is real.

What Survives

Route 66 still has the Wigwam Motel. It survived as a historical attraction, which is the category that personality falls into now, not an active approach to hospitality but a preserved artifact that people drive out of their way to photograph. Chester Lewis is gone. The motel operates as a nonprofit preservation project. You can sleep in a concrete tepee tonight if you want to, which is more than can be said for most of what Route 66 used to offer.

The independent inns and bed-and-breakfasts that survive do so because they found something the brands cannot replicate: a specific place with specific people who know it. The Cape Cod inn operated by the third generation of the same family, the mountain lodge run by the couple who bought it because they wanted to live there, the downtown hotel in a historic building whose owners love the building enough to maintain it properly, these places exist and they're often genuinely excellent because the incentive structure is different. The owner faces you at breakfast. The owner's reputation is the hotel's reputation. The owner cannot extract value and leave.

Family-owned Chatham Bars Inn in Cape Cod maintained service standards across generations because the family's identity was tied to the property's quality. The incentive to cut corners that produces resort fees and staffing devastation at corporate properties simply doesn't exist when the person making the decision has to look the guests in the eye tomorrow morning and explain why the experience was worse than it should have been.

The next time you check into a hotel and the staff seems genuinely helpful, the bill contains no unpleasant surprises, and the room has a window that opens with some personality about where you've ended up, you've found a property that remembers why hospitality matters. Those experiences become more precious as they become rarer.

The Wigwam Motel is still there. The Blue Swallow still runs its neon sign every night in Tucumcari. They survive as exceptions that prove the rule, testaments to what Route 66 was and what hospitality used to mean: a human being, in a specific place, trying to make you feel welcome. That's not a business model that optimizes for quarterly returns. That's why it mostly disappeared.

The Loyalty Program Extraction Machine

Marriott Bonvoy, Hilton Honors, World of Hyatt, IHG One Rewards, the hotel loyalty programs that emerged from the frequent flyer model have become, like their airline counterparts, both a customer retention mechanism and a sophisticated price discrimination and data collection operation.

The programs work by selling points to credit card companies, which offer them as rewards to cardholders. The credit card transaction is where most loyalty program revenue comes from, not from hotel stays. Marriott Bonvoy sold points to credit card issuers for roughly $600 million in 2019. The points are a currency that Marriott controls entirely, whose value Marriott sets and can diminish at will, and which expire or devalue on schedules Marriott determines.

Marriott's 2016 acquisition of Starwood Hotels, which created the world's largest hotel company with over 30 brands and 7,000 properties, also produced the largest hotel data breach in history. The Starwood guest database that Marriott acquired had been compromised by Chinese intelligence hackers for years before Marriott discovered it. Five hundred million guest records were exposed. The records included passport numbers, credit card numbers, and travel histories of guests across decades.

The data breach illustrated what the loyalty programs are beneath their rewards-and-benefits surface: massive databases of personal information about people's travel patterns, preferences, companions, and behavior. The hotel that knows you've stayed 47 nights over two years knows a great deal about you. The hotel that has failed to secure that information has handed it to anyone who managed to breach the system.

Marriott was fined by the UK's Information Commissioner's Office, initially £99 million, later reduced on appeal. The fine represented less than one week of Marriott's annual revenue. The data of half a billion people remained compromised. The loyalty program database that had been assembled to create switching costs and enable price discrimination had become a liability that was born by guests rather than the company that had failed to protect it.

The Private Equity Hotel Play

Private equity discovered hotels as another opportunity to apply the by-now familiar extraction template: purchase a portfolio of properties, implement revenue management systems that maximize short-term returns, cut operating costs through staffing reductions and deferred maintenance, and exit through a sale or REIT conversion before the degradation becomes visible in the returns.

Blackstone's hotel acquisitions, including the $26 billion purchase of Hilton Hotels in 2007, which represented the largest hotel acquisition in history, demonstrated both the scale of private equity interest in hospitality and the consequences of debt-loading properties that run on thin operating margins.

The Hilton acquisition loaded the company with enormous debt right before the 2008 financial crisis devastated hotel occupancy. Blackstone worked with Hilton through the restructuring and eventually generated substantial returns when the company went public in 2013, but the guests and employees who experienced the austerity measures implemented to service the debt were the ones who absorbed the costs of that return.

The sale-leaseback transaction that private equity uses in other industries appears in hotels as the separation of property ownership from hotel operations. A private equity firm buys a hotel, sells the real estate to a REIT (sometimes one it controls), and then operators lease the property back, creating rent obligations on top of the operating costs that squeeze out the discretionary spending, on staff, on maintenance, on the small investments that distinguish a memorable hotel from a forgettable one, that hospitality requires.

The hotel that can't afford to fix the elevator promptly, that runs its housekeeping department understaffed because the REIT payment is due, that eliminated room service because the margin analysis said it cost more than it generated, these are usually hotels where the economics have been engineered by people who have never slept in them.

International Comparison

The Route 66 motel that Chester Lewis built in 1950 was exceptional in America's context for being distinctive. In Japan, distinctiveness is the baseline. The ryokan, the traditional Japanese inn, is built around a philosophy of hospitality that treats the guest's comfort as an end in itself rather than an input to revenue optimization. The room is prepared for the specific guest staying in it. The meal is prepared fresh and presented as an experience. The staff's role is to anticipate needs before they're expressed.

The ryokan model is not economically transferable wholesale to American roadside hospitality, the labor intensity and cultural context are too different. But it illustrates what hospitality looks like when the operating philosophy is service rather than extraction. The ryokan innkeeper is not thinking about resort fees. She is thinking about whether the guest is comfortable.

European boutique hotels, particularly those in family ownership for generations, similarly demonstrate that the boxes-and-fees model is not inevitable. The pension in Austria run by the same family for fifty years, the hotel particulier in Paris where the owner lives on the premises, the small hotel in Edinburgh whose staff has worked there for decades, these places have retained something that American hospitality has largely abandoned: the sense that someone cares whether you had a good time.

The American version of this, the boutique hotel, the independent inn, the historic property restored by owners who love it, exists and is often excellent. It exists as a premium niche rather than a widely available option, and it typically costs more than the brand-standard box that replaced the Route 66 original. The Blue Swallow experience is now a luxury. The Hampton Inn experience is the default.

The Airbnb Disruption and Its Limits

Airbnb arrived as a promised disruption to the hotel monopoly, authentic local experiences, genuine variety, the ability to stay in a real neighborhood rather than a hotel district. For a period in the early 2010s, it delivered on some of that promise. Staying in someone's apartment or guesthouse in a city's actual residential neighborhoods did provide a different experience than the Marriott two blocks from the convention center.

The platform quickly evolved in ways that recapitulated the hotel industry's worst dynamics rather than disrupting them. Professional hosts who operate multiple properties as de facto hotel businesses replaced the original spare-room model. Dynamic pricing algorithms set rates on Airbnb that follow the same logic as hotel algorithmic pricing. Cleaning fees that can exceed a night's accommodation. Service fees layered by the platform. The total cost visible only after significant engagement with the booking process.

The cities where short-term rental platforms achieved significant scale discovered that converting long-term housing to tourist accommodation removed apartments from the housing market, drove up rents for residents, and destabilized neighborhoods. The disruption that was supposed to benefit travelers benefited investors in short-term rentals at the expense of residents who needed housing. New York, San Francisco, Barcelona, and dozens of other cities implemented restrictions on short-term rentals that reduced the platform's scale in those markets.

Airbnb didn't solve the hospitality problem. It created a new extraction model that mimicked the old one's worst elements while adding new forms of opacity and adding housing market distortion to the list of consequences. The Route 66 original was owned by someone who lived there and cared about the place. The Airbnb investment property is managed from a spreadsheet.

What the Boxes Cost

The standardization that franchise brands optimized for comes with costs that don't appear in any brand's financial statements but are real nonetheless. When every city's hotel district looks identical, the same Hampton Inn floor plan, the same Marriott Courtyard lobby, the same Hilton Garden Inn breakfast area, the traveler's experience of arriving somewhere has been diminished. The sense of place that good hospitality communicates is gone. You know you are in Indianapolis or Austin or Charlotte only because the airport said so.

The Route 66 motels that had character told you where you were. The Blue Swallow's neon communicated something about Tucumcari and Route 66 and the

American West that a Hampton Inn's backlit sign cannot. The Wigwam Motel's concrete tepees told you that you had arrived somewhere specific, where a specific person had built a specific thing because he thought it would delight travelers. The Hampton Inn tells you only that Hampton Inns exist here, as they exist everywhere.

That loss is not easily quantified. It shows up in the experience of travel, in the quality of memory, in whether places feel like themselves or like placeholders. The traveler who spent a night in the Wigwam Motel in 1960 has a story. The traveler who spent a night in a Hampton Inn last week has a receipt.

The Wigwam is still there. Chester Lewis's concrete tepees have survived because they are impossible to replicate economically and too distinctive to ignore culturally. They were preserved precisely because they are irreplaceable. The hundreds of other Route 66 originals that weren't distinct enough to achieve landmark status are parking lots and strip malls and nothing at all.

Hospitality was once the art of making a stranger feel at home in an unfamiliar place. The person who ran the Blue Swallow practiced that art. The algorithm that sets the Hampton Inn's resort fee does not practice any art at all. It optimizes.

Grocery Stores - Community Anchors to Self-Checkout Warehouses

Prices keep going up well past what they should be, and the service keeps going down. Self-checkout is a mixed experience depending on where you are. I like it at Publix. I hate it at Walmart. The difference is the machine itself and how much the store has invested in making it work. At Walmart it feels like the store designed the self-checkout to be frustrating enough that you give up and come back when there is a human cashier, except there usually is not one. You are just stuck.

Grocery shopping used to be fun. Not exciting, not glamorous, but genuinely pleasant, the way a good neighborhood errand can be when the people you encounter along the way know what they're doing and seem to care about the place they work.

There was a butcher who could tell you which cut would work best for what you were making and would trim it properly while you watched. A baker who knew what had come out of the oven recently and what had been sitting. A produce person who had been at that stand for years and knew which peaches were going to be perfect tomorrow and which tomatoes to avoid this week. These weren't credentialed experts. They were people who had learned a specific thing through years of doing it and took some pride in the knowing.

Now try finding anyone in a grocery store who knows the store. Find someone who can tell you where the saffron is, or whether the salmon looks good today, or which of the three olive oils on the shelf is worth buying. What you'll mostly find is a scattering of part-timers hired this month who know their assigned section and nothing else, and a customer service desk staffed by someone whose primary job appears to be explaining why the self-checkout machines aren't working.

The stores themselves have changed in a way that tells the story plainly. They used to be stores. Now many of them are effectively real estate operations that lease floor space to vendors and happen to also stock some groceries. The endcaps and premium shelf positions are purchased, not earned by the product's quality. The fresh departments that required skilled staff, butcher, baker, deli counter, have been systematically reduced or eliminated. The person who made the store worth going to has been replaced by a self-checkout machine that treats you as a suspected shoplifter.

That isn't an accident. It's a series of deliberate decisions made by people who calculated, correctly, that customers need groceries badly enough to tolerate a lot of degradation.

The Store That Used to Know You

The grocery store of twenty years ago employed specialists whose knowledge was an actual service. The butcher behind the counter wasn't just slicing meat. He was making decisions about what to order, how to cut for different purposes, how to advise customers whose cooking skill ranged from professional to first-attempt. The relationship between a regular customer and a good butcher was a genuine information exchange, he knew what you cooked and could tell you what was good that week.

The same was true across every fresh department. The produce manager who had been there fifteen years knew which supplier's strawberries were worth buying and which were beautiful at purchase and terrible by dinner. The fishmonger could tell you the difference between the two varieties of snapper on the ice and why it mattered. The cheese counter person could guide you toward something you'd like based on what you'd bought before.

This institutional knowledge was accumulated over years and resided in people. It was not a system asset. It walked out the door when the person left. When grocery chains cut the specialized departments and replaced them with pre-packaged products from centralized distribution facilities, they didn't just reduce labor costs. They eliminated the expertise that had made the store worth visiting rather than ordering online.

The bakery that produced fresh bread in-house required a baker with training and equipment and time. The bakery section that stocks bread from a regional industrial facility requires a shelf stocker. The product is different in ways that matter, freshness, variety, the smell of the store when bread is baking, but the cost structure is dramatically simpler. The chains chose simplicity. The customers got worse bread and found the choice had been made for them.

The Real Estate Operation

The most fundamental change in modern grocery is one most customers never consciously notice: the store's relationship with its own floor space.

A traditional grocery buyer decided what went on the shelves based on what sold and what customers wanted. Good products earned placement. Poor products got cut. The buyer's job was to find items that would make customers want to come back.

In modern grocery, shelf placement is primarily a negotiated commercial transaction. Consumer packaged goods companies pay "slotting fees" for shelf placement, particularly for end caps, eye-level positions, and the premium locations near checkout. They pay "co-op advertising" fees for inclusion in the weekly circular. They pay "new item fees" for the right to be introduced into the store's inventory at all. A new product entering a major grocery chain can cost the manufacturer hundreds of thousands of dollars in fees before a single unit is sold.

The grocery store has become a real estate operation that leases floor space to the manufacturers who can afford to pay for it, then stocks that floor space with whatever those manufacturers provide. The buyer's role has shifted from "find the best products" to "maximize the revenue from our shelf space."

The consequences are visible in any grocery store's layout. The products at eye level are there because someone paid for eye level, not because they're better than the equivalent products on the bottom shelf. The endcap display featuring a product with a "feature price" sticker is there because the manufacturer paid for that endcap, not because the product is a particular value. The store's own private label products, which typically offer better margins, are placed strategically, but their placement is based on the store's financial interest rather than what's best for the customer.

H-E-B's buyers, by contrast, are known in the industry for genuinely evaluating products on merit. The chain's private label program sources locally when possible and genuinely tests quality before shelf placement. The difference between shopping H-E-B and shopping Kroger is partly the difference between a store curating its selection for customers and a store renting floor space to manufacturers.

The Self-Checkout Nightmare

Walk into any Kroger today and witness the full spectrum of cost-cutting degradation. Self-checkout stations dominate the front end, often outnumbering traditional cashier lanes by three to one. The few remaining human-operated lanes move slowly because the company has cut staffing to the minimum required to manage the self-checkout area.

The machines themselves seem designed by someone who has never bought groceries. Try scanning a bunch of bananas and watch the weight sensor have an existential crisis. Buy a bottle of cooking wine and prepare for the age verification system to summon an employee who might be helping customers three aisles away. The bagging area, that mystical zone where items must be placed immediately upon scanning, has the sensitivity of an anxious cat, triggering alerts when you breathe too heavily near your purchases.

This is not incompetence. Kroger's executives understand exactly what they're doing. They've calculated that customers will tolerate significant degradation because people need groceries badly enough to endure self-checkout frustrations. The algorithm has run the numbers on customer tolerance and concluded that the labor savings exceed the customer loss from frustration.

The self-checkout transaction also shifts shoplifting liability toward the customer. The retailer's internal calculations on self-checkout shrinkage, the polite term for customers who accidentally or deliberately fail to scan items, build in an expected loss rate. When that loss rate is exceeded, the retailer's response has sometimes been to install cameras and AI systems that monitor every self-checkout transaction and flag suspected theft. Customers who've done nothing wrong get approached by loss prevention staff. The store that replaced the cashier with a machine has also replaced the cashier's implicit trust with algorithmic surveillance.

According to a 2024 study in the Journal of Business Research, regular checkout with human cashiers makes customers more loyal to a store. Customers feel more rewarded and more valued when a human handles their transaction. The study finding is not surprising, it describes something most people can feel intuitively. What's notable is that the major chains ran the numbers, concluded that short-term cost savings outweighed long-term loyalty effects, and installed the machines anyway.

Major retailers are now backtracking, partially and awkwardly. Dollar General eliminated self-checkout at about 12,000 locations in 2024. Target announced steps to limit self-checkout. Amazon pulled its "Just Walk Out" cashierless system from grocery stores. The retreat is not driven by concern for customer experience. It's driven by shrinkage numbers that came in higher than projected and customer satisfaction scores that fell faster than the labor savings justified.

Private Equity Devours the Pantry

The acquisition of BI-LO and Winn-Dixie by Southeastern Grocers, backed by private equity firm Lone Star Funds, demonstrates the standard extraction template applied to food retail.

Lone Star first bought BI-LO in 2005, ran it into bankruptcy by 2009, then emerged from Chapter 11 in 2010 before acquiring Winn-Dixie in 2012 for $590 million. Between 2011 and 2018, Lone Star extracted $980 million in dividends from Southeastern Grocers while the company accumulated six times more debt than earnings. The company sold $145 million worth of land out from under its distribution centers and grocery stores, then required the affected entities to pay rent on buildings they used to own. The sale-leaseback. Every time.

When Southeastern Grocers filed for bankruptcy in 2018, the private equity owners had already extracted their fees and profits, leaving behind empty buildings and food deserts in the communities those stores had served. The neighborhoods where Winn-Dixie had been a community anchor for decades lost their grocery store. They didn't lose it because it failed to serve the community. They lost it because someone who had never been to those neighborhoods decided that the real estate was more valuable than the service.

The Kroger-Albertsons proposed merger, which would have combined two of the three largest grocery chains in the country, was blocked by the FTC in 2024 after a federal judge found it would likely reduce competition and raise prices. The companies' argument, that the combined entity would be better positioned to compete with Walmart, revealed how thoroughly the grocery industry had come to see scale as its primary value rather than service. Two companies telling a judge that their merger would benefit customers by making it easier to extract value from them was a more honest summary of the industry's direction than their PR materials acknowledged.

The Deli Counter Apocalypse

The deli counter is where the grocery store's transformation from service institution to processing facility is most visible, because it's where the expertise is most obvious in its absence.

A real deli counter employed people who knew about food. Someone who could tell you which cheese would pair with your wine, recommend a mustard to complement the pastrami, explain the difference between the two prosciuttos, slice to the exact thickness you wanted and know why thickness mattered. That knowledge was real and valuable. It made the store worth visiting for the deli section alone.

Today's deli counters, where they still exist, operate with skeleton crews. The person behind the counter knows how to operate the slicer and not much else, because that's all the job requires and all the training provides. Many stores have eliminated in-store bakeries entirely, replacing fresh-baked bread with products shipped from industrial facilities. The cheese selection has been pre-packaged rather than cut to order. The olive bar that required daily maintenance has been replaced by a pre-packaged olive product from a national distributor.

Each of these changes saves money. Each of them removes a reason to shop at a particular store rather than having groceries delivered. The chains have spent twenty years eliminating the experiential advantages of the physical grocery store and then expressed surprise that customers shifted toward online ordering and delivery. The store that has nothing distinctive to offer faces a straightforward question from every customer: why am I here?

Food Deserts and the Geography of Extraction

The grocery industry's enshittification is not distributed evenly. The communities that experience it most severely are the communities with the least political and economic power, in a pattern consistent enough to be a policy.

When Kroger closes a store, it tends to close in lower-income neighborhoods where revenue per square foot falls below the chain's targets. When Albertsons consolidates locations, the stores that survive tend to be in higher-income areas with more purchasing power. The result is that the communities most dependent on accessible grocery stores, those without cars for long-distance shopping, those without financial margin to absorb higher-priced convenience alternatives, are the communities most likely to find themselves without a grocery store at all.

The term "food desert" describes a reality for roughly 23 million Americans who live in low-income areas without convenient access to a full-service grocery store. The communities in these deserts are not geographically remote. They are often inner-city neighborhoods that supermarket chains have decided are less profitable to serve than the suburbs their customers are moving toward.

The corner store and dollar store that fill the gap in food deserts stock shelf-stable, processed food at premium prices, not because that's what residents want to eat but because fresh produce requires refrigeration, skilled handling, and inventory management that small-format retail can't provide. The community that loses its grocery store doesn't just lose convenient access to food. It loses access to fresh food at reasonable prices, which produces measurable effects on health outcomes over the years following the closure.

The Resisters: What Grocery Can Be

H-E-B, the Texas-based chain that remains privately held by the founding Butt family, demonstrates what grocery looks like when the ownership structure aligns with long-term community investment rather than quarterly extraction.

H-E-B stores are staffed at levels that allow employees to know the store and help customers. The produce section has people who know produce. The meat department has butchers who cut to order. The store feels like it has been designed for the people who shop in it rather than for the operational efficiency of the people who run it.

During Hurricane Harvey in 2017, H-E-B stores reopened before other essential services, serving as community gathering points and emergency supply centers. The company hadn't prepared for Harvey because of a regulatory requirement. It had prepared because the people who own H-E-B understand that their company's relationship with the communities it serves is long-term, that their family's name is on the building, and that being the store that shows up when things are hardest is part of what earns the loyalty that keeps the business viable.

Wegmans offers another model. The Rochester-based chain has been named to Fortune's 100 Best Companies to Work For every year from 1998 through 2025, a run so consistent it suggests an actual organizational commitment rather than a good year. Wegmans employees receive training about the products they sell. The produce staff can tell you the difference between apple varieties and which to use for which purpose. The seafood counter employs people who understand how fish should be cooked and can tell you why the salmon looks particularly good this week.

These stores prove that grocery enshittification wasn't inevitable. Every frustrating experience at a corporate chain, the self-checkout machine that won't acknowledge your avocados, the empty deli counter, the customer service person who shrugs and says they don't know the store, represents a deliberate choice to prioritize cost reduction over the experience that makes physical grocery shopping worth doing.

The butcher who knew your order, the baker who knew what was fresh, the produce person who steered you toward the good peaches, they weren't luxuries. They were the service. When grocery chains eliminated them to optimize costs, they eliminated the reason to show up rather than order online. Then they expressed surprise that customers ordered online.

The grocery store that cares is still available to people who live near one. It's getting rarer. And the communities that lose it don't just lose a store. They lose a place where people knew each other and knew the food and took some small pride in providing something worth coming back for.

That used to be normal. Now it's Wegmans or H-E-B, and you have to be lucky enough to live near one.

The Trader Joe's Model

I spent twenty years managing technology at Trader Joe's, which puts me in an unusual position for this chapter: I worked for one of the grocery industry's success stories while watching the industry around it deteriorate.

Trader Joe's works for reasons that are specific and replicable but rarely replicated, because replicating them requires accepting constraints that public companies and private equity-owned operations find intolerable.

The stores are small by design, around 10,000 to 15,000 square feet against the 50,000 to 100,000 of a conventional supermarket. The product selection is deliberately limited, around 4,000 SKUs versus the 30,000 or more at a typical large supermarket. Almost all of those products are private label, developed in-house and sourced directly from manufacturers rather than through the broker and distributor network that adds cost at every step of the conventional grocery supply chain.

The small selection means every product on the shelf was chosen because it met a standard. There are no slotting fees at Trader Joe's, manufacturers don't pay for placement, which means placement decisions are made on the product's actual merit. The buyer's job is finding things worth selling, not selling shelf space to the highest bidder.

The staffing model is structured around paying employees enough that they stay. Trader Joe's wages are substantially above the retail industry average. The turnover rate is a fraction of the industry norm. The crew member who has been in the wine section for three years knows the wine section. The produce person who has been there for five years can answer questions about produce because they've developed actual knowledge. The institutional knowledge that most grocery chains systematically destroy through understaffing and high turnover is actively preserved.

John Shields, who ran Trader Joe's from 1988 to 2001, spent twenty years before that at Macy's learning how retail operations build and maintain quality. His approach to Trader Joe's was to treat the store as a service rather than a processing operation. He would spend days in stores asking employees what the office was doing to make their jobs harder. The answers filled notebooks. The problems got fixed. The employees who knew they were being listened to stayed.

That's not a complicated management philosophy. It's just not compatible with the quarterly earnings pressure that shapes every decision at publicly traded grocery chains.

The Technology Question

Grocery technology done right reduces friction and improves the experience. The inventory management systems that keep shelves stocked, that predict demand patterns, that reduce food waste through better ordering, these are genuine improvements that serve both the business and the customer.

The same technology deployed toward different ends produces self-checkout machines that treat customers as labor and surveillance subjects, algorithmic ordering systems that create predictable out-of-stock patterns at peak times, and dynamic pricing mechanisms that adjust prices faster than human shoppers can track them.

In 2023, Kroger tested dynamic pricing, changing shelf prices electronically based on time of day, demand, and other factors. The technology would allow prices to rise during peak shopping hours, fall during slow periods, and respond to competitor pricing in real time. The company framed this as offering better deals to off-peak shoppers. Consumer advocates framed it as charging higher prices to people who can only shop at certain times, often lower-income workers with less schedule flexibility.

The same electronic shelf label technology that enables dynamic pricing could instead enable greater transparency, showing the price per unit clearly, flagging price increases from the previous week, identifying which products are on genuine sale versus manufactured markdowns. The technology is neutral. The question is what it's optimized to do.

Amazon's "Just Walk Out" system, pulled from its Fresh grocery stores in 2024, was a surveillance technology sold as a convenience. The system used cameras and sensors to track every item every customer touched, building a detailed record of shopping behavior that Amazon could use for its broader data business. The cashierless checkout was the product. The behavioral data was the revenue.

The grocery stores that are getting technology right use it to extend their human staff's capabilities rather than replace them. H-E-B's supply chain technology is among the most sophisticated in the industry, it allowed the company to maintain supply during Harvey and prepare for the specific needs of specific communities in ways that centralized distribution cannot. The technology serves the mission. At chains where the technology serves quarterly metrics, it produces self-checkout machines and surveillance cameras.

The Kroger-Albertsons Aftermath

The FTC's 2024 blockage of the Kroger-Albertsons merger was an unusual moment of regulatory intervention in an industry that had seen almost no antitrust enforcement for decades. The proposed merger would have combined the country's two largest traditional supermarket chains, creating a company with about 5,000 stores across 48 states.

Kroger and Albertsons argued that the combined company would be better able to compete with Walmart, which has become the largest grocery retailer in the United States by volume. The argument was not wrong. Walmart's scale gives it pricing power that conventional grocery chains struggle to match. But the FTC's response was equally accurate: eliminating the competition between Kroger and Albertsons in the hundreds of markets where both operate would raise prices and reduce service for customers in those markets, regardless of how the combined entity compared to Walmart.

The two companies' plan to spin off hundreds of stores to C&S Wholesale Grocers as a remedy, an attempt to address the FTC's competition concerns, was found inadequate by the court. C&S had no experience operating retail grocery stores at scale. The divestiture was structured to satisfy regulatory review rather than to create genuine competition.

The blocked merger left both companies weakened and facing strategic uncertainty. Albertsons pursued legal action against Kroger claiming the company hadn't adequately worked to secure merger approval. The recriminations between two large grocery chains trying to figure out how to survive in a market dominated by Walmart, Amazon, and Costco illustrated how thoroughly the industry had been reshaped by forces that conventional grocery was not designed to address.

The answer that most of the industry has reached, cut costs, reduce staff, install self-checkout, close underperforming locations, makes the individual companies marginally more competitive on cost metrics while making the overall experience worse in ways that accelerate the shift to online ordering and alternative formats. It's the classic enshittification spiral, where each cost cut makes the product slightly worse, which makes customers slightly less loyal, which creates pressure for more cost cuts.

What the Grocery Store Was

The grocery store in its full expression was a striking institution. It employed skilled tradespeople, butchers, bakers, produce specialists, who practiced genuine crafts and transmitted knowledge to customers who couldn't have it otherwise. It served as a community gathering point where you ran into neighbors and caught up on local life. It employed teenagers in their first jobs and provided careers to people who stayed and built expertise. It sponsored Little League teams and held blood drives and closed early on Christmas Eve so families could be together.

These functions didn't generate line items in the financial statements. They didn't show up in same-store sales comparisons. They didn't justify their existence in quarterly earnings calls. So they were cut, one by one, whenever a cost-reduction opportunity was identified.

The grocery store that emerges from this process is cleaner than its predecessor, the floors are more consistent, the lighting is more uniform, the displays are more professionally designed. It is also emptier in every sense that matters. Empty of people who know things. Empty of the small human transactions that made an errand feel like an event. Empty of any reason to prefer it to the app on your phone that will bring the same products to your door.

The butcher who knew what cut you wanted and the baker who knew what had just come out of the oven knew something the algorithm doesn't: that you were a person, not a transaction. The grocery store that treats you as a person gives you a reason to show up. The one that treats you as a processing problem gives you a reason to stay home.

Most grocery stores have made their choice. The self-checkout machine is waiting.

Entertainment and Theme Parks - Magic to Upcharge Everything

I used to go to Disneyland California once a week. Friends and I made it a regular outing. I got into Club 33 twice, which tells you how embedded I was in that world. I knew the park the way you know a neighborhood you have lived in for years. That is gone. I refuse to do anything Disney anymore. The parks are outrageously expensive. The movies are bad. The merchandise is cheaply made. The upsells are insulting. What they built was something genuinely magical. What they turned it into is a machine for extracting money from people who remember what it used to be.

I got into Club 33 twice. For those who don't know it, Club 33 is the private restaurant hidden inside Disneyland, the one Walt Disney himself designed as a place to entertain corporate sponsors and VIPs, with no external signage and an address only members and their guests know to look for. You cannot buy your way in with money alone. You need a membership, and memberships have historically required a connection, a waiting list, and a sponsor. I got in because my ex-boss became a Disney executive and brought me as a guest. It was striking, not because the food was transcendent, but because the access was earned through a relationship, not a transaction. The experience felt earned.

I haven't had a Disneyland annual pass in years. The math stopped working. The park I went to monthly, casually, because it was fun and affordable and I knew it well, has transformed into a premium fee operation where a single day for a family of four can cost over a thousand dollars once you add the Lightning Lane fees that are effectively required to experience the park's main attractions without waiting in two-hour lines. The annual pass program that made me a regular was eliminated entirely in 2020, replaced with tiered memberships that cost dramatically more and include fewer days.

Club 33 memberships now reportedly cost between $25,000 and $100,000 for initiation, plus thousands annually in dues. The thing I experienced through a human relationship is now available to anyone who can pay an initiation fee that exceeds many people's annual salaries. That's not magic. That's exclusivity marketed as magic.

Walt Disney had a clear vision when he sat on that bench in Griffith Park, watching his daughters ride the merry-go-round. "I felt that there should be something built where the parents and the children could have fun together," he said. No carnival barkers hawking overpriced games. No nickel-and-diming families who'd already paid admission. Just a place where magic didn't come with a surcharge.

Walt Disney died in 1966. His vision lasted about as long as he did.

The Numbers Behind the Magic

The transformation of Disney from the park Walt built to what it has become happened gradually and then suddenly, accelerating after the company hired management consultants to "optimize" the guest experience in ways that mostly meant finding new revenue streams.

Disneyland opened in 1955 with a ticket price of $1, about $11 in today's dollars. By the early 1980s, when I was going regularly, the price had increased but remained accessible for middle-class families. The annual pass program made frequent visitors like me economically viable. The park wanted regulars. Regulars spent money, spread word of mouth, and maintained the sense of the park as a community destination rather than a special occasion.

The annual pass elimination during COVID was framed as a pandemic response. What it was is a strategic repositioning: Disney decided it preferred infrequent visitors who spend heavily per visit over frequent visitors who moderate their spending because they know they'll be back next week. The regular who knew the park well and spent modestly was replaced with the occasional visitor who spends extravagantly because this might be the only time.

Today's Disney World represents the triumph of extractive capitalism over childhood wonder. The base ticket runs $119 to $199 per person per day, but that's merely the entry fee for Disney's elaborate fee architecture.

Want to skip the lines your admission supposedly granted you access to? That's $15 to $39 per person for Lightning Lane Multi Pass, but the most popular attractions aren't included. Those require Individual Lightning Lane purchases at $10 to $25 per ride, per person. A family of four trying to experience the major attractions without spending their vacation in line can spend an extra $200 to $400 per day on top of admission.

Hungry? A basic counter-service meal for a family of four runs $80 to $120. Character dining, where children meet Mickey Mouse while eating overpriced chicken nuggets, costs $52 to $62 per adult and $33 to $42 per child. Even parking became a profit center: $25 to $30 per day at theme parks, and resort guests pay additionally to park at their own hotel.

The psychological architecture of this system is what makes it particularly insidious. Disney has weaponized scarcity and parental guilt at the same time. Miss getting a Lightning Lane for the new ride? Your child gets to explain to classmates why they didn't ride the attraction everyone's talking about. The premium options aren't framed as luxuries. They're framed as the baseline experience, and not purchasing them means failing your child. It's guilt-driven upselling that would make a timeshare salesman blush.

The annual family budget that Disney expects, multiple park days, hotel stay, dining, routinely exceeds $5,000 to $10,000. Disney World has priced itself out of the middle-class family vacation it was built for and into the premium vacation market it once competed against. The families who saved for a year to take their kids to Disney are discovering that a year's savings barely covers the entry fees.

The Iger Era and the Optimization Machine

Michael Eisner, who ran Disney from 1984 to 2005, built the modern Disney empire and also began its financialization. He expanded the parks, acquired ABC and ESPN, produced blockbuster films, and introduced the culture of revenue optimization that transformed Walt's park into a pricing laboratory.

Bob Chapek, who briefly succeeded Iger as CEO, accelerated the fee extraction with the ferocity of someone who didn't understand or didn't care what made Disney valuable. Lightning Lane replaced the beloved FastPass system that had been free since 1999. Park reservations required in addition to admission. The annual pass program eliminated. Every guest experience that had been included in the base admission price became a potential revenue line.

Bob Iger, who returned as CEO in 2022 after Chapek's tenure ended in controversy, inherited the apparatus and has made incremental adjustments while defending its fundamentals. Disney has acknowledged that pricing has hurt attendance, particularly among local families and annual passholders. It has modestly expanded pass options. It has not fundamentally rethought the approach. The machine is too profitable in the short term for anyone with a quarterly earnings call to question.

The deeper problem is structural. Disney is now a publicly traded company with institutional shareholders expecting returns. The park that Walt built as a place families could return to regularly, a place designed to build loyal relationships over time, has been converted into a premium destination that maximizes revenue per visit at the cost of the frequency that creates loyal fans. The company is optimizing itself out of the cultural position that made it irreplaceable.

Six Flags: The Art of Managed Decline

Disney's enshittification at least maintains a veneer of polish. Six Flags, after multiple rounds of private equity ownership, abandoned all pretense of caring about guest experience.

Premier Parks acquired Six Flags in 1998 for $1.86 billion with private equity backing and immediately implemented the standard playbook: slash maintenance budgets, reduce staffing, maximize short-term cash extraction. Ride downtime increased as deferred maintenance became policy. Food quality collapsed as contracts went to the lowest bidders. Customer service disappeared as staff levels dropped below functional minimums.

The safety implications of private equity's approach to theme park maintenance are not hypothetical. Ride accidents at PE-owned parks have been documented across multiple properties. Maintenance departments with gutted budgets defer repairs that responsible operators would address immediately. The ride that needs an inspection gets inspected on the schedule the budget permits rather than the schedule safety requires.

Six Flags filed for bankruptcy in 2009, emerged, continued struggling, merged with Cedar Fair in 2024, and continues operating as a chain that offers a substantially worse experience at prices that have steadily increased while the experience declined. The private equity investors who loaded the company with debt have moved on. The families standing in line at Six Flags parks experiencing rides that don't run on time at prices that don't reflect the quality of the experience are the ones who absorbed the cost.

Cedar Fair, the larger and better-run chain that acquired Six Flags, maintains its own properties at higher standards, but Six Flags locations in the combined company are typically identifiable by their operating quality relative to Cedar Fair's legacy parks. The private equity damage to the brand and infrastructure doesn't disappear when ownership changes. It persists in the deferred maintenance, the institutional culture, and the customer expectations that years of underperformance have set.

The Gig Economy Comes to Theme Parks

The staffing model that made Disneyland great when I was a regular visitor was not complicated: pay people well enough that they stay, train them thoroughly, and trust them to use judgment. The cast members who helped guests find their way or made a child's day special were people who had been in the park long enough to care about it. They were not following a script. They were drawing on institutional knowledge and genuine engagement.

Modern theme parks have largely replaced this model with seasonal, part-time, and contract staffing that minimizes labor costs and benefits obligations. The person helping you at the entrance to an attraction may be in their third week on the job. The operational knowledge that would allow them to smooth a problem, suggest an alternative, or make a child feel better about missing a ride is simply not there because the staffing model doesn't create it.

Disney has been more resistant to this trend than most, maintaining higher staffing standards and longer-term employment than competitors. But the pressure is there. As ticket prices have increased and attendance has plateaued, the labor line in the financial statements becomes a target. Each round of cost optimization makes it harder to deliver the experience that justified the price increase that necessitated the cost optimization.

The Universal Challenge

Universal Studios has offered the most credible competitive challenge to Disney's theme park dominance, particularly through its Harry Potter and other immersive environment investments. The Wizarding World of Harry Potter recreated Hogsmeade and Diagon Alley with a level of environmental detail that Disney had pioneered and Universal improved upon.

Universal's approach has been to invest in immersive theming that creates genuine "you are in this world" experiences, then extract through the beverage and merchandise purchases that become irresistible when you're standing in Hogsmeade and the only drink available is Butterbeer. The extraction is real but feels less coercive because the immersion earns it.

The competitive dynamic between Universal and Disney has produced genuine investment in new experiences at both parks. Star Wars: Galaxy's Edge, Avatar Flight of Passage, the Hagrid's Motorbike Adventure, Epic Universe. The parks are competing for the premium vacation dollar with increasingly sophisticated attractions.

The competition that's missing is competition at the accessible end of the market. There is no serious competitor offering a quality theme park experience at prices families with ordinary incomes can afford to visit regularly. Knoebels and Holiday World provide excellent value but are regional parks without Disney's or Universal's cultural cachet. The middle market for family entertainment that Disneyland once occupied, the local park that families visited regularly, that kids grew up in, that created genuine cultural loyalty, has been abandoned.

The Keepers of the Flame

Scattered across America, smaller regional parks demonstrate what entertainment venues look like when community connection matters more than quarterly earnings.

Knoebels Amusement Resort in Pennsylvania has remained family-owned since 1926. The park uses a pay-per-ride system instead of expensive gate admission, letting families control their spending. Free parking. Reasonably priced, genuinely good food. Rides receiving meticulous maintenance because the family's reputation depends on safety and reliability across generations. The park feels like what it is: a place that exists to give families a good time, run by people who live in the community they serve.

Holiday World in Indiana includes unlimited soft drinks and sunscreen with admission, eliminating two of the major sources of vacation nickel-and-diming that make theme park visits feel like an extraction exercise. Their water park comes with the theme park admission instead of requiring separate tickets. The economics work because Holiday World optimized for repeat visitors who feel treated honestly.

Tokyo Disneyland, operated by Oriental Land Company under license from Disney, consistently ranks among the world's best theme parks. The Japanese operators maintained Walt Disney's original vision while applying their own operational standards. Lines move efficiently because the park is properly staffed. Food quality exceeds American Disney parks while costing less. The experience feels like something Walt recognized and designed for, a place where families come to be happy, not to be extracted from.

The difference is not magic. It's what you're optimizing for.

What I Lost When Disney Changed

The Disneyland I went to monthly was not just a theme park. It was a place I knew and that, in the way of places you know well, knew me back. The cast members I recognized from regular visits. The spots I'd discovered over years of attendance. The sense that I was a regular at a good place, not a visitor at a premium destination.

Club 33 was the pinnacle of that experience, not because it was expensive or exclusive, but because access came through a human relationship. My ex-boss who became a Disney executive and brought me as a guest was sharing something he valued with someone he cared about. The experience meant something because it came from a person, not from a transaction.

The current Club 33 has reportedly undergone multiple redesigns to modernize and expand its membership base. The secret restaurant that Walt designed for the inner circle, accessible only through relationship and knowledge, is now accessible primarily through a large check. The magic is still there, probably. But the magic of secret access through human connection has been replaced by the magic of exclusivity purchased at premium price.

Walt's vision was not naive idealism. He understood that creating genuine joy for families could be profitable without being exploitative. He built a company culture that maintained this understanding across his lifetime and into the next decade after his death.

The company that runs Disneyland now is not the company Walt built, except in name. It is a publicly traded entertainment conglomerate whose park operations must justify their capital against alternative investments. The park that was designed to be a place families returned to regularly has been repriced for the premium market. The regular I used to be cannot exist in the current model because the current model has no use for regulars.

The Disneyland of 2026 is objectively more impressive than the one I went to monthly. The rides are more sophisticated. The technology is more advanced. The immersive areas are more detailed. And I haven't been there in years, because the experience of going, the sense of being somewhere that welcomed me, that rewarded my familiarity, that didn't require a financial plan before every visit, is gone.

Walt Disney understood that the most powerful thing his park could be was a place people loved. The company that operates his park now understands that the most powerful thing his park can be is a brand that families associate with childhood wonder and will therefore pay whatever it costs to access.

He would recognize the park. He would not recognize what it's for.

The Acquisition Machine

Disney's modern transformation accelerated through a series of acquisitions that turned the company from a theme park and animation studio into a media conglomerate. Pixar in 2006 for $7.4 billion. Marvel in 2009 for $4 billion. Lucasfilm in 2012 for $4 billion. 21st Century Fox in 2019 for $71 billion. Each acquisition added intellectual property and franchises that could be monetized across theme parks, merchandise, streaming, and theatrical release at the same time.

The strategy is financially logical. Each Marvel character who appears in a new film also appears in a theme park attraction, on merchandise, in a streaming series, and in a video game. The IP compounds across multiple revenue streams at the same time. The customer who buys a Spider-Man ticket has been primed by the films, the park, the toy, and the streaming show to consider the purchase self-evident rather than a choice.

The consequence for the park experience is a physical space increasingly organized around IP rather than around Walt's original vision of themed lands that transported guests to different worlds. Cars Land in

Disney California Adventure is excellent, a beautifully realized immersive environment based on the film. The park also includes areas that feel like merchandise displays for franchises rather than places designed to delight guests. The balance between experience-for-its-own-sake and experience-as-IP-delivery-mechanism has shifted dramatically toward the latter.

The Fox acquisition, the most expensive, also produced the most visible strain. Disney absorbed massive debt, then faced a pandemic that shut its parks entirely, then faced a streaming war where Disney+ had to compete with Netflix, Apple, and Amazon at enormous expense. The financial pressure from the combined debt, the streaming investment, and the pandemic losses produced management decisions, including the Chapek era's aggressive fee extraction, that prioritized short-term revenue recovery over long-term relationship preservation.

The Sports and Concert Venue Extraction

Theme parks are not the only entertainment category where enshittification has transformed what used to be accessible fun into premium extraction experiences. Sports venues and concert halls have followed the same trajectory, driven by the same forces: consolidated ownership, captured audiences, and the realization that people desperate to attend an event they care about will pay more than they rationally should.

The dynamic pricing that airlines introduced and hotels adopted has been applied with particular aggression to concert ticketing. Ticketmaster, which merged with Live Nation in 2010 to create a vertically integrated monopoly controlling venues, ticketing, and artist management, uses algorithms to set prices at what it calculates the market will bear. The "service fees" that can double the face price of a ticket before you've committed to purchasing are the concert industry's version of resort fees, disclosed only after significant engagement with the purchasing process, unavoidable once you've decided to attend.

Taylor Swift's 2023 Eras Tour exposed the dysfunction of the concentrated ticketing system when Ticketmaster's website collapsed under demand for a presale, leaving millions of registered fans unable to purchase tickets before they sold out or became available on the secondary market at multiples of face value. The Congressional hearings that followed produced much concern and no meaningful reform, because Live Nation/Ticketmaster's market control is difficult to legislate away and the company's political influence is substantial.

NBA and NFL ticket prices have increased faster than inflation for decades, driven by the assumption that sports fandom creates a captive market willing to pay escalating prices for access to teams they've followed their whole lives. Personal seat licenses, fees paid for the right to purchase season tickets, can cost tens of thousands of dollars at premium franchises, meaning the cost of attendance must be calculated against a capital investment before the season ticket price itself. The working-class families who provided the cultural base of professional sports are being priced out of the stadiums their taxes often helped build.

The stadium itself has been transformed from a place to watch a game into a luxury hospitality venue where the best sightlines come with premium pricing, club access, and food and beverage packages. The sight lines from the upper deck, where the affordable tickets are, are often legitimately poor, while the suites and club levels where the wealthy fans sit feature excellent views and complimentary service. The physical architecture of modern sports venues has been designed around tiered extraction.

The Movie Theater Parallel

The movie theater industry, covered in its own chapter, has followed the same pattern of premium segmentation that's visible in theme parks and venues. Recliner seats, IMAX and Dolby premium formats, reserved seating, loyalty programs that charge monthly fees for access to regular ticket prices, the movie theater has been transformed from a communal cultural experience into a tiered service where your experience of the same film depends on what you paid.

The art house theaters and repertory cinemas that maintained the movie theater as a community space where people gathered to watch films, rather than to consume a content product, have faced particular pressure from the streaming services that moved theatrical releases online and from the premium multiplex model that has pulled audiences toward bigger screens and fewer showtimes of films that justify the premium format charge.

The 1970s suburban multiplex was a democratic space. Everyone paid the same price, sat in the same seats, and watched the same movie. The movie theater of 2026 has premium recliners at $22 and standard seats at $14, premium large formats at $28, and opening-weekend surcharges that can push a ticket above $30. The democracy of shared cultural experience has been tiered.

The Streaming Paradox

Disney's move into streaming with Disney+ was supposed to democratize access to its content, putting the Disney vault and new releases on demand for $7 per month. For a period it did this, and it was genuinely valuable. Then the economics of streaming required that

Disney+ raise its prices, launch an ad-supported tier, add a password-sharing crackdown, and gradually shift its theatrical releases toward streaming windows that served the subscriber count rather than the theatrical experience.

Disney+ launched in 2019 at $6.99 per month. By 2024 the ad-free plan cost $13.99. The price doubled while the content catalog continued losing titles as licensing agreements expired and studios reclaimed content for their own streaming services. The service that was supposed to make Disney content accessible to everyone had repriced toward the premium range while offering a less complete catalog than at launch.

The streaming wars produced a paradox: the pursuit of paid subscribers at scale required content investment at levels that destroyed the profitability of the services providing it. Netflix, Disney+, HBO Max, Apple TV+, Peacock, Paramount+, and others collectively spent tens of billions annually on content, competing for a subscriber base that could not grow fast enough to support that spending. The streaming services that had disrupted cable bundling created a new form of bundling problem, to access all the content you wanted, you needed subscriptions to four or five services at the same time, at a combined cost approaching cable.

The family that once had a Disney annual pass and went monthly has been replaced by the family managing multiple streaming subscriptions while deciding whether the trip to Disney World is worth a week's vacation budget. Disney has optimized its physical parks for the premium market and its streaming service for the subscription market. The middle, the regular, the fan, the person who loved the place and went constantly, has been left out of the optimization entirely.

What Theme Parks Were For

Walt Disney designed Disneyland for a specific experience: a place where adults could return to something they'd lost and children could discover something new, in the same space, at the same time. The Magic Kingdom was genuinely meant to be a kingdom, a place with its own rules, where the ordinary world's pressures didn't penetrate, where the experience of being there was the point.

That design philosophy required an operational commitment that went beyond ride maintenance and costumed characters. It required staffing the park at levels that allowed every guest to feel attended to. It required pricing the park at levels that allowed families to come back. It required resisting the temptation to extract every available dollar from every interaction, because the experience of not being extracted from was part of what made the place worth returning to.

The Disneyland I had a pass for was that place. It was designed to be revisited, which required it to reward revisiting, which required it to be priced so that revisiting was possible. I was a regular because the park wanted regulars and built itself accordingly.

The Disneyland of now is a better theme park by most technical measures, more sophisticated rides, more detailed environments, more advanced technology. It is not designed for regulars. It is designed for the occasional visitor who will spend as much as possible in a single visit because this may be the only visit. That's a financially rational optimization given Disney's current shareholder expectations.

It is also, as Walt understood and the current management has forgotten, a way of destroying the thing that made Disney valuable. The company that is extracting maximum revenue from childhood wonder is consuming the childhood wonder that makes the extraction possible. The magic that makes people willing to pay is a non-renewable resource if you stop creating it and only extract it.

Walt would have understood this. He built the park to be loved. The company that runs it now knows how to monetize being loved but has forgotten how to be worthy of it.

Movies - From Dreams to Algorithms

For most of my adult life I bought between 200 and 300 movies a year. VHS, then DVD, then Blu-ray. Not because I was a collector in the obsessive sense but because movies were worth owning, worth watching again, worth having on a shelf, worth the money. The 1970s gave us The Godfather, Chinatown, Apocalypse Now, Annie Hall, Taxi Driver, Star Wars, Alien, Jaws. The 1980s gave us Blade Runner, Raging Bull, E.T., Platoon, Blue Velvet, Full Metal Jacket, Die Hard. The 1990s and early 2000s gave us Pulp Fiction, Schindler's List, Fargo, The Silence of the Lambs, L.A. Confidential, Almost Famous, There Will Be Blood, No Country for Old Men.

For me the break came just before the pandemic, around 2019. Disney started releasing those awful live-action remakes, and the franchise disease hit a tipping point where almost everything coming out was a sequel, a reboot, or a spin-off of something that had already been milked twice. I stopped looking at what Hollywood was putting out and started looking for independent films and foreign films instead. That is where the actual filmmaking is happening now. The studios are making content. Someone else is still making movies.

These were movies made by people who cared about what they were making. The directors had vision that came from somewhere real. The writers built characters who felt like humans rather than plot delivery devices. The studios took genuine risks on material that wasn't guaranteed to work because the people in charge understood that the only way to make something great was to occasionally make something that failed.

In 2025, I bought four movies.

Not because I stopped caring about film. Because film largely stopped caring about quality. The directors who should have been developing craft over a decade of progressively ambitious work were handed franchise installments before they'd demonstrated they could handle the responsibility. The writers who should have been learning dialogue and structure in writers' rooms were hired because they checked boxes on a diversity form rather than because they could write. The studios that should have been developing original stories spent their development budgets on IP libraries and franchise extensions because original stories are riskier than known quantities and quarterly earnings calls reward risk minimization.

The result is what you see at any multiplex in America: sequels to sequels, reboots of reboots, adaptations of adaptations, produced by committees optimizing for global box office rather than artistic coherence, reviewed primarily on political criteria, attended by audiences who are running out of reasons to buy the ticket.

Two hundred to four. That's what happened to movies.

The 1970s and What Was Possible

The 1970s Hollywood renaissance was produced by a specific set of conditions that the industry worked for decades to eliminate because they were incompatible with predictable quarterly returns.

The Production Code that had constrained American filmmaking for forty years collapsed in the late 1960s. The studio system that had kept directors on contract and controlled every creative decision had broken down. The old guard was retiring and uncertain what audiences wanted. Into that vacuum walked a generation of directors, Coppola, Scorsese, Spielberg, Kubrick, Altman,

Friedkin, Pakula, Cimino, Cassavetes, who had absorbed European cinema, had opinions about what American film could be, and found studios desperate enough to let them try.

What they made was not safe. The Godfather was a three-hour crime epic that took organized crime seriously as a subject. Chinatown was a film noir that ended with the villain winning. Taxi Driver was a portrait of urban psychological disintegration that offered no resolution. Apocalypse Now was a Vietnam film that dissolved into existential nightmare. These movies worked not because focus groups validated them but because the people making them were trying to say something real about the world they inhabited.

The directors had authority because the studios had decided to give it to them, and the studios had decided to give it to them because the old system had stopped producing films audiences wanted to see. The creative opening was a consequence of institutional failure. When the industry recovered its confidence, it recovered it by finding a more reliable system, the blockbuster, the franchise, the sequel, that restored predictability at the cost of creative risk.

Jaws in 1975 and Star Wars in 1977 were not bad movies. They were extraordinary popular entertainments that happened to demonstrate that a single film could generate returns that dwarfed anything the art cinema moment had produced. The lesson Hollywood drew was not that great popular entertainment was achievable. The lesson was that the blockbuster model was more profitable and less risky than the auteur model, and therefore preferable.

The directors who had flourished in the creative opening found themselves progressively constrained as the industry reconsolidated around the franchise model. Cimino's Heaven's Gate in 1980, a genuine attempt at ambitious historical epic that failed catastrophically at the box office, became the cautionary tale that justified tightening studio control. The lesson Hollywood drew from Heaven's Gate was not that some ambitious films fail. The lesson was that directors with too much creative control produce disasters, and therefore creative control should be taken away.

The 1980s and 1990s: Craft Despite the Industry

The 1980s and 1990s produced extraordinary film despite rather than because of the industry's direction. The blockbuster model had taken hold, and studios were programming increasingly toward it. But the middle market, the $20 to $50 million film aimed at adult audiences that wanted something more than explosions and familiar characters, still existed and was still commercially viable.

This middle market produced the films worth owning in the numbers I was buying them. Scorsese continued making films that took craft seriously: Raging Bull, Goodfellas, Casino, The Age of Innocence, Bringing Out the Dead. The Coen Brothers developed a filmography of genre reinvention and moral seriousness: Blood Simple, Raising Arizona, Miller's Crossing, Barton Fink, Fargo, The Big Lebowski, O Brother Where Art Thou. Paul Thomas Anderson arrived in the late 1990s with Boogie Nights and Magnolia, films of genuine ambition that found audiences.

Independent film in the 1990s created a genuine alternative ecosystem. Pulp Fiction revitalized the artistically adventurous commercial film and made

Tarantino a name. Sundance became a meaningful cultural institution. Miramax under Harvey Weinstein, before its catastrophic collapse, released films that found large audiences for serious material: The English Patient, Shakespeare in Love, Good Will Hunting, Chicago.

The studios were not innocent in this period. The consolidation that would eventually narrow the middle market was already underway. The Disney acquisition of Miramax in 1993 was a harbinger of the IP-driven consolidation that would follow. But the middle market still had oxygen, and the films made for it were made by people who had developed craft over years of working in progressively more demanding projects.

The DVD revolution that accelerated in the late 1990s and early 2000s made owning films economically accessible in a way that VHS hadn't quite been. I was buying 200 to 300 movies a year because 200 to 300 movies a year were worth buying, and because owning a Blu-ray of Chinatown meant having Chinatown available whenever you wanted it. The home library made sense as an institution when the films going into it were worth returning to.

What Happened to the Writers

The writers' room of a 2025 prestige television series is staffed differently than the writers' room of a 1995 equivalent. The difference is not about quality. It's about how the economics of content production streaming restructured, and what that restructuring did to the conditions that allow craft to develop.

The Writers Guild of America strike of 2023 made this visible in a way the industry would have preferred to keep quiet. The studios' position was that they intended to staff writers' rooms with the minimum number of writers for the minimum duration possible, using AI-generated material to fill the gaps. The writers' argument was not primarily about wages. It was about the development pipeline: the difference between a writers' room where junior writers spend years learning how stories work, absorbing the craft from people who had already learned it, and a system where every project starts from scratch with whoever was cheapest to hire on the shortest possible contract.

The traditional writers' room was an apprenticeship model. The junior writer who spent five years in a room eventually became the senior writer who could run their own show. That pipeline produced the writers who wrote the television worth watching, the same way the low-budget film circuit produced the directors worth watching. Netflix, Hulu, and the rest of the streaming services disrupted that pipeline by treating content as a volume problem rather than a craft problem. They needed more shows faster at lower cost, which meant shorter rooms, shorter contracts, and no time for anyone to develop into something better than they already were.

The minimum staffing requirements and contract protections the WGA won in 2023 were an attempt to restore some of the conditions that made development possible. The studios accepted them under duress and have been working around them since. The pressure toward cheaper, faster production hasn't changed. The pipeline that produced the writers worth hiring continues to get shorter.

The result is what you see in the output: competent execution of familiar formulas, occasional genuine talent in a project where someone had authority and time, and a consistent absence of the specificity and earned surprise that comes from writers who have spent years learning how stories break and why. The streaming service that can generate forty shows a year is not developing the writers who could have made four striking ones. It is consuming the talent that exists and producing nothing to replace it.

The Franchise Trap

The franchise model that now dominates studio output is not intrinsically incapable of producing good films. The first Avengers film, The Dark Knight, Spider-Man: Into the Spider-Verse, Logan, these demonstrate that franchise constraints can produce genuine craft. What they share is not the franchise structure but the presence of creative talent with authority to execute a vision within that structure.

What the franchise model has produced in bulk is the opposite: films made by directors chosen for their ability to execute corporate requirements rather than their distinctive vision, scripts developed by committee to satisfy brand standards rather than narrative logic, and casting decisions driven by contract obligations from previous installments rather than what the specific film needs.

The Marvel Cinematic Universe produced twenty-two films in its first three phases that maintained coherent quality because Kevin Feige exercised genuine creative authority and attracted directors who had something to contribute. The subsequent phases have produced increasingly inconsistent work as the universe expanded beyond the story's natural scope, the directors capable of the earlier work moved on to other projects, and the institutional obligation to keep the franchise going overrode the creative questions of whether specific films needed to exist.

The Star Wars sequel trilogy produced by Disney after the Lucasfilm acquisition is the most visible failure of franchise management in recent memory: three films made without a coherent plan, with the second film actively contradicting the first, the third film abandoning the second film's character and narrative decisions, and the whole project ending in a story that satisfied no one because there was no story, there were only marketing schedules and IP activation plans.

The directors involved, J.J. Abrams, Rian Johnson, and Abrams again, are not incompetent. Johnson's The Last Jedi, whatever you think of its narrative choices, is a film made with genuine intention and craft. The problem is that a franchise installment is not a film. It is a chapter in a corporate publishing schedule, and no amount of individual directorial talent survives the absence of a plan for the larger work.

Private Equity's Hostile Takeover

The Paramount-Skydance merger exemplifies the financialization of Hollywood, with private equity firms RedBird Capital Partners and KKR investing over $8 billion to acquire control of the legendary studio. These firms do not care about cinematic legacy or artistic vision. They care about extracting maximum value from intellectual property assets through sequels, spin-offs, and merchandising opportunities.

Employment in the film industry fell by 26% between August 2022 and the end of 2023. Writers, directors, and production staff who specialized in developing original content found themselves unemployed as studios prioritized franchise management over creative development. The development executives whose job was finding and nurturing new material, reading scripts, meeting writers, taking bets on unproven concepts, were among the first casualties of cost reduction programs.

MGM's journey through bankruptcy and eventual acquisition by Amazon illustrates the destructive cycle. The studio that produced The Wizard of Oz and the James Bond franchise was stripped for parts, with its valuable intellectual property becoming just another asset in a tech giant's content portfolio. Amazon acquired MGM primarily for the Bond franchise and the MGM library, not to continue the studio's function of developing and producing films. The acquisition completed the transformation of a studio from a creative enterprise into an IP holding company.

When Streaming Ate Cinema

Netflix's emergence as a film distributor was supposed to democratize access to adventurous filmmaking by providing budgets and distribution for films that traditional studio economics couldn't support. For a period it did this, the company funded Scorsese's The Irishman, Alfonso Cuarón's Roma, David Fincher's Mank and The Killer, and genuinely ambitious work from established directors who valued Netflix's lack of interference and large budgets.

The model required subscriber growth to justify the content spending, and subscriber growth plateaued. As it did, Netflix's approach to film production shifted from ambitious development toward volume production: a high-speed assembly line of films with recognizable elements, designed to generate social media buzz for two days before being forgotten. The company's internal metric is completion rate, what percentage of viewers finish the film, which rewards accessible mediocrity over challenging work and teaches the algorithm to recommend more accessible mediocrity.

The theatrical experience itself has been degraded alongside the films being shown. Concession prices have reached levels that require a significant secondary budget for the family that already paid for tickets. The previews run for twenty minutes before the feature. The sound systems malfunction, the projectors show dim images. The chain theaters that control most American theatrical exhibition have not invested in the experience at rates that justify the prices they charge.

The art house theaters and repertory cinemas that maintained film as a cultural experience rather than a content delivery mechanism have faced existential pressure. The theaters that once showed foreign films, classic revivals, and adventurous independent work have closed in most American cities, replaced by entertainment multiplexes and premium large format venues that price the theatrical experience out of the range of regular attendance.

What It Costs

The number is 200 to 4. That's the story.

Two hundred to three hundred films a year worth owning means an industry producing at a rate that justified the investment of time and money to watch carefully, keep, and return to. It means a steady flow of films that rewarded serious attention. It means directors and writers who cared enough about what they were making that the finished work repaid caring.

Four means almost nothing worth owning. It means a year of theatrical releases, streaming content, and home video releases has produced four things I wanted to watch again. Not four disappointing films in an otherwise strong year. Four that qualified at all.

The films that justified 200 to 300 purchases a year were made by people who had spent years learning craft. Scorsese had spent the 1960s and early 1970s developing before Taxi Driver. The Coens had made Blood Simple before anyone gave them a real budget. Spielberg had made Duel and Sugarland Express before Jaws. The directors who made the films worth owning had earned the authority to make them through demonstrated ability in progressively demanding work.

The industry that produces four films worth owning in a year has not simply suffered a dry spell. It has restructured its creative pipeline in ways that prevent the development of the craft that made the earlier films possible. The junior writer who would have spent five years in a writers' room absorbing how stories are built and broken is now hired for a single project and let go. The director who would have made three or four modestly budgeted films before being trusted with something large is handed a franchise installment before she knows what she's doing. The studio executive who would have spent a career learning which material was worth developing has been replaced by an algorithm identifying IP with existing audience awareness.

Great films are hard. They require people who have learned to make them, who are given the resources and time to do it properly, and who are trusted with creative authority rather than managed toward a predetermined result. The industry has organized itself against all three conditions at the same time. The result is a year that produced four films worth buying.

The other 196 were not made by people who didn't care. Most of them were made by reasonably talented people working under conditions designed to prevent quality. Insufficient development time. Inadequate budgets. Creative interference from executives optimizing for global marketing compatibility. Franchise constraints that required specific outcomes regardless of what the story needed. Hiring decisions made on criteria other than demonstrated ability.

The movies of the 1970s, 1980s, 1990s, and early 2000s were not uniformly great. The era produced enormous amounts of forgettable material alongside the films worth owning. The difference is that the conditions that allowed greatness also existed, directors with authority, writers with time, studios willing to take risks on original material, an industry that understood that craft required development.

Those conditions are not gone forever. A24, Neon, and a handful of other distributors are producing and releasing films that still reward serious attention. The directors who came up in the art house and independent ecosystem of the past decade include genuine talents developing genuine vision. The filmmakers and writers who survived the streaming expansion with their artistic integrity intact are still making work worth watching.

But they're fighting against an industry structure that has systematically defunded the conditions that allow quality. Until that changes, the number will stay close to four.

The Theater as Extraction Machine

The movie theater was once a democratic institution. Everyone paid the same price. The screen was big and the sound was loud and the experience of watching a film with a room full of strangers, the collective gasp, the shared laughter, the silence when something landed, was itself part of what film was. You couldn't replicate it at home because home didn't have a room full of strangers.

The chains that control most American theatrical exhibition have spent the past decade discovering how many layers of premium they can add before audiences stop showing up. IMAX tickets. Dolby Cinema tickets. Premium large format tickets. Reserved seating fees. Dynamic pricing for opening weekend. The $18 ticket that seemed expensive a decade ago has been replaced by the $26 ticket for a premium format that may or may not justify the premium.

Concessions, which are the primary profit center for most theaters, have reached the level of an acknowledged joke. The $8 water. The $15 popcorn. The family that spends $100 on tickets and another $60 on food for a two-hour film. The theaters know customers resent the concession prices. They charge them anyway because the alternative, charging enough for the ticket to cover costs without the concession margin, would require honest pricing that would reduce attendance.

The previews that precede the feature have extended from a few minutes to twenty or more minutes of advertisements. You have paid for a seat, arrived on time, and are now watching advertising before the film you came for begins. The advertisements include ads for the streaming services that are competing with the theater you're sitting in. The theater shows these ads because the streaming services pay for placement. The customer experiences them as an additional extraction on top of the ticket price and the concession prices.

The major chains, AMC, Regal, Cinemark, have invested in premium formats and recliner upgrades as a response to competition from home streaming. The investment is real and the recliners are genuinely more comfortable than the seats they replaced. The investment was also funded partly by reducing the number of seats per auditorium, which means the theater that previously showed a film to 300 people now shows it to 150. The economics of theatrical exhibition required by the premium model mean fewer screenings and fewer tickets available for the same film.

The art house theaters that showed foreign films, classic revivals, and adventurous independent work have largely closed in markets outside the largest cities. The Landmark chain, which operated a network of art house theaters across the country, filed for bankruptcy in 2023. The Alamo Drafthouse, which combined theater exhibition with food service and a curated programming philosophy, has gone through bankruptcy and significant contraction. The middle of the theatrical market, the non-multiplex, non-art-house exhibition space that served general adult audiences with a range of film rather than exclusively franchise product, has largely disappeared.

The International Distortion

The global box office is now the primary driver of studio production decisions, and the global box office has different requirements than the domestic one. Chinese audiences represent a substantial portion of global theatrical revenue and have demonstrated preferences, for spectacle over dialogue, for action over character drama, for absence of elements that would require Chinese censors to approve additional cuts, that have materially influenced what American studios produce.

The Marvel films' increasing reliance on spectacle over character and their consistent avoidance of political content that might complicate Chinese distribution is not entirely coincidental. The absence of morally complex historical drama, the preference for globally legible visual storytelling over culturally specific material, the increasing budget allocation toward visual effects over writing and performance, these tendencies serve global marketing needs.

The films that were worth buying in the 1990s and early 2000s were largely films made for domestic audiences by filmmakers with something specific to say about a specific world. Fargo was about Minnesota. Boogie Nights was about the San Fernando Valley pornographic film industry. L.A. Confidential was about 1950s Los Angeles. These films succeeded internationally, but they were not made for international audiences. They were made by filmmakers who cared about their subjects.

A film made for global audiences must be legible to audiences in markets with different cultural contexts, different censorship requirements, and different narrative traditions. The process of making a film globally marketable tends to remove the cultural specificity that makes films worth returning to. The globally optimized film is the cinematic equivalent of the Hampton Inn, recognizable everywhere, distinctive nowhere, designed to satisfy adequately rather than delight.

The Craft That Takes Time

The directors whose films are worth owning spent years learning to make them. Scorsese's first feature was Who's That Knocking at My Door in 1967. Taxi Driver was 1976. Nine years of developing vision and technique between a student film and a masterpiece. The Coens made Blood Simple in 1984 and spent the next decade making progressively more ambitious and accomplished work before No Country for Old Men in 2007. PTA made Hard Eight in 1996 and spent the following decade developing the vision that produced There Will Be Blood.

The career development arc that produced these filmmakers, early low-budget work, progressively more ambitious films as craft developed, eventually the authority and resources to make fully realized visions, has been largely replaced by two alternatives: the fast track to franchise installments for directors who show social media presence and marketable demographics, and the slow grind of independent film that pays poorly and distributes narrowly.

The fast-track director handed a franchise installment before they've developed is not being given an opportunity. They're being given a rope. The franchise structure requires execution of corporate requirements, not development of artistic vision. The director who does this successfully has learned to execute, not to create. The films that result reflect that learning.

The slow-grind independent filmmaker develops craft through constraint, making something with no money forces creative problem-solving that lavish budgets prevent. The independent ecosystem has produced real filmmakers in this generation: Barry Jenkins, Boots Riley, Eliza Hittman, Chloe Zhao before the MCU absorbed her, Robert Eggers, Ti West. These directors have developed genuine vision through the demanding conditions of low-budget filmmaking.

What's largely absent is the middle path, the modestly budgeted studio film that allowed directors to develop craft with professional resources before being trusted with large ones. That middle path was where the Scorseses and the Coens and the Andersons developed in earlier decades. Its disappearance from the studio landscape means that the directors who will make the next generation of films worth owning are developing primarily in independent film, if they develop at all.

The Four Films

I'm not withholding the titles. In 2025, four films were worth buying and returning to. That number is not a complaint about a single bad year. It is the result of two decades of structural decisions that have degraded the conditions necessary for quality, implemented by an industry that has chosen the reliable extraction of franchise value over the uncertain returns of genuine craft.

The films worth owning in a given year are produced by people who care about what they're making and work in conditions that allow caring to matter. Those conditions still exist in corners of the industry. The directors and writers who maintain them are doing so against structural pressure that discourages everything that makes films worth returning to.

Two hundred to four. The industry did that. Not the audience.

Part III: The Resistance

What Protects Against Enshittification

Walking through downtown Portland on a drizzly Tuesday, you might notice something peculiar. While the Starbucks on every corner serves burnt coffee from automated machines, there's still Powell's Books sprawling across an entire city block, its employees knowing where to find that obscure poetry collection you're seeking. While the chains have turned shopping into a sterile march through identical gray boxes, Powell's remains gloriously chaotic, stuffed with books from floor to ceiling, and staff who treat literature like a calling instead of inventory to move.

Powell's isn't an accident. It's what happens when a business stays in the hands of people who care about what they're selling.

The question isn't whether enshittification can be stopped, it's already happening everywhere you look. The question is what makes some businesses immune to it while others succumb faster than a tourist's ice cream cone in Phoenix.

The Ownership Shield

Private ownership, especially family ownership, acts like a vaccine against enshittification. When the Nordstrom family recently took their company private in a $6.25 billion deal, they couldn't exactly strip-mine their own legacy for quarterly gains. Their name is literally on the building. Try explaining to your grandmother why you destroyed the business she helped build so some hedge fund could buy another yacht.

Compare this to Sears, where Eddie Lampert turned a once-proud retailer into his personal cash machine. Lampert didn't grow up folding clothes in a Sears stockroom. He didn't have family dinners where Grandpa talked about serving customers with dignity. To him, Sears was just a collection of assets to be monetized, real estate to be sold, brands to be liquidated. The difference between vandalism and stewardship often comes down to whether someone's name and family history are on the line.

In-N-Out Burger remains privately held by the Snyder family, and it shows. While McDonald's has turned food preparation into a factory process, In-N-Out still cuts fresh potatoes for fries daily, pays employees well above minimum wage, and maintains quality standards that would horrify a cost-cutting consultant.

The math here is simple but profound. Public companies answer to shareholders who can dump their stock at any moment. Private equity firms have exit timelines measured in years. But family owners are stuck with their creation for generations. That changes everything about how they think about the future.

Trader Joe's, which remained under the Albrecht family's private ownership after Joe Coulombe sold it in 1979, demonstrates this across fifty years of consistent quality. The family has never taken Trader Joe's public, never sold it to a private equity consortium, never subjected it to the quarterly earnings pressure that would require raising prices, cutting staff, or compromising the product selection that makes the stores worth visiting. The business decisions that look inefficient from a financial engineering perspective, paying crew members substantially above retail industry wages, maintaining small stores that limit throughput, refusing slotting fees that could generate millions in vendor payments, are precisely the decisions that built and preserved the brand's value. You can't extract your way to a line at the door.

The Cooperative Advantage

Cooperative ownership creates an even stronger immune system. When customers own the business, extraction becomes literally impossible, you'd be stealing from yourself. REI's member structure means every major decision gets filtered through the question of whether it's good for people who use outdoor gear.

Credit unions operate on this principle. While Wells Fargo creates fake accounts to hit sales targets, credit unions focus on serving their member-owners. Navy Federal Credit Union doesn't have shareholders demanding maximum extraction from checking account fees because the account holders are the shareholders. The overdraft fees that generate billions for national banks are constrained at credit unions by the same logic, the people being charged are the people who own the institution. The incentive to extract from customers disappears when customers are owners.

Agricultural cooperatives have operated on this model for over a century. Land O'Lakes, Ocean Spray, Sunkist, cooperatively owned enterprises that have resisted financialization precisely because their owners are farmers and growers who depend on the cooperative's long-term health rather than investors seeking short-term returns. The cooperative model doesn't eliminate competitive pressure or require operational inefficiency. It eliminates the specific pressure to extract value from the customer base, which is the pressure that produces enshittification.

Worker cooperatives extend the model further. Mondragon Corporation in Spain, a federation of worker cooperatives employing over 80,000 people across multiple industries, has operated since 1956 on the principle that the people doing the work should own the enterprise. The cooperative's wage ratio between highest and lowest paid employees is capped, executives cannot earn more than a certain multiple of the lowest worker's wage. Not because this is morally required by the model, but because the workers who own the enterprise vote on it and prefer it that way.

The Mission Fortress

Organizations with deeply embedded missions create another layer of protection. Patagonia's environmental mission isn't just marketing, it's baked into their business model in ways that make traditional private equity approaches nearly impossible.

Try explaining to Patagonia employees why they should start making clothes designed to fall apart quickly. Try convincing them to move production to the cheapest possible factories regardless of environmental impact. The mission acts as an immune system, rejecting changes that contradict core values. When Yvon Chouinard donated the company to fight climate change, he made it extraction-proof forever. The legal structure he created, a trust controlled by the Holdfast Collective, a nonprofit dedicated to environmental causes, means that no future management team can take the company public, sell it to private equity, or redirect its profits away from the mission. The extraction route is simply closed.

Healthcare organizations built around genuine mission demonstrate the same protection. The Mayo Clinic's nonprofit structure and century-long commitment to patient care over profit has consistently produced better patient outcomes and higher satisfaction than the private equity-owned hospital chains that optimize for profitable procedures. The mission is not separate from the business model, it is the business model. Organizations that exist to provide a service rather than to extract returns from customers providing that service make different operational decisions at every level.

The Regulatory Moat

Strong regulatory environments can force good behavior even when ownership structures don't naturally encourage it. European airlines, operating under stricter passenger rights regulations, somehow manage to treat customers like human beings instead of cargo. Canadian banks, operating under stricter oversight than their American counterparts, avoided the worst excesses of the 2008 financial crisis, not because Canadian bankers are morally superior but because the regulatory environment made the riskiest extraction strategies illegal rather than merely inadvisable.

The telecommunications industry shows the flip side. Where regulatory capture has eliminated meaningful oversight, companies like Comcast operate with customer service standards that would be illegal in most of the developed world. Where municipal broadband creates actual competition, the big providers discover they can offer better service at lower prices. The competition was always possible. It took regulatory permission for alternatives to exist.

Germany's co-determination law requires worker representation on corporate boards for companies above a certain size. The workers who sit on these boards vote against the most aggressive cost-cutting and extraction strategies because they are the ones who bear the costs of those strategies. The law doesn't prevent businesses from being profitable. It prevents businesses from being profitable at the exclusive expense of their workers. German manufacturing has remained competitive globally for decades under this model, not despite worker board representation but partly because of it.

The Technology Fork

The same technology that accelerates enshittification when deployed against customers can prevent it when deployed for them. This is the most underappreciated protection mechanism because it requires conscious choice rather than structural constraint.

Every AI-driven customer service system that routes callers through endless loops to exhaust them into abandoning complaints uses the same underlying technology as a system that identifies customer problems early and resolves them proactively. Every algorithmic pricing system that detects customer desperation and raises prices accordingly uses the same data infrastructure as a system that offers customers discounts when they're struggling. Every self-checkout machine that treats every customer as a potential shoplifter uses the same sensor technology as a system that could genuinely speed up the shopping experience.

H-E-B's supply chain technology is among the most sophisticated in the grocery industry. The company uses it to predict demand patterns, reduce waste, and ensure shelves stay stocked, including during natural disasters when centralized distribution systems fail. The technology serves the mission of keeping communities supplied with food. The same technology deployed at a chain optimizing for margin would be used to identify which stores to close and which customers to deprioritize.

Trader Joe's technology investments focus on what their product development teams call "fearless buying", using data not to optimize vendor payments or shelf placement fees but to find products that will genuinely delight customers at prices they can afford. The data serves the product, which serves the customer. This sounds obvious. In most of American retail, it is not how the data gets used.

The Culture Fortress

The strongest protection against enshittification is an organizational culture that values craft, service, and long-term thinking. These cultures take decades to build and can be destroyed in quarters, which makes them both powerful and fragile.

Wegmans grocery stores built a culture around food expertise and customer service that makes employees feel like artisans instead of replaceable cogs. The company's investment in employee training, running its own culinary school, sending produce buyers to farms in other countries to understand the products they sell, creates staff who know things that can't be scripted. A Wegmans cheese buyer who has visited the farms that produce the cheese on the shelf knows something that no algorithm can replicate.

The vulnerability of culture-based protection is real. When Amazon acquired Whole Foods in 2017, the cultural clash was immediate and visible. The company that had built its brand on knowledgeable staff and quality sourcing found itself subject to Amazon's logistics efficiency imperatives and cost-reduction culture. The stores that had felt like they were run by people who cared about food began to feel like distribution centers with produce. Culture can't survive when it conflicts with parent company values and those parent company values are backed by sufficient financial leverage.

The Time Horizon Defense

All these protection mechanisms share a common thread: they extend the time horizon for decision-making beyond the next quarter. When you're planning for decades instead of months, customer satisfaction becomes more important than customer extraction. Employee development becomes more valuable than employee replacement.

Private equity operates on 3-7 year exit timelines, which makes long-term relationship building irrelevant. Why invest in employee training when you're selling the company next year? Why maintain quality standards when you can cut costs and let the next owner deal with the reputation damage?

The Japanese concept of shokunin, the master craftsperson who has dedicated a lifetime to perfecting a specific skill, is culturally embedded enough to produce institutions that have operated for hundreds of years on the principle that doing something well for its own sake is sufficient justification for the enterprise. The oldest restaurant in the world, Honke Owariya in Kyoto, has been serving soba noodles since 1465. It has survived feudal Japan, the Meiji restoration, two world wars, and the rise and fall of multiple economic systems by doing one thing extraordinarily well and refusing to compromise on it.

American businesses are not going to achieve 560-year lifespans, and the Japanese business culture that produces them is not transplantable wholesale. But the underlying principle, that the point of a business is to provide something genuinely worth having, and that this is sufficient justification for keeping it running well, is not culturally specific. It's just been optimized out of the American system.

Across all these protection mechanisms, the pattern becomes clear: enshittification isn't a natural law or technological inevitability. It's a choice made by people operating under specific incentive structures. Change the incentives, and you change the outcomes. The businesses that have resisted extraction have done so through ownership structures, missions, cultures, and regulatory environments that make extraction either impossible or less rewarding than service. Building more of those structures is not utopian. It's the plainest possible description of what works.

The True Cost of Extraction: What We Really Lost When the Vultures Came Home to Roost

There's a Toys"R"Us in Paramus, New Jersey, that closed in 2018 and still hasn't found a new tenant. The building sits empty, a 40,000-square-foot monument to extraction capitalism, weeds growing through cracks in the parking lot where kids once begged their parents for just one more toy. The sign is gone, but the ghost outline remains on the brick facade, a faded rectangle where Geoffrey the Giraffe once smiled down at families.

The private equity firms that killed Toys"R"Us, KKR, Bain Capital, and Vornado, walked away with hundreds of millions in fees and dividends before the company collapsed under the debt they'd loaded onto it. But they didn't account for what economists call externalities: the unmeasurable damage that radiates outward when you strip-mine a community's gathering places.

The true cost of enshittification isn't measured in jobs lost or stock prices fallen. It's measured in the slow unraveling of the social fabric that held American communities together.

The Death of Third Places

Sociologist Ray Oldenburg coined the term "third places", spaces that aren't home or work, but the informal gathering spots where community life happens. Barbershops where men argued about baseball. Diners where shift workers grabbed coffee and gossip at 3 AM. Bookstores where strangers became friends over shared literary obsessions. Hardware stores where neighbors compared notes on home repair projects and the conversation turned, inevitably, to everything else going on in town.

These places served functions that no app replicates. They mixed people from different economic circumstances who would not otherwise interact. The diner at 3 AM served truck drivers, nurses coming off shift, college students, and insomniacs with nowhere else to go. The mixing was not incidental. It was the mechanism through which communities understood themselves as communities rather than as collections of people sharing a zip code.

Private equity has systematically eliminated these third places, turning them into "underperforming assets" that needed to be optimized or liquidated. When you eliminate enough third places, you eliminate the infrastructure of democracy itself. Local politics happens in coffee shops and community centers, not just in city halls. Social movements start in bookstores and churches, not just on social media. The community that loses its gathering places loses the informal civic infrastructure that allows it to organize around shared interests.

When Alden Global Capital acquired newspaper chains across the country, they didn't just cut reporters and slash budgets. They eliminated the only institutions in thousands of small towns that covered city council meetings, school board elections, and local corruption. Research by economists at the University of Notre Dame found that municipalities where local newspapers closed saw significant increases in municipal borrowing costs, investors required higher interest rates to lend to governments whose operations were no longer subject to journalistic scrutiny. Democracy dies in darkness, and private equity has been turning off the lights for profit.

The Collapse of Local Knowledge

Every small business that gets enshittified takes with it decades of accumulated local knowledge. The pharmacist who knew which customers needed extra help reading prescription labels. The hardware store owner who could diagnose engine problems by sound alone. The restaurant owner who knew half the town's dietary restrictions and family histories.

This knowledge can't be replicated by corporate training manuals or customer databases. It's the product of years of relationships, passed down through generations of local ownership. When Olaf, who ran the independent pharmacy for thirty years, retires and CVS takes over the building, the institutional knowledge of three decades of patient relationships doesn't transfer. The new pharmacist is new. The algorithm doesn't know that Mrs. Alvarez's blood pressure medication needs to be explained slowly, or that Mr. Chen sometimes skips refills when money is tight and a call from the pharmacist helps.

This is not sentimentality about the past. It is a description of a specific kind of human capital that has economic value, lower readmission rates, better medication adherence, fewer preventable emergency room visits, that the current system does not measure or compensate for, and therefore systematically destroys.

The replacement is algorithmic customer service designed to maximize throughput while minimizing human contact. Self-checkout machines that assume you're stealing. Phone trees that route you through eight automated menus before connecting you to someone reading from a script. Chat bots programmed to exhaust you into giving up your complaint. The efficiency gains are real and measurable. The losses are real and invisible to any metric the spreadsheet class has learned to track.

The Economic Multiplier in Reverse

When economists talk about the multiplier effect, they usually mean the positive ripple effects of local spending. Independent businesses keep 60-70% of their revenue in the local economy, compared to 15-30% for chain stores. They hire local accountants, local lawyers, local suppliers. They advertise in local newspapers. Their owners live locally and spend locally. The money circulates.

Enshittification reverses this process. When private equity extracts wealth from local businesses, they're breaking the circulation system that keeps money flowing through communities. The local restaurant that used to buy vegetables from area farms gets replaced by a franchise that sources everything through corporate supply chains. The local bank that funded small business expansion gets replaced by a national institution whose lending decisions are made by algorithms in another state. The local newspaper that provided the connective tissue of community information gets replaced by a website operated from a distant city by people who have never been to the community they claim to cover.

When private equity destroyed Sears, they didn't just eliminate 125,000 jobs. They eliminated the foot traffic that supported mall ecosystems, the small retailers, food court vendors, and service providers who depended on Sears customers wandering through their spaces. The malls that depended on Sears as an anchor tenant lost their anchor and subsequently lost their other tenants and in the end became the dead malls that now dot American suburbia, giant empty buildings consuming property tax revenue from cities that can't afford the police calls they generate.

The cumulative effect of this extraction on regional economies is substantial but diffuse. No single closure produces a measurable economic disaster. The aggregate of thousands of closures over decades produces communities that have lost their economic circulation systems without any single cause being visible enough to address.

The Destruction of Career Ladders

One of the most insidious effects of enshittification is how it eliminates the career ladders that once allowed working-class Americans to build middle-class lives. Department stores didn't just employ cashiers, they employed buyers, managers, and specialists who could earn decent livings without college degrees.

A Sears appliance salesperson might start part-time in high school, work their way up to full-time sales, become a department manager, and eventually move into corporate buying or store management. These career paths created stability for millions of families. They provided a mechanism for economic mobility that did not require a college degree or the debt that comes with it.

Private equity systematically destroyed these pathways by eliminating middle management, outsourcing specialized functions, and replacing career employees with part-time contractors. The result is a generation of workers trapped in gig economy jobs with no clear path to economic stability. The 45-year-old who was a Sears department manager does not have a comparable opportunity waiting. The skills she accumulated over twenty years, inventory management, staff supervision, vendor relationships, customer service, are real skills that the economy no longer has a place for, not because the functions disappeared but because the functions have been either automated or concentrated in the corporate headquarters of chains that hire only from specific educational backgrounds.

The Democratic Deficit

The community newspaper that covered the school board election provided something that social media cannot: professional verification of claims, institutional accountability for accuracy, and a shared informational baseline from which disagreement could proceed. When the paper is gone, each community member's information environment becomes self-selected and unverified. The disagreements that were once mediated by shared facts become irresolvable because the parties are operating from incompatible information.

The civic participation that local newspapers supported is measurable. Research published in the American Journal of Political Science found that local newspaper closures were associated with lower voter turnout in local elections, fewer candidates running for office, and higher incumbency rates as challengers lacked the coverage that would make them viable. The extraction of news organizations from communities doesn't just reduce information availability. It reduces democratic participation in ways that compound over time as civic muscles atrophy.

The local businesses that once sponsored Little League teams, donated to the food bank, and provided venues for community meetings are gone or replaced by franchises whose charitable giving is determined by corporate headquarters according to national priorities rather than local needs. The informal community support infrastructure that depended on local business ownership has been extracted along with the businesses.

The Health Care Cascade

When private equity firms buy hospitals and medical practices, they slash staffing, reduce services, and optimize for profitable procedures while eliminating community health programs. But the health impacts extend beyond the medical system.

When Walmart moves into a community and drives out local grocers, residents often lose access to fresh food and gain access to food deserts filled with processed options. The stress of economic uncertainty itself becomes a public health crisis. Research published in the American Journal of Epidemiology has found that community-level unemployment is associated with increased rates of depression, anxiety, substance abuse, cardiovascular disease, and suicide that persist for years after employment recovers.

Communities that lose their economic anchors see increases in all of these outcomes, not because losing a Sears or a Boston Market directly causes depression but because the economic disruption, the loss of community gathering places, and the sense that the community's institutions are being systematically dismantled produces chronic stress that manifests in physical and mental health consequences.

The Path Forward

Case Study: How Glass-Steagall Was Built and Lost

The history of Glass-Steagall is the most useful case study in American financial regulation, because it demonstrates both how reform gets built and how it gets dismantled.

Carter Glass had been working on banking legislation since 1908. The Federal Reserve Act of 1913 was largely his work. He had spent two decades watching commercial banks gamble depositor funds in speculative markets and had concluded the practice would eventually produce a crisis. The crisis arrived in 1929. Glass was ready.

The Pecora Commission hearings of 1933 produced months of public spectacle. Bankers were questioned under oath about practices that had been hidden from public view: bonuses to executives whose banks had failed, preferred stock allocations to politically connected customers, mortgage loans to family members of bank officers, securities fraud committed by the institutions that were supposed to be protecting depositor savings. The hearings did not just shame the bankers. They built the political pressure that made reform possible.

Glass-Steagall passed in June 1933. The act separated commercial banking from investment banking, established federal deposit insurance, prohibited interest payments on demand deposits, and gave the Federal Reserve new tools to constrain speculation. The financial industry fought every provision. The industry lost because the political moment, public anger combined with documented abuses combined with a President willing to confront the bankers, was too strong to resist.

The protection lasted sixty-six years. The American banking system did not produce another systemic crisis between 1933 and the savings and loan failures of the 1980s, when the deregulation that culminated in Gramm-Leach-Bliley in 1999 was already well underway. Six decades of stability allowed the construction of the largest middle class in human history. The reform worked.

The dismantling took thirty years. The financial industry never accepted Glass-Steagall as legitimate. Beginning in the 1970s and accelerating through the 1980s and 1990s, the industry funded academic research arguing that the separation was inefficient, lobbied for regulatory interpretations that gradually weakened the boundary between commercial and investment banking, and supported political candidates who would vote for repeal. The 1999 Gramm-Leach-Bliley Act formalized what had already been mostly accomplished through interpretation and exemption. Eight years later, the financial crisis the original act had prevented for sixty-six years arrived.

The lesson is that reform requires constant defense. The coalition that produced Glass-Steagall did not maintain itself. The labor unions weakened. The progressive economists retired. The state-level reformers moved on to other issues. The financial industry, by contrast, never moved on. It maintained its lobbying infrastructure, funded its academic supporters, and waited for the political moment to dismantle what had been built. The reform that took years of organizing to win took decades of organized effort to lose.

Case Study: How States Are Building Worker Ownership

Italy's Marcora Law, passed in 1985, gives workers the right to purchase their company when it is sold or closed, with state-backed financing for the buyout. The law has produced thousands of worker-owned conversions of failing businesses over four decades, in a country that experienced its own version of corporate consolidation in the 1980s. The model exists. American states have begun adapting it. Maine, Vermont, Colorado, and several other states have passed employee ownership tax incentives that exempt the gain on sales to ESOPs or worker cooperatives from state income tax, reducing the cost of selling to employees compared to selling to outside investors. The legislation is incremental rather than transformative, but it has produced a measurable increase in employee ownership conversions in the states that have implemented it.

The coalition behind these state-level reforms has been built over years by the Cooperative Development Institute, a nonprofit that has been working on cooperative business models in New England since 1994, and similar organizations across the country. CDI provided the technical infrastructure, financial models, and policy expertise that the political coalitions required. State legislators have introduced employee ownership legislation repeatedly across multiple sessions. The PE industry has not paid much attention to most of these state-level efforts because they are small and incremental. By the time the industry recognizes the cumulative threat, the legal infrastructure for worker ownership will already exist.

The Maine tax credit, in effect since 2021, has supported worker-cooperative conversions including Liberty Graphics in rural Liberty, Maine, where the longtime owner sold the business to its employees in 2019 rather than to an outside buyer. The conversion preserved the jobs and the company's presence in a small rural town that would have lost a meaningful employer if the sale had gone to an acquirer planning consolidation. Similar conversions have happened in dozens of communities. Each is small. The cumulative effect is a parallel track of business succession that does not run through the extraction model.

Vermont, Colorado, New York, and several other states have implemented or are considering similar legislation. Federal legislation, including the Workplace Democracy Act, has been introduced repeatedly without passing. The state-by-state accumulation is producing more reform than the federal effort, which is a pattern consistent with how reforms have historically been built in American policy: state experimentation builds the political case for federal action, and federal action eventually follows when enough states have demonstrated that the policy works.

Case Study: How Massachusetts Won Right to Repair

The Massachusetts Right to Repair ballot initiative passed in November 2020 with seventy-five percent of the vote. The campaign that produced that vote is worth examining in detail because it represents a model of how a constituency that lacks corporate funding can defeat well-funded opposition through organized public pressure.

The constituency was specific. Independent automotive repair shops were being progressively locked out of servicing modern cars by manufacturers who restricted access to diagnostic data. The lockout was not gradual. It was systematic. Manufacturers required certified equipment costing thousands of dollars, ongoing software subscriptions, and authorization protocols that effectively eliminated independent repair as a competitive alternative to dealer service. The mechanics knew exactly what was happening to them.

The campaign also organized farmers who could not repair their John Deere tractors without proprietary software, electronics enthusiasts who had been fighting Apple over similar restrictions on phones and laptops, and consumer advocates who had been documenting the broader pattern of repair restriction across industries. The campaign brought these constituencies together around a single specific policy: manufacturers would be required to provide independent repair shops with the same diagnostic data they shared with their dealer networks.

The auto industry spent over $26 million fighting the initiative. The Right to Repair Coalition, funded by aftermarket parts companies, spent roughly $24 million in support. Both sides were well funded. The industry's arguments centered on cybersecurity. The campaign's arguments centered on the actual experience of trying to fix your car. The industry argument was vague. The campaign argument was specific. The voters chose specific.

The implementation has been contested. The auto industry sued in federal court, arguing that the state law was preempted by federal vehicle safety regulations. The litigation has continued for years. The industry has used the legal challenges to delay implementation while the technology evolves further from what the law was designed to address. The Maine version of the law, passed in 2023, faced similar challenges.

The lesson is that winning the political fight is necessary but not sufficient. The implementation is also a fight, conducted through litigation, regulatory interpretation, and the slow erosion that has characterized the dismantling of every reform of corporate extraction in American history. The coalition that won the ballot initiative has had to maintain itself through the implementation phase, which has been longer and harder than the original campaign. The reform exists. Its survival depends on the coalition continuing to defend it.

The true cost of enshittification can't be calculated in quarterly earnings reports because it's measured in lost possibilities: the businesses that won't be started, the communities that won't form, the innovations that won't be discovered, the civic organizations that won't coalesce because the gathering place that would have hosted them is a vacant storefront.

The empty Toys"R"Us in Paramus might seem like just another retail casualty, but it's a choice point. That 40,000 square feet could become a community center, a maker space, a food hall featuring local vendors, an indoor farmer's market. The question is whether communities have the vision, the resources, and the regulatory environment to create those alternatives, and whether Wall Street will allow it, given that community-oriented uses generate lower returns per square foot than the next chain store.

The ghosts of Geoffrey the Giraffe are haunting more than empty parking lots. They're haunting the American dream itself, demanding to know why we chose efficiency over community, optimization over opportunity, and shareholder value over human values.

We made those choices. We can unmake them.

It Doesn't Have to Be This Way

A fair accounting requires acknowledging what this book is not about. There are forms of private equity that provide genuine capital to businesses that need it, that create operational value rather than extract it, that leave companies stronger than they found them. These exist. They are not the subject of this book.

The pension fund paradox is real: some of the capital extracted from the businesses documented here flowed into retirement accounts for teachers and firefighters, into university endowments funding scholarships, into the savings of ordinary Americans. That money went somewhere, and some of where it went was genuinely useful. Acknowledging this is not a concession. It is an accurate description of how the system launders its returns.

The counter-examples are real too. H-E-B and Wegmans and Costco and In-N-Out and Alaska Airlines and credit unions and community newspapers prove every day that the alternative is viable. Businesses can serve their communities, pay their employees well, and remain profitable without loading themselves with debt, gutting their operations, and abandoning the customers who made them worth acquiring in the first place.

This book is about the dominant model, the debt-loading, fee-extracting, short-exit playbook applied to healthy businesses serving communities, and the people who designed and run it. They are identifiable. Their names are on the letterhead of the firms that did the damage. Their choices are documented in bankruptcy filings and congressional testimony and the empty storefronts of American Main Streets.

The distinction between legitimate capital allocation and deliberate extraction matters. The damage from the latter doesn't.

How to Cage the Vultures Before They Strip the Carcass Clean

In 1933, a Democratic senator from Virginia named Carter Glass stood on the floor of the U.S. Senate and delivered a speech that would reshape American capitalism for the next fifty years. The country was drowning in the Great Depression, and millions of Americans had lost their jobs and savings to what Glass called "the money changers in the temple of our civilization."

Glass wasn't calling for revolution. He was calling for regulation. The Glass-Steagall Act didn't eliminate banking, it just prevented banks from gambling with depositors' money. For half a century, that simple rule prevented another financial crisis and helped build the most prosperous middle class in human history.

Then in 1999, Congress repealed Glass-Steagall. Eight years later, the housing bubble burst and nearly took down the global economy.

Today, we face a similar choice. Private equity firms are strip-mining American businesses with the same reckless abandon that investment banks showed before 2008. The policy solutions aren't complicated. Most of them already exist in other countries. The obstacle isn't imagination. It's the political will to implement rules that constrain an industry that has spent decades building the political relationships necessary to prevent exactly that.

Private Equity Transparency

The first rule of private equity is that nobody talks about private equity. These firms operate behind a wall of secrecy that makes other financial industries look positively forthcoming. They hide ownership structures through layers of shell companies. They use non-disclosure agreements to silence everyone from employees to pension fund managers. They structure their operations to avoid the disclosure requirements that apply to public companies while enjoying the same access to capital markets and regulatory protection.

When Apollo Global Management bought Chuck E. Cheese, they didn't want parents to know that their kids' birthday parties were funding a firm that also owned predatory payday lending operations. When Blackstone acquired thousands of single-family homes after the 2008 crash, they didn't want tenants to know their rent money was flowing to the same firm that lobbied against tenant protection laws. The opacity is not incidental. It is structural.

The solution is to require private equity firms to disclose their ownership structures, portfolio companies, and key financial metrics, just like public companies do. The European Union's Alternative Investment Fund Managers Directive already requires this level of disclosure for large private equity firms operating in Europe. American pension funds that invest trillions in these firms often know less about where their money goes than European regulators do.

Real transparency would also require disclosure of fees. When KKR, Bain Capital, and Vornado loaded Toys"R"Us with debt and paid themselves hundreds of millions in management fees, those numbers only came to light during bankruptcy proceedings. By then it was too late to save the company or its 33,000 jobs. Disclosure requirements that surface these arrangements while companies are operating, not after they've collapsed, would at minimum allow the pension funds, creditors, and workers who bear the costs of extraction to make informed decisions about their exposure.

The Debt Loading Limit

The heart of the private equity playbook is debt loading: buying companies with borrowed money, then forcing the companies to pay back the debt. It's like buying a house with someone else's credit card and then making them pay the bill while you collect the rent. The interest payments that service this debt crowd out every other investment the company might make, in employees, equipment, product quality, or customer service. The debt is not incidental to the extraction. The debt is the mechanism.

Germany limits leveraged buyouts to 60% debt financing. France's equivalent is roughly 70%. The companies acquired under these rules don't routinely collapse under interest payments because they're not drowning in artificial debt from the moment of acquisition. Retailers, hospitals, newspapers, and restaurants operating in these regulatory environments do fail, market forces remain real, but they fail for market reasons rather than because a private equity firm loaded them with debt they never incurred and cannot service.

The United States could implement similar rules. Require that at least 40% of any acquisition be financed with actual equity, money the acquirer has raised and committed, not debt pushed onto the target. This doesn't prevent leveraged buyouts. It prevents the most destructive version, where the acquirer contributes minimal equity and maximizes the debt burden on the company being acquired.

The private equity industry would argue this constrains deal activity and reduces returns. That's accurate. It's the point. The returns that private equity generates from debt loading accrue to the fund investors. The costs accrue to the employees, customers, communities, and creditors of the acquired companies. Constraining that transfer through leverage limits is not anti-market. It's a correction of a market failure in which the people bearing the costs are not the ones making the decisions.

The Clawback Revolution

When Toys"R"Us went bankrupt, the private equity firms that killed it kept every penny of the hundreds of millions they'd extracted in fees and dividends. When Payless Shoes collapsed under private equity ownership, Golden Gate Capital walked away with $175 million in profits while 16,000 employees lost their jobs. When Sears was systematically dismantled over thirteen years, Eddie Lampert's various entities extracted billions before the company filed for bankruptcy. In each case, the people who made the decisions that destroyed the companies were financially insulated from the consequences of those decisions.

This heads-I-win-tails-you-lose dynamic is what makes private equity so reliably destructive. Clawback provisions would change the calculation: if a private equity-owned company goes bankrupt within five years of acquisition, or lays off more than a specified percentage of its workforce within three years, the PE firm should be required to return the management fees and dividends they extracted, or at minimum, a significant portion of them.

Investment bankers already face clawback provisions when their deals go bad. Financial advisors are subject to clawback requirements in their compensation structures.

Private equity firms have argued successfully that their carried interest and fees are compensation for services rendered, not returns subject to clawback. The argument is creative. The policy case for exempting them evaporates when you look at the pattern of extraction and collapse.

Antitrust Revival

Private equity has become a monopoly-creation machine operating below the traditional antitrust radar. The "rollup" strategy, acquiring multiple companies in the same industry to achieve pricing power, has been applied to everything from physician practices to funeral homes to veterinary clinics to car washes. Each individual acquisition may be too small to trigger antitrust review. The cumulative effect creates regional or national monopolies that raise prices and reduce quality with the same dynamics as traditional monopolies.

Veterinary care costs have increased dramatically as private equity firms have assembled regional networks of clinics that effectively eliminate price competition for pet owners who need emergency services. Funeral home prices have increased substantially as Service Corporation International and other consolidators have assembled near-monopolies in many markets. Physician practice consolidation has given hospital systems enormous leverage over insurance companies in contract negotiations, leverage that shows up in higher costs for patients.

Current antitrust enforcement focuses on consumer prices, but private equity rollups often maintain or decrease prices while degrading quality, the classic enshittification pattern. We need antitrust enforcement that examines quality degradation alongside price increases, that looks at the cumulative effect of multiple acquisitions across time, and that scrutinizes rollup strategies with the same rigor applied to traditional horizontal mergers.

Tax Policy

The tax code rewards financial engineering over business building in ways that compound the damage from private equity extraction. Carried interest, the share of profits that private equity managers receive as compensation for running their funds, is taxed at the capital gains rate of 20% rather than the ordinary income rate of 37%. This is a subsidy for financial extraction paid by everyone who pays taxes at ordinary income rates, which is most people.

The argument for the carried interest treatment is that PE managers share the downside risk with their investors. In practice, the fund structures that generate carried interest are designed to ensure that managers collect substantial compensation in fee income even when funds perform poorly. The downside sharing is theoretical. The upside capture is structural.

Closing the carried interest loophole would raise tens of billions in revenue over a decade while removing a direct subsidy for the extraction that produces enshittification. It would not end private equity. It would end the tax advantage that makes private equity returns look better than they are on a pre-tax basis, potentially shifting capital toward investment forms that generate returns through value creation rather than extraction.

Additional tax policy tools include: accelerated depreciation for businesses that make capital investments in their operations (penalizing the asset stripping that sells buildings and equipment); tax treatment of debt interest deductibility that doesn't reward excessive leverage; and potential transaction taxes on rapid asset transfers that make short-term extraction strategies less profitable relative to long-term value building.

Supporting Alternatives

Government policy shouldn't just constrain destructive private equity, it should actively support business models that resist enshittification. Employee ownership, cooperative structures, and long-term private ownership all resist extraction more effectively than public company or PE ownership. They deserve policy support commensurate with the public benefits they provide.

Several states have begun building the legal infrastructure for employee ownership. Maine, Vermont, Colorado, and others have passed tax incentives that exempt the gain on sales to ESOPs or worker cooperatives from state income tax, reducing the cost of selling to employees compared to selling to outside investors. The laws have produced a measurable rise in employee-ownership conversions where they are in effect. The Italian precedent discussed in the previous chapter, the Marcora Law, demonstrates what is possible at scale when worker buyouts are paired with state-backed financing. Federal legislation modeled on that approach could extend the benefit to companies in states without their own legislation.

The SBA's existing loan programs could be explicitly extended to employee buyouts, with favorable terms that reflect the demonstrated stability of employee-owned businesses. Community Development Financial Institutions could receive additional federal support targeted at financing cooperative development and employee buyouts in communities that have experienced significant extraction through PE activity.

The Pension Fund Problem

Here's the cruel irony that runs through the entire private equity story: much of the funding comes from pension funds representing the same workers whose jobs these firms eliminate. Teachers' retirement funds invest in firms that close schools. Police pension funds back companies that lay off security guards. The workers who bear the costs of extraction are often, through their retirement accounts, providing the capital that funds it.

CalPERS, the largest public pension fund in America, has reduced its private equity allocation in recent years after internal analysis found that the returns, adjusted for fees and risk, were not significantly better than public market alternatives. Other large pension funds have reached similar conclusions. The financial case for pension fund investment in private equity is weaker than the industry's marketing suggests, once you account for the full fee structures and the illiquidity premium.

Federal policy could require pension funds that invest in private equity to disclose the employment effects of their portfolio companies alongside the financial returns. A pension fund for teachers that invests in PE firms closing schools should be required to explain that relationship to its beneficiaries. This transparency would not prohibit pension funds from investing in PE, but it would create accountability for those investments that currently doesn't exist.

The Path Forward

Carter Glass understood that financial markets need guardrails to prevent them from destroying the productive economy they're supposed to serve. The private equity industry has spent the last forty years removing those guardrails and capturing the regulatory agencies that might restore them.

The results speak for themselves: shuttered Main Streets, eliminated career ladders, degraded customer service, and extraction of wealth from communities to financial centers. The experiment in unregulated private equity has failed as completely as the experiment in unregulated banking failed in the 1920s.

None of these policy solutions requires economic revolution. They require the political will to implement rules that other developed countries have already implemented, with documented results. The obstacle is not ignorance about what works. It's the political power of the industry that benefits from the current rules and has invested substantially in keeping them.

Time to bring back the guardrails before the whole system crashes into the ditch.

How to Fight Back When the Vultures Circle Your Town

In 2019, when private equity firm Fortress Investment Group tried to close nursing homes across the country, communities fought back. Instead of accepting the closures as inevitable, residents organized protests, contacted state regulators, and found alternative operators willing to take over the facilities.

Most communities would have shrugged, complained on social media, and watched their neighbors get shipped off to facilities an hour away. But scattered across America, a different response was emerging. Local activists were learning that enshittification isn't a natural disaster, it's a business model. And business models can be changed.

The communities that fight back effectively share a quality that is easy to describe and difficult to sustain: they refuse to accept extraction as inevitable. They understand that the private equity firm circling their hospital or newspaper or grocery store is making a calculation about whether the resistance will cost more than the extraction is worth. Communities that organize, publicize, and persist change that calculation.

Know Your Enemy

Before you can fight enshittification, you need to understand who's driving it. Most people see a deteriorating business and blame the workers, the managers, the economy, or foreign competition. They don't see the private equity firm that loaded the company with debt three years ago and has been extracting management fees ever since.

Learning to identify the actual owners of the businesses that serve your community is the first step. When a local hospital starts reducing services, check who owns it. When a regional newspaper starts laying off reporters, check the ownership structure. When a grocery chain starts closing stores in your neighborhood while opening premium locations in wealthy suburbs, find out who's on the board.

The Private Equity Stakeholder Project maintains databases of PE-owned companies and their performance records. Americans for Financial Reform tracks which firms are targeting which industries. SEC filings, which are public documents, reveal ownership structures for companies above certain asset thresholds. State insurance filings reveal hospital and healthcare system ownership. The information is available. It requires effort to find, but the effort is worthwhile because strategy depends on knowing who you're dealing with.

The difference between a business failing because the market has changed and a business being deliberately degraded for extraction is not always visible from the outside. But the signs accumulate: sudden management changes after an acquisition, sale-leaseback transactions that convert owned real estate to leased real estate, systematic staff reductions accompanied by increased management fees, a pattern of cost-cutting that degrades the product while extracting cash. Once you know what to look for, the playbook is recognizable.

Vote with Your Wallet (Strategically)

Individual consumer choices matter more than the extraction industry would prefer to acknowledge, but they matter most when they're strategic rather than reflexive. Boycotting a PE-owned chain accomplishes less if the only alternative is a different PE-owned chain. Knowing who owns what allows consumer choices to reinforce the businesses worth reinforcing.

Start by identifying businesses in your community that resist enshittification: employee-owned companies, long-term family businesses, cooperatives, locally-owned independents. These businesses typically provide better service and better products precisely because their incentive structures reward service rather than extraction. Supporting them isn't charity. It's rational consumer behavior that happens to align with community benefit.

Local bookstores and independent music stores, credit unions and community banks, independent restaurants and locally-owned hardware stores, these businesses often provide the local knowledge and genuine service that their national competitors have optimized away. The experience of shopping in a store where someone knows the inventory, cares about the customer, and will still be there next year to answer for their recommendations is qualitatively different from the experience of navigating a self-checkout machine in a store optimized for throughput.

Making these choices visible amplifies their effect. When you choose an independent bookstore over Amazon, tell someone why. When you move your accounts to a credit union, explain the reasoning to your friends. The individual consumer choice matters less than the culture of preference it contributes to, and cultures of preference, over time, affect the investment decisions of even the most extraction-oriented enterprises.

Build Alternatives Before You Need Them

The most powerful response to enshittification isn't just opposing bad businesses, it's building good ones before the bad ones arrive. Employee ownership is one of the most effective defenses against PE acquisition because it creates a legal and structural barrier to the kind of ownership transfer that enables extraction.

When workers own their companies through employee stock ownership plans, worker cooperatives, or other structures, the path to PE acquisition runs through a vote of the owners, the workers themselves. Workers who understand what PE acquisition means for their jobs, their benefits, and their community are not going to vote to sell to firms with documented track records of mass layoffs and service degradation. The structural barrier is not perfect, sufficiently attractive acquisition offers can overcome worker resistance, but it dramatically raises the cost of extraction compared to acquiring a family business or a public company.

Cooperative grocery stores have successfully filled gaps left by chain store closures in dozens of American communities. The Cooperative Grocers Network and the National Center for Employee Ownership provide resources for communities interested in these models. Several foundations and CDFIs provide patient capital for cooperative development and employee buyouts. The infrastructure for building alternatives exists. It requires community awareness and early action, cooperatives take time to establish, and starting the process after the chain has already announced closure is usually too late.

The Local Government Lever

Local governments have more tools than most residents realize, and more political accountability to use them than state or federal governments. City councils can't regulate private equity directly, but they can create conditions that make extraction less profitable and community ownership more viable.

Zoning and land use decisions profoundly affect which businesses can operate in a community. Cities that designate commercial corridors for independent businesses, that limit formula retail (chain stores with standardized designs and merchandise), and that create small business incubator spaces are actively shaping the economic environment. San Francisco, Portland, and several other cities have implemented formula retail restrictions that limit chain store density in specific neighborhoods. The restrictions don't eliminate chains, but they preserve space for independent businesses that would otherwise be priced or crowded out.

Procurement policies offer immediate leverage for any local government. Purchasing from locally-owned, employee-owned, or cooperative businesses, rather than defaulting to the largest national vendor, directly supports the businesses most resistant to enshittification. The cumulative effect of municipal procurement choices across thousands of local governments is substantial.

Community benefit agreements attached to development permits, tax incentives, and zoning variances can require that large commercial developments include affordable commercial space for local businesses. When a national retailer wants a zoning variance to build a large format store, negotiating community benefit requirements as a condition of approval is a legitimate use of municipal authority that communities underutilize.

Organize Your Community

Individual consumer choices and individual political pressure accomplish less than collective action. The organizing that has produced meaningful change, worker cooperatives that saved businesses, municipal broadband systems that broke cable monopolies, community land trusts that preserved affordable commercial space, required sustained collective effort over years.

Labor unions remain one of the most effective checks on private equity extraction in workplaces. Unionized workplaces are significantly harder for PE firms to restructure through mass layoffs, because collective bargaining agreements create legal obligations that complicate the cost-cutting that makes PE deals profitable. Workers who are considering whether to organize should factor in the protection against PE acquisition that union status provides, not as the primary reason to organize, but as a genuine benefit.

Faith communities, neighborhood associations, and civic organizations already have the trust and organizing infrastructure that effective campaigns require. The local pastor who has credibility with fifty families has more capacity to change community behavior than a thousand social media posts. Channeling existing community organizations toward economic justice issues, which directly affect their members' economic wellbeing, is more effective than building new organizations from scratch.

Success Stories

The success stories of communities that have fought back against enshittification are more numerous than the dominant narrative of inevitable decline suggests. They are less visible than the failures because failures are dramatic and successes are quiet, but they exist and they demonstrate what is possible.

Pittsburgh, East End Food Co-op.

When the supermarket chain that had served the neighborhood for years announced it would close, residents had a choice. They could accept that the neighborhood was now a food desert. Or they could build their own grocery store. They built their own grocery store. The East End Food Co-op now serves thousands of members in a neighborhood a chain had abandoned as insufficiently profitable. The co-op pays its workers, sources from local farms, and operates on the cooperative model where members vote on major decisions. None of this is innovative. The co-op model has been around for over a century. What is notable is that an ordinary American community in 2025 can still build one when extraction makes the alternative unviable. The infrastructure exists. The capital is available through cooperative development funds. The legal framework is established. What is required is the community will to do the work, and the willingness to start before the crisis becomes irreversible.

The Bronx, Cooperative Home Care Associates.

Cooperative Home Care Associates began in 1985 with twelve home health aides who decided to organize themselves as worker-owners. Forty years later, CHCA employs over two thousand staff, more than half of whom are worker-owners, providing home health services across New York. The workers earn higher wages than the industry average. They have benefits. They participate in governance through cooperative structures. The clients receive more consistent care than is typical in the industry, with measurable effects on hospitalization rates and patient outcomes. The competitive home health agencies in the same market, several of them owned by private equity firms, have higher worker turnover, lower wages, worse client outcomes, and less stable operations. The cooperative model produces better results for workers and clients while remaining economically viable in a market the private equity firms have actively tried to consolidate.

Chattanooga, EPB.

Chattanooga's municipal broadband system, EPB, started as a fiber network the city built to manage its electric grid more efficiently. The fiber network had excess capacity. The city decided to use the excess capacity to provide internet service to residents. The result was a gigabit fiber network that served the entire city for $68 per month. Comcast, which had previously charged significantly more for substantially slower service in the same market, was forced to compete or lose customers. The competitive pressure that EPB created produced lower prices and better service across the entire Chattanooga market. The economic development effects of the fiber network were substantial: businesses relocated to Chattanooga specifically to access the gigabit infrastructure, the city's tech sector grew dramatically, and the network has been credited with contributing billions in economic value to the region. Chattanooga's success has been replicated in Wilson, North Carolina; Longmont, Colorado; Ammon, Idaho; and dozens of other cities. The model works. The only thing preventing wider adoption is the laws that twenty-three states have passed, almost all written by telecommunications industry lobbyists, restricting municipal broadband.

Maine, employee ownership tax incentives.

Maine passed legislation in 2019 creating tax incentives for business owners who sell their companies to ESOPs or worker cooperatives instead of to outside investors. The law exempts gains from such sales from state income tax up to a substantial threshold and excludes interest income on financing the sale. The state has subsequently expanded the program to include the Maine Center for Employee Ownership, a state-supported entity that provides technical assistance to retiring business owners considering employee ownership as a succession option. Companies that have converted to worker ownership through this framework include Liberty Graphics in rural Liberty, where Tom Opper sold the company to its employees in 2019 rather than to an outside buyer. The workers who became owners did not have substantial capital. They financed the purchases through cooperative development funds, ESOP loans, and seller financing arranged with the previous owners, with the tax exemption making the seller financing more attractive. The framework works because the previous owners often prefer selling to their own workers, when given the option, over selling to a private equity firm whose track record is closing the business and selling the parts. The framework has not eliminated PE acquisition in Maine. It has produced a meaningful alternative path. Vermont, Colorado, and several other states have implemented similar tax incentive frameworks. The model is replicable. Federal implementation would extend the incentive to companies in states without their own legislation.

Indiana, the SEIU and the nursing homes.

SEIU's organizing of nursing home workers in Indiana documented systematic abuses in PE-owned facilities, including the staffing reductions, deferred maintenance, and resident neglect that have characterized PE healthcare ownership. The campaign produced state-level reform legislation that established minimum staffing ratios and required PE owners to disclose their financial structures. The reforms passed because the workers, the residents' families, and the public health professionals organized into a coalition that elected officials could not ignore. The PE firms fought the legislation. The coalition won. The lesson is that PE-owned operations are not invulnerable. They are vulnerable to the same kinds of organized pressure that has historically constrained other extractive industries.

These success stories share common elements: early mobilization before the crisis became irreversible, broad community support that crossed demographic and political lines, alternative financing that did not depend on the same capital sources as the extraction industry, and persistence through the inevitable setbacks and obstacles. None of them happened quickly. None of them happened without organized effort. All of them happened in places that had been told the extraction was inevitable and decided not to accept that.

The Long View

The enshittification of American business happened over decades. Reversing it will take decades. The policy reforms, the alternative institutions, the cultural shifts in what Americans expect from the businesses they patronize, none of these happen quickly, and none of them happen without sustained effort.

But the trajectory is not fixed. The businesses that have resisted extraction demonstrate that the alternative is viable. The communities that have organized and built alternatives demonstrate that collective action produces results. The policy frameworks that other countries have implemented demonstrate that different rules produce different outcomes.

The private equity vultures are circling communities across America. But vultures are scavengers, not predators. They feed on things that are already dead or dying. Communities that are alive, organized, and fighting back can drive them away and build something better.

The Route 66 I drove as a child is gone, but what it represented, businesses that knew their customers, communities that knew each other, commerce that built connection rather than extracted from it, is not gone. It exists in the credit union that knows your name, the independent pharmacy that remembers your prescriptions, the bookstore whose staff knows what you'll like. It exists in every business that has chosen service over extraction and found that the choice sustains them.

The vultures are betting you'll accept enshittification as inevitable. The evidence says otherwise. The choice remains ours.

Carter Glass did not pass the Glass-Steagall Act by writing about it. He passed it through a coalition that had been building for years, against an industry that fought it every step of the way, in a political moment that finally allowed it. Every successful reform of corporate extraction in American history has followed the same pattern. The diagnosis comes first. The organizing comes second. The political moment comes third. The reform comes fourth. Skipping any of the steps means the reform does not happen.

This book has been the diagnosis. The diagnosis is not enough. The next step is the organizing, which is harder, slower, and less rewarding than the diagnosis but is the only thing that has ever produced reform.

How the Glass-Steagall Coalition Was Built

The Glass-Steagall Act did not pass because Congress decided one day to regulate banks. It passed because of a sustained organizing campaign that began before the 1929 crash and continued through the early years of the Depression. The Pecora Commission hearings of 1933, named for chief counsel Ferdinand Pecora, provided the public spectacle that made reform politically possible. Pecora questioned bankers under oath about practices that had been hidden from the public. The hearings produced front-page newspaper coverage for months. The bankers, accustomed to operating with minimal scrutiny, were caught defending practices that ordinary Americans found indefensible.

The hearings were not spontaneous. They were the product of organized pressure that had been building for years. Progressive economists had been documenting the abuses of the banking system since the Pujo Committee hearings of 1912. Labor unions had been arguing for financial reform throughout the 1920s. State-level banking reformers had built networks across the country. Carter Glass himself had been working on banking legislation since 1908. When the political moment arrived, the coalition was already in place.

The lesson for the present is that the political moment does not produce its own coalition. The coalition has to exist before the moment, ready to act when the moment arrives. The diagnosis without the coalition produces nothing. The coalition without the diagnosis produces nothing. The coalition with the diagnosis, ready to act when the next financial crisis or political opening arrives, produces reform.

How the Consumer Movement Forced the Agencies

The Federal Trade Commission of the 1970s was not the agency that the FTC of the 1960s had been. The transformation came from outside the agency. Ralph Nader and his network of researchers had spent the 1960s documenting consumer harm with a level of specificity that Congress could not ignore. The Nader Report on the FTC in 1969 found the agency had become essentially captured by the industries it was supposed to regulate. The report did not just criticize. It named individuals, documented specific failures, and provided a roadmap for reform.

Congress responded. The FTC's enforcement authority was expanded. The Magnuson-Moss Warranty Act of 1975 gave the agency new tools. The Consumer Product Safety Commission was created in 1972. The Environmental Protection Agency in 1970. The Occupational Safety and Health Administration in 1970. None of these agencies existed before the consumer movement created the political pressure to require them.

The infrastructure for this work was specific. The Public Interest Research Groups, the consumer organizations, the labor coalitions, the environmental groups, the legal aid networks. Each of these organizations had been built over years of organizing. Each had specific competencies, specific constituencies, and specific leverage. When the political opportunity arrived, they had the people and the materials to push reform through.

How the Right to Repair Movement Won Massachusetts

The Massachusetts Right to Repair ballot initiative passed in 2020 with seventy-five percent of the vote, requiring automakers to provide independent repair shops with the same diagnostic data they share with their dealer networks. The campaign that produced that vote was organized by independent repair shops, agricultural equipment owners, electronics enthusiasts, and consumer advocates who had been working for years to build public awareness of how manufacturers were locking customers out of repairing the products they had purchased.

The campaign won because it was organized at the level of the actual constituency. The independent mechanic who could not service modern cars without paying the manufacturer's licensing fees had a direct economic interest in the outcome. The farmer who could not repair his John Deere tractor without proprietary software had a direct interest. The phone owner who could not get her screen replaced for under $300 had a direct interest. The campaign brought these constituencies together around a specific policy that addressed their specific harms.

The fight became the most expensive ballot question in Massachusetts history. The auto industry spent over $26 million fighting the initiative. The Right to Repair Coalition, funded by aftermarket parts companies including AutoZone, O'Reilly, and Advance Auto Parts, spent roughly $24 million in support. Both sides were well funded. The campaign won because the issue connected to lived experience in a way the industry's arguments could not match. The mechanic explaining what he could no longer do for his customers was more persuasive than the industry's claims about cybersecurity. The campaign also won because the constituency had been organized in advance. The Right to Repair groups had existed for years. They were ready when the political opportunity appeared.

How the PBM Reform Movement Is Building

The PBM reform fight is currently ongoing and offers a working example of how a reform coalition is built in real time. The coalition includes independent pharmacy associations, patient advocacy groups, state attorneys general, and a bipartisan group of legislators who have noticed that PBM practices generate constituent complaints across political lines. The coalition does not have major industry support. It has built power instead through documentation, public testimony, and the steady accumulation of state-level reforms that have demonstrated PBM constraints can be implemented without breaking the prescription drug system.

Arkansas was the first state to pass meaningful PBM reform in 2018, requiring PBMs to reimburse pharmacies at rates at or above the cost of the drug. The PBMs sued. The litigation traced through multiple courts. The Supreme Court ultimately ruled in Rutledge v. Pharmaceutical Care Management Association in 2020 that state regulation of PBMs was permitted under federal law. The ruling unlocked a wave of state reforms that have continued through 2025.

The federal FTC investigation that produced the 2024 reports on PBM practices was driven by sustained pressure from this coalition. The reports document what the coalition had been arguing for years: that PBMs steer patients to their affiliated pharmacies, squeeze independent pharmacies through below-cost reimbursements, and inflate drug prices through opaque rebate structures. The reports gave federal policy makers the documented basis for action that the coalition had been requesting.

Federal PBM reform legislation has not yet passed. The fight is ongoing. The lesson is that reform takes time, that state-level victories accumulate into federal momentum, that documentation is necessary but not sufficient, and that the coalition has to be patient enough to keep working through the multi-year timelines that meaningful reform requires.

What the Movement Looks Like

The movement that would constrain private equity extraction at the scale documented in this book does not currently exist. It has elements. The SEIU campaigns against PE-owned nursing home chains. The worker cooperatives that have organized buyouts of threatened businesses. The consumer protection coalitions that have backed antitrust enforcement. The academic and policy networks that have produced the research base. What is missing is the coordination among them, the shared narrative that connects them, and the political infrastructure that converts the diagnosis into demands politicians have to respond to.

Building that movement is the work that this book cannot do. The book can name the problem and document the harm. The movement has to be built by the people who experience the harm directly. The pharmacists who watched their stores close. The newspaper reporters who watched their bureaus shut down. The healthcare workers who watched their hospitals collapse. The retail workers who watched their careers disappear. The pension fund beneficiaries who discovered their retirement security was being used to fund the destruction of their communities.

These constituencies exist. They are not currently coordinated. They could be. The movements documented above all started with constituencies that were not coordinated, that did not see themselves as having shared interests, that had to be brought together through years of organizing. The PE reform movement has the same potential and the same requirement.

What Reform Looks Like When It Wins

Glass-Steagall lasted sixty-six years. The protection it provided was not theoretical. The American banking system did not produce a major financial crisis between 1933 and the 1980s, when the deregulation began that culminated in the 1999 repeal. The reform produced six decades of relative stability that allowed the construction of the largest middle class in human history.

The current period of unconstrained financial extraction has produced the documented harm in this book. It has also produced the political conditions for reversal. The same conditions that produced the 1929 crash, concentrated wealth, weakened regulation, captured oversight, public anger looking for direction, are present now. The political moment will arrive. The question is whether the coalition will be ready.

The lesson of every previous reform is that the coalition has to be built before the moment, not during it. The book that you have just read is part of building the coalition. The book on its own does nothing. The book combined with the organizing it might support is the difference between this period of extraction lasting another forty years and ending in the next decade.

The choice is not between markets and regulation. The choice is between markets that serve communities and markets that serve extraction. The reforms that produce the first kind of market have been won before. They can be won again. The work required to win them is specific, documented, and available to anyone willing to do it.

Conclusion: I Drove It Again

I drove Route 66 again in 2006.

Started at Santa Monica Pier, where the End of the Trail sign marks the western terminus, and made it as far as Flagstaff before I had to turn around. Two days through what used to be the spine of the country.

What I saw was the country I had described in the opening chapter of this book, with the past tense made literal.

Most of the original road is gone. Where it survives, it survives mainly as a tourist nostalgia route, with brown historical markers and the occasional preserved relic and people in vintage cars taking photographs in front of buildings that once were. The bypassed stretches, the parts of the original alignment that the interstates left behind, contain what remains. Most of it is closed.

Roy's Motel and Cafe at Amboy, with its giant retro sign rising out of the Mojave, was a ruin. The motel rooms were uninhabitable. The cafe had been closed for years. Someone had bought the place with restoration plans, but in 2006 it was a documented memory more than a functioning business. The same scene played out across the desert. Closed gas stations with the original signage still standing. Diners that had become storage. Motels with their neon broken and their pools filled in. The road had once been the main commercial artery between Chicago and Los Angeles. By 2006 it was a series of empty lots interrupted by occasional preserved relics.

I hiked up Amboy Crater that afternoon. It is an extinct volcano about a mile from Roy's, 250 feet of cinder cone with a trail that loops to the rim. From the top, Route 66 is a thin strip of asphalt cutting across the lava fields, and the human commerce that had once depended on the road, the gas stations and the cafes and the motor courts, looks small against the size of the desert it crossed. The Mojave will be there when whatever replaced Roy's also closes. The buildings I had just walked through were already in the process of being reabsorbed.

The chains were there. Hampton Inn, McDonald's, Chevron, Holiday Inn Express, all the recognizable names of modern American commerce. They were not on Route 66. They were on the interstate service road that ran parallel to it, in the towns large enough to support an interstate exit. The original road and what was on it had been left to die.

A few places were holding on. Seligman, Arizona, was the exception. Angel Delgadillo, the barber whose campaigning had produced the historic designation that protected Route 66 in Arizona, had turned the town into a destination for people who wanted to remember what the road had been. His barbershop was still open. The Snow Cap Drive-In his family ran was still open. The town had decided to be the keeper of the memory, and the memory was paying enough bills to keep the lights on. Oatman did the same thing on a smaller scale, with the wild burros wandering the streets and the storefronts dressed up for tourists. These places were exceptions because they had committed to being exceptions. Most other towns had not made that decision, or had not made it in time.

I drove up Essex Road that morning to Mitchell Caverns. Jack and Ida Mitchell had built the place in 1934 as a Route 66 attraction, sixteen miles up a side road into the Providence Mountains, where the limestone caves they had developed offered something nothing else on the desert stretch could match: a guided tour through caves at forty-three hundred feet of elevation, in a desert so empty the silence was its own feature. They sold it to the state in 1954. By 2006 it was a state park, run by California State Park rangers who led tours through the same caves the Mitchells had begun showing seventy years earlier. The visitor center was the Mitchells' original house. The porch Jack Mitchell had built to catch the desert breeze was still there. The tour was excellent. The ranger knew the geology, the history, the names of the formations. The place felt continuous in a way little else on the route did.

In January 2011, the state of California closed Mitchell Caverns because of the budget crisis. The closure was supposed to be temporary. It was not. During the seven years the park sat empty, vandals broke in repeatedly, stole the copper wire, and damaged the visitor center the Mitchells had built. The state did not have the money to protect what it had stopped operating, and what it had stopped operating got stripped. The park reopened in November 2017 after four hundred thousand dollars of repairs and the work of a volunteer committee that refused to let it die. The place still exists. The ranger still gives the tour. The seven-year gap is its own kind of monument, and it is a reminder that the extraction documented in this book is not the only mechanism that hollows out the institutions Americans depend on. Public stewardship can fail in its own way, and what it fails to protect gets stripped just as surely as what private equity acquires.

The interstates killed Route 66, mostly. Eisenhower's Federal-Aid Highway Act of 1956 authorized the system that became I-40 across the desert, I-44 across Missouri and Oklahoma, I-55 between Chicago and St. Louis. Each new interstate segment bypassed the original Route 66 alignment and routed the traffic to a parallel corridor that did not pass through the small towns the original road had served. The cars stopped coming. The motels and diners and gas stations that had been built around the assumption that travelers would stop in those towns lost the travelers. Most of them closed within a decade of being bypassed. By 1985, Route 66 was officially decommissioned because the interstates had replaced essentially every section of it.

What killed Route 66 was not the same thing that killed Toys"R"Us. Route 66 was bypassed by a federal infrastructure decision made by people who never visited Holbrook or Tucumcari. Toys"R"Us was loaded with debt by a private equity firm whose partners never visited the stores. Different mechanisms. Similar results. The communities served by Route 66 lost their economic anchors when the federal government decided to route the interstates a few miles to the north. The communities served by Toys"R"Us lost their anchor when KKR decided that loading the company with debt was more profitable than running it. In both cases, decisions made far from the affected communities, by people who would not bear the consequences, dismantled institutions those communities depended on. The book you have just read is about the second mechanism. The road I drove in 2006 was a monument to the first.

By the time I reached Flagstaff, what I had seen was an architectural elegy. The country that had been built around small businesses and roadside originality had been replaced by a country running on franchises. The road I drove with my father in the early 1970s does not exist anymore. What replaced it is what most of America looks like now: chain hotels, chain restaurants, chain gas stations, identical everywhere, distinctive nowhere.

The original plan was the full length, Santa Monica to Chicago. I made it to Flagstaff. The heat had made the decision for me by then. So had the desert, which had made the same point made all the way back at Roy's.

I had not gone back to be sad. I had gone back to see if the country I remembered was still there. Some of it was. Most of it was not. The drive answered the question I had not entirely wanted answered.

I thought about who had made the choices that had produced what I had just driven through. Stephen Schwarzman. Leon Black. Henry Kravis. Names I have spent the last two hundred and fifty pages writing about. The same handful of men appear over and over in the destruction of American institutions, and they are not hiding. They are public figures who give speeches and donate to museums and serve on advisory councils. Their names are on letterhead. Their wealth is documented in Forbes. Their decisions are recorded in SEC filings. The destruction has authors. The authors are knowable.

What I want for the people who read this book is for the destruction to stop being invisible. The Toys"R"Us that closed in your neighborhood did not close because parents stopped buying toys. The Pan Am terminal did not get demolished because air travel went out of style. The Boston Market that became a vacant storefront in your town did not become one because nobody wanted roasted turkey anymore. Each of those losses had specific causes, specific actors, and specific consequences. Naming them is the prerequisite for changing them.

I do not know if the next forty years will look like the last forty. The forces that produced the destruction documented in this book are still operating. The political conditions that produced the deregulation of the 1980s and 1990s are still in place. The pension funds are still investing in the firms that are still extracting from the businesses that are still being acquired. The pattern is still operating.

What I know is that the pattern can be broken because patterns like it have been broken before. Glass-Steagall lasted sixty-six years. The Sherman Antitrust Act broke up Standard Oil. The consumer protection movement of the 1970s produced agencies that still exist. The right to repair movement won in Massachusetts. The PBM reform movement is winning state by state. The history of American business is not a one-way slide into extraction. It is a recurring contest between institutions that build and institutions that strip, and the contest has been won by the builders before, and can be won by them again.

The America that produced the institutions documented in this book still exists. It exists in Trader Joe's and H-E-B and the Storm Lake Times and Navy Federal Credit Union and the Wigwam Motel and Costco and In-N-Out and Wegmans and the independent pharmacies that survived and the family restaurants that never sold to the spreadsheet. It exists in the people who work at those places and the families who shop there. It is rare enough that finding it feels like luck. It is not luck. It is the choice that some people made, decades ago, to build institutions that would last because they were worth lasting. The choice is still available. The institutions can still be built. The people who would build them are still here.

I turned around at Flagstaff. The road home was I-40, the interstate that had killed the road I had just driven. There is no escape from the system this book has documented while operating inside it. The choice is what to do with the knowledge.

That system is not the only system possible. We built it. We can rebuild it. The book ends here. The work begins now.

Afterword: Is This Evil?

The question hangs in the air like barbecue smoke that got doused with lighter fluid. After walking through thirteen industries that have been systematically stripped for parts, after seeing how private equity transforms working businesses into extraction machines, we have to ask: is this evil?

It's a weird question for a business book. We're supposed to discuss market forces and competitive dynamics. We're not supposed to use words like "evil" because that sounds unserious.

But when you watch a perfectly good toy store get murdered so some suits can extract a few billion dollars, when you see local newspapers destroyed not because they're failing but because a hedge fund can make more money selling the real estate, unserious seems appropriate.

Evil traditionally requires intent. You can't accidentally be evil. By that standard, most enshittification falls short. The private equity partners loading Toys"R"Us with debt weren't trying to hurt children or destroy communities. They were trying to make money. That their money-making process demolished a beloved institution was just an externality.

But here's where the moral math gets interesting.

After the first few dozen times this exact playbook destroys functioning businesses and devastates communities, ignorance stops being an excuse. When you've seen what happened to Circuit City and Sports Authority and Brookstone and dozens of other retailers, when you've watched the same debt-loading, cost-cutting, cash-extraction dance play out repeatedly, you can't claim surprise when it happens again.

Willful blindness becomes a choice.

The executives who implement these strategies aren't stupid. They know what happened to the last ten companies that got the private equity treatment. They do it anyway because the math works for them. They extract their fees and profits upfront. By the time the business collapses, they've moved on to the next target.

If you design a system that consistently produces harm, and you keep operating that system because it produces profits for you personally, what do we call that?

Maybe the right word isn't evil. Maybe it's sociopathic. A sociopath isn't necessarily malicious. They just can't empathize with other people's pain. They see other humans as objects to be manipulated instead of fellow beings deserving consideration.

But most of the people implementing these strategies are perfectly normal humans who love their families, donate to charity, and probably consider themselves decent people. They just happen to work in systems that reward them for treating everyone outside their immediate circle as expendable.

This might be the most disturbing part. Evil we can fight. Sociopathy we can identify and contain. But what do we do with systems that turn normal people into agents of destruction simply by aligning their incentives properly?

The answer, depressingly, is that we probably call it capitalism. Not the capitalism of small businesses competing to serve customers better. The financialized capitalism of asset stripping and rent extraction, where making money matters more than making anything useful.

This version of capitalism doesn't just tolerate enshittification. It requires it. When publicly traded companies have a legal obligation to maximize shareholder returns, when private equity firms raise money by promising double-digit returns, when Wall Street rewards cost-cutting more than customer satisfaction, degradation becomes inevitable.

The businesses that resist enshittification prove every day that the alternative is viable. They optimize for different things: customer satisfaction, employee wellbeing, community benefit, long-term sustainability. They prove that capitalism doesn't have to mean extraction.

The question was answered at the beginning of this book. The evidence for the next two hundred and fifty pages was the proof.

It's wrong.

About the Author

Richard Lowe is a professional ghostwriter with 113 published books to his credit, including works for Fortune 50 executives, technology founders, and industry leaders across finance, healthcare, and enterprise software. His clients have raised over $30 million in venture capital, built platforms reaching millions of readers, and landed TEDx speaking invitations, outcomes that typically follow from being known as the person who wrote the definitive book on their subject.

Before ghostwriting became his primary work, Richard spent two decades as Director of Computer Operations at Trader Joe's, where he built the technology infrastructure that supported the company's growth from regional curiosity to national brand. That experience, running systems at a company that consistently resisted the cost-cutting playbook destroying its competitors, gave him an insider's understanding of what separates businesses that serve their communities from businesses that extract from them.

His earlier technology career included developing fraud detection systems that pioneered the behavioral analytics now standard in modern AI platforms, managing digital transformation at a $16 billion retail chain, and building infrastructure for major water utilities. He understood how systems worked before he started writing about what happens when the wrong people get control of them.

That combination, twenty years inside a company that got it right and a decade listening to executives describe why they got it wrong, produced this book. The patterns he documents are not theoretical. He watched them operating in real time, from both sides of the ledger.

Richard's books have been adopted as university textbooks, translated into seven languages, and featured on podcasts reaching millions of listeners. He lives in Florida and works with business leaders who have a story worth telling and want it told well.

About This Series

https://enemiesofyou.com

Something is working against you. Not in the abstract. Not against society or the culture or the country in general. Against you, specifically. Your ability to think. Your ability to pay attention. Your ability to understand what's happening in the world and make good decisions about your own life inside it. Your ability to pass something worth having on to the people who come after you.

This series documents what that something is.

Not one thing. Several things, operating at the same time, from different directions, with different tools. Some of them are commercial. Some of them are political. Some of them are foreign. Some of them were designed specifically to do what they're doing and some of them are just the predictable outcome of systems nobody was watching carefully enough. The result is the same regardless of the cause. Something is eating your capacity to think, to participate, to resist, and to build. This series is about what that something is and what you can do about it.

Each book in the series identifies a specific enemy operating against a specific capacity. The Death of Thinking is about what AI dependency does to your mind when you let it think for you. Turn Off the TV is about what passive consumption does to your time and attention when you let platforms have both. The Birth of the Augmented Human is about the path back to your own capability. Stuck in the Middle is about the geopolitical forces reshaping your world without your knowledge or consent. The Enshittification of America is about the financial engineering that stripped the institutions your daily life depended on and left hollow shells in their place. The Emasculation of America is about the deliberate foreign campaign to demoralize and neutralize the men who would otherwise resist. The Villainization of America is about the psychological operation that turned a nation against its own story.

Nineteen books. Nineteen enemies. One argument running through all of them: none of this happened by accident, none of it is inevitable, and all of it can be countered by people who understand what they're actually dealing with.

You can read them in any order. Each one stands on its own. But if you read them together, something becomes visible that isn't visible in any single book: the pattern. The way cognitive erosion feeds civic collapse. The way civic collapse feeds cultural vulnerability. The way cultural vulnerability feeds foreign exploitation. The way foreign exploitation feeds the economic extraction that makes everything else worse. These aren't separate problems. They're the same problem operating at different scales.

The series is written for normal people living normal lives who suspect that something is wrong but can't quite name what it is. Not for academics. Not for policy people. Not for the already-converted on either side of any political argument. For people who are smart enough to understand the world but haven't been given the information in a form that respects their intelligence without requiring a PhD to decode it.

Every book is written at a ninth-grade reading level. On purpose. Not because the ideas are simple. Because clarity is a form of respect. If you can't explain something clearly, you probably don't understand it yourself.

The series is also optimistic. That will surprise you after a few hundred pages of documented disasters, structural failures, and deliberate attacks. But the optimism is earned, not performed. The tools exist to counter every one of the enemies documented in these books. The examples exist. The knowledge exists. The only thing standing between the current situation and a dramatically better one is the decision to act on what you now understand.

That decision is yours.

Enemies of You Series

The Death of Thinking: The Enslavement of Humanity

A diagnosis of what happens to human cognitive capacity when practitioners consistently outsource the parts of their work that require genuine thinking to AI tools. Not in one session or one project, but across months and years of daily practice that removes the demands that were quietly building something. Following composite characters through the specific moments where the pattern becomes visible, this book traces the mechanisms of cognitive erosion: the convenience trap, the illusion of understanding, the death of the wrong answer, and the transfer of epistemic authority that occurs when humans stop standing outside the AI's framing and examining it.

The Birth of the Augmented Human: The Freeing of Humanity

The companion to The Death of Thinking maps the other path. A notebook before the AI is opened. A paragraph written before the structure is requested. A hypothesis formed before the diagnostic tool is consulted. Small choices in sequence that accumulate, over months and years, into a practitioner who is more capable, more original, and more able to surprise themselves than the practitioner who did not make them. The other path is available. This book is the map.

Turn Off The TV, Get Off Your Ass, and Do Something

Most people complain about not having enough time while spending hours every day staring at screens. This is not an anti-technology book and not a minimalism guide. It is an anti-passivity book built around one specific argument: every platform has a consuming side and a contributing side. The device is identical either way. The relationship to it is not. This book is about crossing that line and what waits on the other side.

Stuck in the Middle: Wars, Weapons, and the Forces That Will Shape the Next Thirty Years

Written against the backdrop of a US-Israel strike on Iran that exposed the hollowness of American military industrial capacity, this book connects cognitive decline, civic collapse, private equity extraction, and great power competition into one argument about where the world is heading. Covering missile math, carrier vulnerability, demographic collapse, the Belt and Road as strategic colonization, and the technologies that could solve every crisis on the horizon, this is the book that ties everything else into one coherent warning. And one earned, hard-won optimism.

The Enshittification of America: How Private Equity Destroyed the Things We Love

A documented investigation into how private equity firms systematically acquired beloved American institutions, loaded them with debt, stripped out everything that made them worth visiting, and walked away wealthy while leaving communities with hollow shells of what they once had. Airlines. Restaurants. Department stores. Newspapers. Hospitals. Pharmacies. This book names the firms, documents the playbook, and makes the case that the degradation of American commerce was not inevitable. It was deliberate.

The Emasculation of America: How Russia's Long War Against the American Male Is Destroying the Nation From Within

Beginning with a KGB defector's 1984 warning that nobody heeded, this book traces the deliberate Soviet and Russian strategy to defeat America not through military force but through cultural subversion. Seeding an ideology through universities, amplifying it through social media, delivering it through institutions that now enforce it as policy. Applying academic cult identification criteria to gender ideology, documenting the biological attack through endocrine disruption, and tracing China's acceleration of the same strategy through TikTok, this is not a culture war book. It is a national security argument.

The Villainization of America

America ended slavery, defeated fascism twice, rebuilt its enemies after defeating them, created the largest middle class in human history, and produced more medical and technological breakthroughs than any nation that ever existed. Somehow a significant portion of its own citizens have been convinced it is the primary source of evil in the world. This book documents how that happened, who executed it, and why the psychological campaign to make Americans ashamed of their own country is inseparable from the economic and cultural attacks documented in the two preceding volumes.

Watch the Other Hand: Politics as Cover for the Kleptocracy

While Americans argue about culture war flashpoints and election outcomes, a quieter operation has been moving wealth and power from public hands into private ones at a scale most citizens never see. The political theater is real and exhausting and often deeply felt. It is also doing work for the people whose interests would not survive a population paying attention to what was actually happening. This book documents the kleptocratic capture happening behind the visible politics, names the mechanisms, and traces how the visible politics functions to keep attention pointed elsewhere.

Manufactured Fear: How Crisis Becomes Profit

Every era has its emergencies. The current era has manufactured ones, engineered to maintain a state of generalized anxiety that benefits specific industries and political coalitions. The fear is not invented. The proportions are. This book traces how a healthy capacity for legitimate concern was converted into a permanent state of alarm, names the actors who profit from it, and documents what happens to a population that lives at sustained emergency pitch for years on end.

The Death of Privacy: They Know Everything, You Know Nothing

The surveillance system that the citizens of free societies were promised would never be built has been built. Not by a single state with a single agenda but by a coalition of corporate platforms, advertising infrastructure, data brokers, and government agencies that share the substrate even when they do not coordinate the use. This book documents what is actually known about each individual user, who knows it, what they do with it, and what the absence of meaningful privacy means for political freedom in a society that depends on individuals being able to think and act without continuous monitoring.

The Wrong Fight: How the Climate Response Became the Climate Problem

The climate is changing, the consequences are real, and the response that was supposed to address them has been captured by interests that are using the response as a vehicle for their own purposes. The result is a policy regime that produces consequences which would be unacceptable on their own terms but become acceptable because the alternative is framed as denial. This book separates the science from the policy capture, names the specific failures of the current response, and argues for what an honest climate strategy would look like.

The Quiet War: How America's Adversaries Attack Without Firing a Shot

The hot wars of the twentieth century have been substantially replaced, against the United States in particular, by sustained operations that operate below the threshold of military response. Information operations. Cultural subversion. Economic coercion. Cyber penetration of critical infrastructure. Strategic drug supply campaigns. These are the instruments of the quiet war, and they have been working. This book documents the campaigns currently underway against the United States, names the state actors directing them, and explains why the inability to recognize them as warfare is itself one of the campaigns' objectives.

The Dumbing Down: How American Schools Stopped Teaching Children to Think

American schools have been progressively converted from places where children were taught to think into places where children are processed for credentials. The conversion was not an accident or a failure of execution. It was the predictable outcome of policy choices that prioritized measurable outputs over the difficult work of cognitive development, and that defined educational success in ways that did not require it. This book documents what was lost in the conversion, when the choices were made, and what would have to change to teach thinking again.

The Pattern: How the Enemies of You Work Together

The enemies named across this series are not parallel items on a list. They are a system. Cognitive erosion makes civic collapse possible. Civic collapse creates the conditions for kleptocratic capture. Kleptocratic capture funds the manufactured fear that legitimizes the surveillance state. The surveillance state runs on the educational system that produced citizens who cannot evaluate what is being done to them. Each enemy reinforces the others. None of them can be addressed in isolation. This book is the synthesis: how the system operates as a system, why the standard frame of fix-this-one-problem is itself part of the problem, and what counter-strategy looks like for someone who can finally see the whole shape of the attack.

The Debt Trap: How the Financial System Was Designed to Extract From You

Student loans that cannot be discharged in bankruptcy. Credit cards engineered to keep balances revolving. Mortgages structured so the first ten years of payments are mostly interest. Buy-now-pay-later services that have re-engineered impulse purchasing to operate on an installment basis. Auto loans that now run seven years and underwater within twelve months. Each financial product looks like a service. Each one is a specific design choice about who pays whom over time, and the design has consistently moved in the same direction. This book traces the architecture of consumer debt as a wealth extraction system, names the policies and corporate decisions that built it, and explains why the standard personal-responsibility framing is the cover story that lets the system continue.

The Sick Industry: How American Medicine Profits From Keeping You Sick

The American healthcare system spends more per capita than any other developed nation and produces worse outcomes on most measures that matter. The reason is structural. Chronic illness is more profitable than cure. Symptom management is more profitable than prevention. The food industry produces the conditions that the pharmaceutical industry then medicates. The hospital system bills by procedure, not by health. The medical research apparatus is funded primarily by entities with financial interests in particular conclusions. This book documents the architecture of medical extraction, names the specific incentive structures that produce it, and explains why the conversation about fixing healthcare has been confined to the question of who pays rather than what is being paid for.

The Gambling Machine: How America Made Predatory Gambling the Default

In 2018, sports betting was illegal in nearly every U.S. state. By 2024, it was legal and aggressively advertised in most of them. The expansion was not driven by public demand. It was driven by industry lobbying that succeeded because the public attention was on other issues. The new gambling environment is engineered with the full machinery of behavioral psychology: variable rewards, push notifications, free credits that require deposits, in-game betting that runs faster than judgment can keep up with. The financial outcomes are predictable and documented. The social outcomes are accumulating. This book traces how the legalization happened, who profited, and what is now being done to the people the new system has captured.

The Loneliness Engine: How American Life Was Structured to Isolate You

The third places where Americans used to encounter each other are gone. Bowling leagues, fraternal organizations, churches, neighborhood bars, civic clubs, parent-teacher associations: all measurably smaller, in many cases by orders of magnitude, than they were thirty years ago. The replacements are commercial products that provide the appearance of connection while delivering its opposite. This book documents the destruction of the institutions that made American social life functional, names the economic and policy forces that did the destroying, and traces the consequences for mental health, civic participation, and the basic human capacity to be known by other people.

The Theft of Childhood: How American Kids Stopped Becoming Adults

Children spend more time on screens than in any previous generation, less time outdoors than any previous generation, and reach standard milestones of independence later than any previous generation. The teen mental health collapse that accelerated after 2012 is not mysterious. The mechanism is documented. Phone-based childhood, helicopter parenting, the elimination of unsupervised play, the medicalization of normal developmental difficulty, and the school system's drift toward credentials over capacity have produced a generation that is anxious, fragile, and structurally unprepared for adulthood. This book names what was taken, who took it, and what would have to change for the next generation to get a different result.

Books by Richard Lowe

See books by Richard Lowe at

https://masterofworlds.com

Get free publishing insights and industry updates at

https://thewritingking.substack.com

For ghostwriting and book coaching services see

https://thewritingking.com

Index

H

I

Y

www.ingramcontent.com/pod-product-compliance
Lightning Source LLC
Chambersburg PA
CBHW020906060726
47591CB00004B/1104